Mastering
Strategic Management

Palgrave Master Series

Accounting
Accounting Skills
Advanced English Language
Advanced English Literature
Advanced Pure Mathematics
Arabic
Basic Management
Biology
British Politics
Business Communication
Business Environment
C Programming
C++ Programming
Chemistry
COBOL Programming
Communication
Computing
Counselling Skills
Customer Relations
Database Design
Delphi Programming
Desktop Publishing
Economic and Social History
Economics
Electrical Engineering
Electronic and Electrical Calculations
Electronics
English Grammar
English Language
English Literature
Fashion Buying and Merchandising Management
Fashion Styling
French

Geography
German
Global Information Systems
Human Resource Management
Information Technology
Internet
Italian
Java
Management Skills
Mathematics
Microsoft Office
Microsoft Windows, Novell NetWare and UNIX
Modern British History
Modern European History
Modern United States History
Modern World History
Networks
Organisational Behaviour
Pascal and Delphi Programming
Philosophy
Physics
Practical Criticism
Psychology
Shakespeare
Social Welfare
Sociology
Spanish
Statistics
Strategic Management
Systems Analysis and Design
Theology
Visual Basic
World Religions

www.palgravemasterseries.com

Palgrave Master Series
Series Standing Order ISBN 0–333–69343–4
(outside North America only)

You can receive future titles in this series as they are published by placing a standing order.
Please contact your bookseller or, in case of difficulty, write to us at the address below with
your name and address, the title of the series and the ISBN quoted above.

Customer Services Department, Macmillan Distribution Ltd
Houndmills, Basingstoke, Hampshire RG21 6XS, England

Mastering
Strategic Management

Tim Hannagan

Business Series Editor: Richard Pettinger

palgrave

First published 2002 by
PALGRAVE
Houndmills, Basingstoke, Hampshire RG21 6XS and
175 Fifth Avenue, New York, N.Y. 10010
Companies and representatives throughout the world

PALGRAVE is the new global academic imprint of
St. Martin's Press LLC Scholarly and Reference Division and
Palgrave Publishers Ltd (formerly Macmillan Press Ltd).

ISBN 0-333-92746-X

This book is printed on paper suitable for recycling and made from fully managed and sustained forest sources.

A catalogue record for this book is available from the British Library.

Library of Congress Cataloging-in-Publication Data
Hannagan, Tim.
   Mastering strategic management / Tim Hannagan.
      p. cm. – (Palgrave master series)
   Includes bibliographical references and index.
   ISBN 0-333-92746-X
      1. Strategic planning. 2. Management.   I. Title.   II. Series

HD30.28 .H3672 2001
658.4'012 – dc21   2001036987

10   9   8   7   6   5   4   3   2   1
11   10   09   08   07   06   05   04   03   02

Printed and bound in Great Britain by
Creative Print & Design (Wales), Ebbw Vale

Contents

◼ ◢ Preface and plan of book

This book is an introduction to strategy and strategic management for both students of management and business subjects and for practising managers. It is designed to provide a comprehensive foundation and appreciation of management and the formation of strategy for readers with a very limited prior knowledge of either, and provides a range of examples and case studies to illustrate the concepts and practices which are discussed. It is packed with actual and theoretical examples and illustrations in order to enable readers to understand the practical consequences of the theories and management techniques which are introduced. It leads the reader from an understanding of the place of strategic management in the role of managers through the processes involved with strategic analysis, to the choices and options open to organisations and the application of strategic change.

Mastering Strategic Management focuses on the challenges of strategy formation and developing a structured approach to it through a combination of basic management skills, practical techniques and relevant theory. The chapters include questions which need to be asked in the formation of strategy, and give answers to them – from 'what is strategic management?' and 'how do we analyse strategic needs?' to 'what are the strategic options?' to 'how do we manage strategic change?' There is not, of course, any one correct answer to each of these question, because management is not a series of questions and answers or techniques which always work. It is an approach to problems, with better and worse solutions, and managers have to 'position' themselves as much as they have to create a strategy for 'positioning' their organisation and its products and services.

An understanding of organisational resources is an essential element in strategic management along with a consideration of organisational structure. These form part of the strategic choices open to an organisation as reflected by the mergers, take-overs, downsizing, outsourcing and restructuring that have taken place in recent years. In order to understand its present position and to consider actions to change it, an organisation needs to know its markets, the needs of its customers and how it can maintain a competitive advantage.

Strategy is analysed mainly at the business level, although this analysis can be applied to corporate management and to functional, unit and team management. The dimensions of strategy are discussed in terms of its context, content and process so that a particular approach can be applied to actual situations. Strategic options are considered along with the problems of selecting a strategy, and the differences between strategy and strategic planning are emphasised to lead into an introduction to producing a strategic plan. Marketing strategy is seen as an essential element in strategic management, leading into a focus on the needs of customers and strategy to maintain a competitive advantage. The influence of strategic leadership and strategy in different organisational cultures is explored as well as the whole process of managing strategic change.

This book is designed for students on business and management courses and for those studying business and management on a range of other courses such as engineering, social sciences and business administration, as well as for managers and potential managers. It can be applied to both the private and the public and voluntary sector and the term 'organisation' is frequently used in order to make it clear that strategy does not only apply to profit-making businesses even though it is an essential element in their management. There are references for further reading, a glossary of terms and assignments to assist in learning and discussion.

The structure of the book works through:

- the meaning of strategy and strategic management;
- strategic analysis and choices;
- the processes of developing strategy in terms of marketing;
- meeting customer needs;
- maintaining a sustainable competitive advantage;
- the importance of culture and leadership;
- the expectation of continual change.

What is strategic management? – *the meaning of strategic management (Chapter 1) – analysing the internal structure and the external environment of organisations (Chapter 2)*

What are the strategic options? – *strategic resources and organisational strategic options (Chapter 3) – planning organisational strategy (Chapter 4)*

How is strategy decided? – *markets and marketing (Chapter 5) – focusing on customers (Chapter 6) – beating the competition (Chapter 7)*

How is an organisation's strategy changed? – *strategy and organisational culture (Chapter 8) – strategic leadership (Chapter 9) – managing strategic change (Chapter 10)*

Tim Hannagan

◪ Acknowledgements

Many thanks to all those people who helped in the production of this book, and in particular Yvonne for her patience.

The author and publishers wish to thank Richard Pettinger for the use of Figures 2.1, 4.7, 6.4 and 6.10 from his book *Mastering Management Skills* (Palgrave, 2001).

◤ Introduction

Case studies

In order to help the reader understand and appreciate strategic management in practice, two case studies run through the book. One company is a new service company founded as a result of the boom in information technology, the other is an old, long-established manufacturing company that is facing the challenges of the modern economy. (If it is felt that there are gaps in the narrative in relation to these companies, they could be filled by the knowledge and imagination of the reader!)

'The Communications Company'

'The Communications Company' was founded without a carefully thought out strategy. The people involved knew that they had a high-quality product for which there was a demand, but they did not test the market by carrying out market research before they founded the Company. They did not know what the demand for their product would be so they decided to 'test the water' by launching it and seeing what happened. Although they knew that they might lose all the investment they had put into this launch, and this included all their savings, they thought that they had a great deal to gain and they had a 'hunch' that their product would sell well.

They were right ... for a time! Then market forces began to come into play as others, including more established companies, recognised the opportunity that 'The Communications Company' had identified. The rival companies introduced updated versions of 'The Communications Company' product, which included more features and satisfied customer needs more directly. As a result, 'The Company' had to adapt and develop if it was to survive. This meant that it had to introduce a well thought out business plan based on a strategy which would enable it to develop new offerings and provide benefits for the needs of a wider range of customers. This involved carrying out market research, creating a marketing strategy, developing new products and searching for a competitive advantage.

This process required 'The Communications Company' to develop its strategic management and leadership, to analyse its options, to become a learning organisation and to acquire the structures of an established company. It would be interesting and useful to consider the parallels between the development of 'The Communications Company' and the history of some dot com and e-commerce companies, and to consider how 'The Communications Company' has survived and to speculate on its future.

'The Engineering Company'

'The Engineering Company' is a long-established manufacturing company producing machinery and equipment supplied to a number of areas of industry. It was originally founded by an entrepreneur who started by manufacturing one machine in his spare time using his garage as a workshop. He was able to sell this machine, and the interest raised in it as a result from other firms in the industry encouraged him to move into an industrial unit on a local trading estate and to work on the production of this machine full-time. In order to meet demand he had to employ friends and acquaintances, first on a part-time basis and then full-time. He then saw opportunities in other areas of industry and over a period of years the company expanded into a factory and employed four hundred people.

When the founder of the Company retired, his son took over. He had been groomed to take over by working in every area of the Company from cleaner, to skilled operative to office administrator. He turned the Company into a public company, although he maintained a controlling interest, and introduced an investment programme in order to modernise the factory and introduce new technology. Although he knew the business inside out, his interest in it waned and a few years ago he handed over the day-to-day running of the Company to his Assistant Managing Director, the present Managing Director, and he became Chairman of the Board. His own children show little interest in the Company.

The present MD has been in post for some years and he has tended to run the Company on similar lines to his predecessors. There is still a feeling that it is a family business because the Chairman of the Board is the son of the founder and is still involved in important business decisions. Many of the workforce have been with the Company for many years and some of them remember the founder.

Until recently, changes have been introduced gradually on a step-by-step incremental basis. Now all the indicators, such as profit and sales figures, returns to shareholders and industrial indicators, suggest that a dramatic change is necessary if the Company is to survive. Both domestic and overseas competition has increased and the MD has convinced the Board that the required changes involve alterations to the Company strategy. The Company needs to make changes in order to survive and he is convinced that these are strategic changes.

⚙ ▌ What is strategic management?

OBJECTIVES

To define and describe strategic management
To provide an understanding of the role of the strategic manager
To consider a range of strategic issues
To introduce strategic analysis

The nature of strategic management – Differences between strategic management and strategic planning – The manager's role – Operational management and strategic management – Identifying strategic issues – Strategic decisions – Strategy as 'scope', 'fit' and 'stretch' – Strategic analysis – The dimensions of strategy – Levels of strategy – Definition of strategic management

1.1 The nature of strategic management

Strategic management consists of the decisions and actions used to formulate and implement strategies that will provide a competitively superior fit between the organisation and its environment, to enable it to achieve organisational objectives. It can also be described as the process of management needed to enable an organisation to move from where it is now to where it wants to be in the future. It is about a sense of direction and aligning this with an organisation's aims. Setting a strategic direction for an organisation is the most complex task facing a management team because:

- strategy direction is established in an unknown future;
- there are a range of choices for the management team;
- organisations operate in a volatile and dynamic environment;
- strategic management involves people, including the managers and everybody else in the organisation.

Strategic management is not the same as strategic planning, although it may include it. Strategic planning is associated with an activity carried out a little apart from the line management of the organisation and reviewed at periodic well-defined intervals. Strategic planning tends to be associated with medium or long-term planning which extrapolates trend lines for the key business variables and assumes a known future point at which the organisation will arrive. On the other hand, strategic management is concerned with establishing a competitive advantage, sustainable over time, not simply by tactical manoeuvring, but by taking an overall long-term prospective.

While strategic management is involved in all areas of management, it is not the same as day-to-day management because it is concerned with the issues affecting the fundamentals of the organisation. It can be argued that setting the strategic direction for an organisation can be the most complex task facing any top management team because strategy is about an unknown future, there are many ways forward that the organisation can follow and the competitive environment for organisations is a dynamic one, not one that is 'standing still' or entirely predictable. Superior organisational performance over a period of time is not a matter of luck, it is determined by the choices made by managers.

'The Engineering Company' is a long-established firm manufacturing machines for a number of areas of industry. The Managing Director of 'The Engineering Company' arranges a meeting with his most experienced Divisional Product Manager. 'I want to discuss the basics,' the Managing Director (MD) of 'The Engineering Company' tells his most experienced Divisional Product Manager (DPM). 'At present,' he continues, 'as you know, we make products supplying machinery to five different areas of industry. You also know that this has developed over a period of years as we have diversified. This was a successful strategy in the past, but the problem we face now is that there are specialised firms in each of these industries competing against us with lower costs than us, at least partly because they are specialised.' The Divisional Product Manager nods his head in agreement. 'We are beginning to lose out against this competition and we have to do something about it. What do you suggest?' the MD asks. After a pause the DPM replies, 'I don't know, we've always done all right in the past.' 'Yes, in the past.' 'My division is very efficient,' the DPM adds, 'I don't know anything about overall company strategy.' The MD leans forward. 'That is all very well,' he says, 'but whatever we do it will affect your Division. You know why we diversified in the past, how do we decide what to do next?'

ASSIGNMENT

Discuss the statements made by the Divisional Product Manager of 'The Engineering Department' that his division is very efficient and that he does not know anything about company strategy. Why should he be concerned with factors to make sure that the whole Company is viable?

1.2 The manager's role

A manager's role is to organise, supervise and control people so that there is a productive outcome to work. Organisations of one type or another, small or large, are essential for productive work because they bring people together with raw materials and equipment in order to achieve a variety of goals. Combining people's talents and energy with resources can often achieve more than by individuals working on their own. People who are working on their own still have to have management skills in order to 'manage' themselves, for example they need to be self-disciplined in organising and controlling their work so that there is a productive outcome. Managers are responsible for:

'The process of planning, organising, leading and controlling the efforts of organisation members and using all organisational resources to achieve stated organisational goals.'

(Mescon, Albert and Khedouri, 1985)

Operational management provides for organisation, control and supervision, while strategic management provides a sense of purpose. Companies, schools, universities, hospitals, football teams and so on are all organisations which have a purpose, whether this is to make profits, maintain a market share, promote educational achievements, provide good health or win football matches. Operational management is essential because if these basic management functions are not carried out, productive work is unlikely and an organisation will only achieve its purpose or purposes if these aspects of management are present. If a football team is to be successful it has to be organised and controlled so that the players combine their skills in the best possible way, so like any other organisation there is a need for these elements of management.

1.3 Operational management and strategic management

As well as operational management there is at the same time other aspects of management which can be seen as 'dynamic', innovative and risky. Managers who start football teams from scratch rather than taking over established teams are taking a great risk. They have to bring together players, equipment, pitches and fixtures against other teams, with no guarantee that even after a great deal of work the team will be successful. Starting a company is both risky and innovative, but once the team or company has become established and has survived for a time this innovation and risk may become a less prominent part of the manager's role, and supervision and control may become more important.

A manager's role will partly depend on his or her position in the organisation. Junior managers will be mainly responsible for supervising and controlling

Figure 1.1   Management.

non-managerial employees, while middle management will take on more responsibility for planning innovation and innovating (see Figure 1.1). Senior managers are responsible for the overall direction of the organisation and company-wide co-ordination, planning, organising and directing. They will establish company strategy (see page 17).

Strategic management emphasises that the role of modern managers is to maintain dynamic roles even after the organisation has become established, because the greatest challenge to management skill now is the speed of change in the environment of present-day organisations. **The 'environment' of an organisation is everything around it that affects it and that can influence its success or failure**. These are the so-called STEP factors (see Chapter 5) which are the social, technological, economic and political factors which have an effect on the success or failure of an organisation. These may also include competition from other companies, uncertainty about raw material supplies, price fluctuations, government legislation and natural disasters. The speed of change means that managers have to be prepared to constantly redevelop and reconstruct their company so that, as well as being operational, they also have to plan, innovate and lead. The difficulties facing Marks & Spencer in the period after 1999 illustrate the problems an established company can still meet.

'The maxim "managing means looking ahead" gives some idea of the importance of planning in the business world, and it is true that if foresight is not the whole of management at least it is an essential part of it.'

(Henri Fayol, 1949)

Strategic management today is about 'looking ahead' and although it may include planning, it is more complicated than simply planning a journey in order to travel, or to escape, or to arrive at one destination. Figure 1.2 summarises the differences between operational management and strategic management.

Strategic management		Operational management
A sense of direction	—	Organising
Positioning	—	Supervising and controlling
Ambiguous and complex	—	Routine
Long-term implications	—	Short-term implications
Organisation-wide	—	Operationally specific
Fundamental	—	Operationally specific

Figure 1.2 Strategic and operational management.

A manager may be heavily involved in organising and controlling people, making sure they know what to do and are doing it so that their targets are achieved. There may be a variety of tactics used to achieve these targets which are short-term and operationally specific. At the same time there has to be an underlying strategy designed to make sure that these targets are the ones which will help the organisation achieve its overall objectives. In this sense, tactics can be seen as the methods used to carry out a particular policy to arrive at a particular result, while the strategy is concerned with choice of the operations selected. The Divisional Product Manager in the example of 'The Engineering Company' may be right in claiming that his division is very efficient, but does he know how effective it is in comparison to competitors?

Strategic management is ambiguous and complex because the objective of a company may be very clearly defined, but the way to achieve it may not be obvious. A company may have as its objective 'to make a profit', and this may be given greater clarity by identifying a particular level of profit. The way to arrive at this objective may be obvious to start with but changes in the environment, such as increased competition or government legislation, may provide obstacles to its achievement. It is at this point that an underlying strategy is necessary. This is more complicated than simply having contingency plans, although these plans may be part of the strategy. Strategy must be fundamental, with long-term implications, because it is about the basic survival of the organisation.

'The Communications Company', an information technology-based company, was started as a result of a 'good idea' which proved to be saleable because other people wanted it. It introduced a new computer software package to improve company communications. At first the company expanded as a result of increasing demand for its innovative product. Other companies sought after the package and 'The Communications Company' needed to do the very minimum of marketing. However, its very success attracted other people into the market and soon other companies were producing similar packages. These tended to have more features and they were better marketed. In time, the very need that the original 'good idea' had met was overtaken by

(Continued)

advances in information technology so that the communication software package was no longer needed.

In order to survive, the Company needed a new 'good idea'. It designed a new package with a new application and for a time there was an increasing demand for this product, but in due course this product suffered the same fate as the first one. For long-term survival the Company needed a strategy which would provide a more fundamental sense of direction than a series of 'good ideas'. The founders of the Company thought that this could be to service the information technology needs of a particular section of industry.

ASSIGNMENT

Are the founders of 'The Communication Company' thinking on the correct lines?

1.4   Identifying strategic issues

In military terms, 'strategos' is the Greek for 'general' – the strategist who plans the whole campaign; while lower ranks in the army are the people who use tactics in order to put troops and equipment in the right places to make sure that the campaign is successful. Strategic management can be described as providing an organisation with a 'sense of purpose', a mapping out of the future direction to be taken, and developing policies and actions in order to put the purpose into practice.

> 'Corporate strategy is the pattern of major objectives, purposes or goals and essential policies or plans for achieving these goals, stated in such a way as to define what business the company is in or is to be in and the kind of company it is or is to be.'
>
> (Drucker, 1955)

It can be argued that in the environment in which managers work today, change is the natural order of things and the important management skill is the management of change. Once a company is established the management role may appear to be one of supervision and control, but in practice there are so many changes taking place in the manager's environment that every organisation needs a strategy in order to deal with this. An organisation, whether it is a private sector company or a public sector corporate body or for that matter a voluntary sector organisation, needs to make strategic decisions if it is to survive. Companies such as Marks & Spencer, public sector corporate bodies such as universities and colleges, and voluntary sector organisations such as charities, all need a sense of direction and a sense of purpose. The owners or shareholders in private companies and the stakeholders in public bodies want to know that there is a future for their organisation if they are to continue to support it.

'The Communications Company' at first needed to concentrate on management functions such as those of producing its products in quantities which were matching demand, distributing them and selling them. The role of the managers was to supervise and control these functions. The future of the Company was assumed to be assured, and strategic management did not play a part in management thinking in the Company until it experienced difficulties.

Strategic issues address such questions as 'who are our customers?', 'what changes and trends are occurring in the competitive environment?', 'what products or services should we offer?' and 'how can we offer these products and services most efficiently?'. These questions raise issues which help to focus a manager's attention on how to position the organisation in relation to rival organisations. A manager's strategic decisions affect the long-term direction of a company and they are usually concerned with gaining some advantage for the company. It may be that a decision which were thought to be strategic appears, in hindsight, to be a 'tactical decision'. This means that although at the time they were made such decisions were thought to alter the 'position' of the company in a fundamental way, the changes introduced were of a more superficial or cosmetic nature.

Reports in the financial press described the High Street retailer, Marks & Spencer, as 'struggling', with its share price being half its peak value and with reduced profits in 1999. Christmas sales were down by 3 per cent compared with the previous year and the Company's performance was redeemed only by strong food sales. There had been attempts earlier in the year to revive Company fortunes by revamping sales lines, but the Autumn sales and Christmas sales had not shown a turnaround in the downward trend.

Competing companies such as Next and John Lewis had seen rises in Christmas sales of 17 per cent and 18 per cent respectively. M&S were reported to be working with leading design consultants in order to provide a fundamental revamp of its image during the year 2000. As well as shifting its source of supplies of clothing products from the UK manufacturers to international suppliers, there has been pressure on the Company to change its policy on the use of credit cards in its stores.

Strategic decisions can be thought of as the search for an effective 'positioning' in relation to competitors so as to achieve an advantage. 'Positioning' means where the business sees itself in its market (see Chapter 5). This may be in terms of market share, but also involves positioning each of its 'offers', that is its products and services, in terms of value and price. The attempts by M&S during 1999 to alter its appeal to customers by revamping its sales lines, may be considered to be tactical rather than strategic; while a fundamental revamp of its image – changing suppliers in order to reduce costs and prices, and alterations in its financial arrangements – could prove to be strategic decisions, because these decisions may effectively reposition the company in the market. Tesco is a good example of the strategy of 'positioning'. In the 1970s it was a company selling goods at the lower end of the price range in order to meet the needs of the large number of low-income families. As prosperity has increased throughout the population, the company has made a strategic move so that it now sells a wider range of goods than before at prices which the majority of families are able to afford and concentrates on 'value for money', and this strategy has been successful.

1.5   Strategy as 'scope', 'fit' and 'stretch'

Strategy is concerned with the 'scope' of an organisation's activities, whether it concentrates on one area of activity or whether it is concerned with many. This question of the 'scope' of activities is an indication of the organisation's boundaries, the number and range of its offers of products and services (see the chapters that follow). M&S may be thought of as mainly a clothing retailer, but it also sells a wide range of food and other commodities, such as furniture, and has moved into providing financial services. Tesco may be considered to be mainly a food retailer, but it also sells a range of other goods such as clothes and hardware commodities. Strategic 'fit' is the attempt by managers to develop strategy by identifying opportunities in the environment of the business and organising its resources to take advantage of these, that is trying to match the resources and capabilities of the organisation to the opportunities open to it. Strategic 'stretch' is the process of innovation and development involved in finding new opportunities and creating a competitive advantage from an organisation's resources and competencies (see Figure 1.3).

Fundamental	Long-term
A sense of direction	Looking ahead
A sense of purpose	A search for competitive advantage
Positioning	Scope of activities
Strategic fit	Stretching and leverage

Figure 1.3   Characteristics of strategic management.

The Managing Director of 'The Engineering Company' discusses the problems of the Company with the Assistant Managing Director (AMD). 'Our difficulties are becoming clear, in that our profits have fallen again and orders are down. We need to know why this is happening and what we should do about it.' 'Our strategy in the past,' says the AMD, 'has been to diversify by moving into new areas of industry, but while this has increased the scope of our activity it may be that we have over-extended ourselves.' 'Yes, we have expertise and skills which we must use in the best possible way,' the MD agrees, 'we must work from our strengths.' 'I can see the problems but I am not sure how we solve them,' the AMD admits. 'Well, we must have a strategy which matches the needs of the areas of industry we serve,' the MD tells him. 'What I would like you to do is to carry out a strategy survey which analyses our internal structure, our use of technology, the way we work and also provides an analysis of our competitors and the overall economic climate. The Marketing Manager should be able to help at least with information on our customers and potential customers.'

ASSIGNMENT

Is the MD's instruction to the AMD a good idea?

Strategy is involved with matching the activities of an organisation to the environment in which it operates so that there is a 'strategic fit' in which there is an attempt to identify the opportunities in the environment in which the organisation works, and then tailoring the strategy of the organisation to capitalise on these. This is again a question of 'positioning', for example this may take the form of making sure that the company is producing goods or services which meet market needs and also has the resources of people and materials to maintain production at the correct level. **Strategy can also be seen as 'stretching' an organisation's resources or applying 'leverage' to an organisation's resources to create opportunities or to capitalise on them**. This involves identifying the 'core competencies' that an organisation requires in order to optimise its ability to meet the opportunities and challenges it faces. The 'core competencies' are those competencies which are necessary to underpin the organisation's competitive advantage. This is not only a question of making sure that the correct resources are available, but also of identifying existing resources and competencies which can be used as a basis for creating new opportunities in the future.

1.6 Strategic analysis

It is not sufficient to consider strategic management as the process of strategic decision-making. **It involves the complexity arising out of ambiguous and non-routine situations with organisation-wide rather than operationally specific implications**. Managers are most often responsible for operational control, such as managing a sales force, marketing particular products or services, and monitoring financial performance, so that managers may tend to see problems in terms of their particular speciality, whether it is sales, production finance or

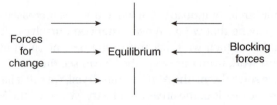

Figure 1.4   Forcefield theory.

marketing. Strategic management is characterised by complexity and an organisation-wide approach. Decisions and judgements have to be based on the conceptualisation of difficult issues and situations which are not clear-cut. An example of this conceptualisation is 'strategic fit', which emphasises the importance of managers identifying opportunities arising from an understanding of the environmental factors acting on an organisation, and adapting resources so as to take advantage of these. There should be 'fit' among a company's activities, so that it manages to do many things well and provide integration between them.

'**Forcefield theory**' (Lewin, 1951) **suggested that there were forces for change and forces resisting and restraining change in any organisation** (Figure 1.4). Forces for change include new technology, better raw materials, management factors, as well as competitive pressures (see also Chapter 10). Forces for maintaining the status quo include the fear of change, complacency, well-learned skills, and economic and social factors. At the beginning of change, the organisation can be said to be in a state of equilibrium in which the forces driving for change and forces resisting change just balance each other. The 'unfreezing' of this balance is the result of some environmental change which causes internal change and unbalances the 'forcefield'. Managers seek a new equilibrium and once this has been identified, there is a 'refreezing' as people in the organisation are converted and persuaded to accept the new situation.

If the organisation is to survive, this new equilibrium has to be one that is more appropriate to the new environment and the organisation would have to develop by mean of a plan to strengthen the driving forces for change to match the environment and to weaken the blocking forces.

The view of 'strategic fit' has been questioned by Hamel and Prahalad (1993). In their study of successful companies at that time (such as Honda and Canon) as against the ones that were less successful at the time (such as General Motors and Xerox), they found that a distinguishing factor was the different mental models of strategy guiding their respective actions. They observed that less successful companies followed the conventional approach to maintaining strategic fit, by matching their resources to the changing environment. They believed that this caused a trimming of ambitions to those that could be met by available resources. Consistency in these companies was preserved through requiring conformity in behaviour and a focus on achieving financial objectives. On the other hand, more successful companies use the resources they have to meet the requirements of the environment and push to achieve 'stretching' goals while aiming to continually renew and transform their organisations.

'Leveraging' resources means using the resources that a company already has in new and innovative ways in order to reach new 'stretching' goals which require a company to use resources to the full. It can be argued that organisational success arises from an organisation-wide 'strategic intent' based on a shared vision of the future of the organisation. This would be secured less by long-term plans than by achieving a broad and challenging intention to build 'core competencies'. These are skills and intentions which enable the company to lever resources and stretch towards new goals as the environment changes.

It is suggested that traditional 'management frames of reference' need to be broken. Ideas acquired from educational experience, business schools, peers and business experience determine a company's senior managers' view of what is meant by 'strategy'. In this sense these 'frames of reference' affect companies' approaches to competition. At the same time, global trade has altered the nature of competition. Managers have shared frames of reference because competition is often between companies whose managers have similar backgrounds and experience. With the expansion of the global business community, competition is not simply in products but in 'mind-sets' and 'managerial frames of reference'.

'Positional' advantage is familiar to military strategists, chess players and diplomats. **In business strategy it is the process a company goes through in order to define which industry, market and business it is currently in and where it fits in them**. At any one time, the company may want to strengthen its existing position, or may prefer to reposition itself in either the current, or a newly defined industry, market or business. A company may concentrate on positioning itself within a market, so that it targets a product or brand at a particular group of customers. The key issue is to meet customer demands in a different manner from that of alternative products or services. In these circumstances, the emphasis is on the need for the company to be market-driven.

A company that more generally distinguishes itself from other firms producing similar goods or services, is positioning itself within an industry. This is a broader view than that of individual products and markets because a company is comparing itself with other firms making a similar type of product or providing a similar service.

> 'A company can outperform rivals only if it can establish a difference that it can preserve. It must deliver greater value to customers or create comparable value at a lower cost, or do both.'
>
> (Porter, 1996)

1.7 The dimensions of strategy

The distinction between strategy process, strategy content and strategy context are the three dimensions of strategy that can be recognised in real-life strategic problems. **The process is the manner in which strategies come about, the 'how' of strategy, in the sense of how strategy is formulated, implemented and controlled**. It is also about 'who' is involved in this process and 'when' the necessary activities take place. There is usually an 'analysis' stage in this process when managers identify the opportunities and threats in the environment, as well as the internal strengths and weaknesses of the company. This may include considering the 'position' of the company in its market and its industry, and the way it uses its resources.

The content is the product of a strategy process, it is about the 'what' of strategy – what is or will be the strategy for the company and its various sections and parts? The content of strategic management can be considered at functional, business and corporate levels. Strategy issues at a functional level are concerned with functional aspects of a company such as marketing, finance and operations. At the business level there is an integration of functional level strategies for a distinct set of products and services that are intended for a specific group of customers. At the corporate level, strategy requires the alignment of the various business level strategies. Many organisations are in only one business so that their corporate and business level strategies will be the same (see section 1.8 below).

The context is the set of circumstances under which both the strategy process and the strategy content are determined – the 'where' of strategy, that is in which company and which environment. It can be argued that the context determines the process and content which are largely the result of circumstances over which managers have little control. On the other hand, it can be argued that managers have a large measure of freedom to decide on a course of action and can to a large extent determine their own circumstances. In practice, both of these arguments may be important in that an organisation may have freedom to act within boundaries established by the particular circumstances of the time. For example, government legislation may control or limit the freedom of a company in one way or another.

In practice, although it is possible to distinguish these three dimensions of strategy, they are not different parts of strategic management. **Each problem that arises in strategic management is three-dimensional in the sense of having characteristics of process, content and context – how, what and where**. In every problem a manager has to consider how the strategy is to be resolved, what it will be and in what circumstances is it being decided. The three dimensions also interact in that, for example, the process may influence the content, and the content may influence the future strategy process.

At the same time, an over-emphasis on separating these three dimensions may suggest a very clear-cut approach to strategic management. This is also suggested by splitting strategy between the analysis stage, the formulation stage and the implementation stage. In the analysis, strategic managers identify the threats and weaknesses in the environment, as well as strengths and weaknesses of the organisation. At the formulation stage, managers decide which strategic options are open to them, evaluate each and choose one. At the implementation stage, the selected strategy is translated into a number of specific activities.

Managers may work through these strategic steps one by one and take into account each of the strategic dimensions in turn, but they may have a more intuitive and chaotic approach to strategy where analysis and logic are felt to be less important than a general feeling about the correct strategy. Strategic management may be a well-organised activity or it may be messy with the activities of analysis, formulation and implementation going on at the same time, thoroughly intertwined with one another.

An extreme view is based on **'chaos theory', which argues that the organisational world is so turbulent and chaotic that it is not possible to predict what is going to happen or when**. This suggests that strategic management is of little use in these circumstances. Managers do need to take into account the problems of realising any process or plans when they are put into practice. The work situation does not neatly fall into categories and is to some extent a rough and tumble with a constant 'noise' arising from the day-to-day detail of working. The problems of working with other people and the practical problems involved in working combined with 'office politics', or 'factory politics' for that matter, are factors for possible 'chaos' in most people's working lives. This does not make an analysis of the situation and planning for the way ahead redundant, but it is another factor to be taken into account. For a successful journey, it is not only important to know where you are going but also it is worth plotting a route and planning how you are going to travel.

1.8 Levels of strategy

It is possible to distinguish three levels of strategy: corporate, business and functional. **Corporate strategy** applies to large companies which are divided into a number of discrete and fairly autonomous units. Holding companies are typical of this type of organisation in which a number of companies are grouped together, usually for financial reasons such as the efficient allocation of capital and investment. Corporate strategy is the responsibility of the corporate head office, with the fundamental issue based on the reason for the different businesses being collected together.

Corporate strategy may be based around investment, the economies of scale or the sharing of core competencies, and in particular what should be its portfolio of businesses. In practice, the corporation may adopt a hands-off approach to the individual companies or units under its control, so long as they fulfil the corporate objectives. These can be concerned with levels of profit or market share, or may be about levels of investment or cash flows.

The critical issues for **business strategy** will be in terms of which markets to focus on, the critical factors required in order to compete successfully, the organisation of the business and overall competitive strategy. The chapters that follow are mainly focused on this level of strategy, although many of the concepts and practices can be applied to corporate and functional strategy. For example, marketing strategy can be viewed at a functional level, but in fact it must further the achievement of the business objectives and also meet the needs of the corporation.

Functional strategies are those which involve the functional departments or divisions of organisations. Most companies have some elements of a functional or divisional structure in which people focus on a particular specialisation such as finance, marketing, manufacturing, quality assurance, information systems, customer care, or a specialisation such as a product or market. The overall business strategy has to be reflected and linked into the functional level strategies, such as marketing strategies, human resource strategy and financial strategies. The organisational structure of a business needs to assist the business level strategy in one way or another, otherwise responsibilities for parts of the strategy may not be picked up by the functional units. At the same time, the functional departments may interpret the business strategy in ways that suit them rather than reflecting the needs of the whole business. The Divisional Product Manager in 'The Engineering Company' is responsible for a particular product in the company's portfolio of products and he should understand the overall company strategy because it will affect his division, and he needs to make sure that the way his division is managed supports this company strategy if the company and his division within it are to be successful.

1.9   So what is strategic management?

Strategic management is about a sense of purpose, looking ahead, planning, positioning, strategic fit, leverage and stretching. It is the creative part of management, the part which makes sense of organising, supervising and controlling – it is the result of innovative thinking. **It is about the purpose of the organisation, the direction it is to take and the way it forms and prepares itself to face competition**. It informs and influences every aspect of management from leadership, to marketing, to financial control, to organisational culture.

Strategic management consists of elements of analysis, of choice and of implementation. Strategic analysis is concerned with the organisation itself, its environment, its expectations and purposes, and its resources and capabilities. Strategic choice is a question of considering options and evaluating and selecting, while strategic implementation is about the organisational structure and design, resource allocation and control, and managing strategic change. In order to analyse its strategy effectively, an organisation has to understand itself and to understand the market, or situation, in which it is working; it then has to make choices between a variety of options for meeting the needs of its customers and maintaining a competitive advantage. It has to be able to implement strategy in relation to all these factors and its own organisational culture, and it has to have leadership in order to manage the constant changes it faces in its attempts to be successful.

Not all managers are involved directly with strategic management. Although aspects of management are part of the simplest task, a person becomes a manager when they start to organise and supervise the work of other people. One person digging a hole has to 'manage' the task, even though someone else may have decided where the hole is to be dug. The 'digger' has to decide what tools to use from those available, where and how to start and so on. However, someone is not described as a manager until they supervise other people's work. A 'supervisor' may even be described as a 'junior manager', with 'middle managers' in charge of them and 'senior managers' organising and controlling them.

As Figure 1.1 illustrates, at the junior end of management, where there are the most managers, supervision, organisation and control are by far the most important functions. As a manager is promoted, the amount of planning and innovation expected increases and strategic decisions become a greater part of a manager's task. Part of the role of middle or senior managers is to implement strategic decisions as well as to make them at an appropriate level. A team, unit or section manager has to interpret and apply organisational strategy for the team or unit, while a senior manager may be concerned with developing organisational strategy and also applying it to a major area of the organisation.

SUMMARY OF CONCEPTS

Nature of strategic management – Strategic management and strategic planning – Manager's role – Operational management and strategic management – Identifying strategic issues – Strategic decisions – Strategy as 'scope', 'fit' and 'stretch' – Characteristics of strategic management – Strategic analysis – Forcefield theory – Leveraging – Positional advantage – The dimensions of strategy – Context, process and content – Chaos theory – Levels of strategy – Definition of strategic management

---

ASSIGNMENTS

1. Discuss the role of strategic management in a company.
2. Consider the differences between a strategic issue and an operational issue.
3. What is meant by 'strategic fit' and 'positioning'?
4. What is meant by 'stretching an organisation's resources' and 'applying leverage', and in what way are these concepts important in developing strategy?
5. Who is responsible for strategy in an organisation that is known to you (whether it is a company, public service or sports or social club)?
6. What strategic decisions have been made by 'The Communications Company' and 'The Engineering Company' so far?

▼ 2 Strategic analysis

OBJECTIVES

    To discuss strategic options
    To understand strategic choices
    To consider strategic fit
    To analyse strategic decisions

Strategic models – Strategic options – Strategic choices – Strategic pathways – Strategic fit – Market extension/positioning – Competitive advantage – Sustainability – Acceptability – Crisis management – Strategic decisions – Market-based strategic options – Resources-based strategy – Strategic analysis

2.1   Strategic models

Strategic management involves making choices in what are usually complex situations. Managers are faced with a huge range and a considerable variety of information coming at them from different directions, while each day in their working lives they are surrounded by the 'noise' or 'interference' which arises from the day-to-day business of the workplace.

> The Sales Manager for 'The Communications Company' walks into the reception area of the Company office building, expecting to spend the day checking through yesterday's monthly sales figures by product, salesperson, branch, area and region, comparing these with the results for last month and for the same month last year, checking the results against targets established in the organisation's strategic plan and then talking to each Area Sales Manager about these results. The day is clear-cut and falls into a neat pattern which the Sales Manager has planned out on the journey to work. The first part of the morning will be spent on comparing results, then after a break for coffee there will be a discussion of the results with the

Assistant Sales Manager. The Area Sales Managers will then be telephoned or left e-mail or voice-mail messages to contact the Sales Manager. This process will continue after lunch until the Sales Manager has a clear idea why sales are up in some areas and down in others. In the late afternoon, the Sales Manager will discuss the results with the Sales Director.

What actually happens is that when the Sales Manager arrives in the reception area of the office building, the lifts are not working so the day starts with a long walk up the stairs. In the office, the Sales Manager's computer has crashed so that the monthly sales figures are not available. Other computers have also closed down and the IT department thinks it might take all day before normal service is resumed. Luckily, hard copies have been taken of the weekly figures for each area, so that the Sales Manager will still be able to work on them once the Personal Assistant has retrieved them from the filing system. Unfortunately the Sales Manager's Personal Assistant has a dental appointment that morning and is not going to be in the office until lunch time, so that it is coffee time before the Sales Manager has found all the figures required. This means that all the Area Sales Managers who had expected telephone calls before lunch have moved on to their afternoon appointments before the Sales Manager is ready to talk to them. The afternoon is spent in damage control, not least with the Sales Director. So what appeared on the journey to work to be a well-organised and orderly day ends, late in the evening, in wondering how far the damage had been controlled.

A manager's well-planned day may be interrupted by all sorts of matters – some practical, some personal or to do with personnel, some financial and some to do with office politics. Although managers may have organised their day in an orderly way, the demands of other managers, both more senior and more junior, and other staff in the organisation, will interfere with this. Their diaries may include an entry which does not appear in the Sales Manager's diary which reads 'see the Sales Manager'. At the same time, crises do arise from time to time: computers have been known to malfunction, staff on whom a manager depends may not be available and senior managers may make unexpected demands. This is the 'noise' of the work situation that makes it different from the controlled conditions of a laboratory.

A strategic management decision about the direction of the organisation should ideally be taken in a calm, well-ordered atmosphere with clear information on the past and present performance of all the organisation's products and services, the performance of competitors and potential competitors in the organisation's markets, certainty about government economic policy, and stability in exchange rates and levels of inflation. In practice, strategy will be formulated as part of the day-to-day business of an organisation with inadequate information about the organisation's own products and services,

a) Progression

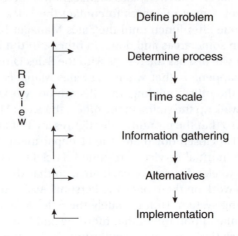

b) Process

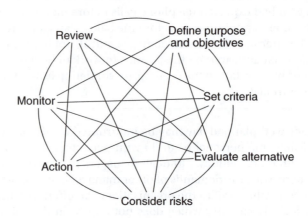

Figure 2.1 A decision-making model.

limited information about the policy and practice of competitors and potential competitors, and in an environment where government policy may change at any time and where exchange rates fluctuate.

Strategic managers will need to make decisions through a process of defining the situation or the problem, and determining the process they are going to follow to arrive at a decision (Figure 2.1). Then, knowing the time scale they have to make the decision, they gather the information needed, consider the alternatives, make a decision and implement it.

The **progression** from defining the problem to implementing the decision is involved in a **process** which sets the objectives which the decision is aimed to achieve, and the criteria on which it should be based, considers the risks involved in a number of alternatives, and monitors and reviews the objectives, the criteria, the alternatives, the risks and the actions taken (Figure 2.1). The options available to the strategic manager are considered further in Chapter 3, the strategic planning process in Chapter 4, information gathering in Chapter 5, and the evaluation of alternatives, risks and decisions in Chapters 6, 7 and 8.

In making strategic decisions about the direction of an organisation, managers will in fact receive a range of stimuli which they will have to simplify if they are not to be swamped. This simplification of reality can be described as a model. **Models are simplifications of reality with unnecessary detail discarded so that the fundamentals can be seen clearly**. Maps showing bus and train routes are good examples of models. Compared with Ordnance Survey maps they are highly simplified, often showing routes in straight lines and leaving out all the other features of the area covered, apart from the train or bus routes. These maps show which trains or buses travel between different places and they do not confuse this fundamental message by showing twists and turns in the route or the times of the service.

Such maps are descriptive models in that they describe the links between train or bus networks but they do not show how the system could change with different inputs. Scientific models tend to be prescriptive because the situations in which they are developed, such as a laboratory, can be controlled, so that particular events under these circumstances can be predicted to arrive at particular outcomes. Strategic management models tend to be descriptive in providing the fundamentals on which the detail of a particular situation can be considered. Strategic plans can fulfil this function in that they set out the underlying vision and objectives of an organisation, moving from general fundamentals to levels of detail in the action plan. They can support strategy implementation by providing a route map in terms of the direction in which the organisation wishes to travel and when and how it intends to arrive.

2.2   Strategic options

Strategy is concerned with the objectives of an organisation and the means of achieving them. Managers are faced with a set of options in terms of which products or services to offer to customers and which resources to use in order to provide these products and services, and these options constitute a strategic pathway or a strategic route. **The strategic options are the broad choices open to a business and those that are selected by a business are its strategic pathway**. The choice of a strategic pathway is a very important aspect of leadership in strategic management. In making this choice the strategic manager must consider what products and services the organisation wants to offer and in what quantity it wants to offer them. Consideration has also to be given to the organisation's position in the market in terms of market share and also to the positioning of its products and services. This process can be seen as a sequence from decisions about the organisation's vision and objectives,

Portfolio of offers (products and services)
Offer positioning
Resources required
Access to resources
Sources of funds
Expectations of return

Figure 2.2   The development of a strategic pathway.

through its portfolio of products and services, through to decisions about funding and expectations of returns.

When a company starts operating, its objectives and its portfolio of offers may be restricted to the reason for starting the company in the first place. The internet (dot com) companies have often been established on a single idea such as providing travellers with cheap flights, or providing a computer-based book shop, in the same way as computer software companies have been established in the last two or three decades based on providing a solution to a single business problem. These companies may have a single product offer or portfolio; their mission and objectives may be as 'simple' as being successful, or being the biggest, but they still have to work out a strategic pathway (Figure 2.2). Once they expand into more complex offers and once they have established their offers, the strategic choice is based around the present situation and whether to extend or reduce their offers.

Strategic pathways in the 'dot com' sector

Clickmango.com, for example, was established to provide natural health products by two friends who after working for other companies wanted to start their own business. They were lucky enough to do this at a time when investors were looking for internet companies in which to invest. They first met their investors at a 'First Tuesday' party, 'events that let a few hundred hungry venture capitalists meet keen entrepreneurs with ideas for dot com businesses. At that time we had no pitch, no business plan and no company name.' (Toby Rowland and Robert Norton, *Sunday Times*, 13th August 2000, p. 5). The following day they moved into an office in an old brewery in the East End of London; this cost £60 a week, had an area of 100 square feet and was equipped with only two telephone lines and two power sockets. 'The mice came free with the rent and would sometimes sit in on meetings.' They then wrote their business plan and started cold calling potential investors. 'We raised three million pounds in eight days ... nobody then had any idea it could be so short-lived.'

Six months later the Clickmango.com site was launched and the founders sought new investment. By this time, investors were no longer particularly interested in dot com companies and after 80 days of pitching for funds a new strategic pathway had to be identified. The one chosen was to cut costs, stop spending on marketing and most significantly to 'set the record straight'. 'We wanted people to know that although our survival prospects were poor we were solvent and we would continue trading.' As a result 'we received hundreds of e-mails. Traffic to the site had quadrupled and we are setting new weekly records for online sales.'

Clickmango can be seen as an example of a newly formed company established on the basis of a good idea and a single range of products. It did not have a clear strategy, although the hurriedly written business plan would have provided a strategic pathway in including a portfolio of offers (the natural health products), their positioning in the market (presumably cheaper than in shops), the resources required (the two founders plus expert assistance, an office and an established website) and sources of funding (the dot com investors) (Figure 2.2). It was when it wanted to generate new funds and to convince potential investors, old and new, of the expectations of returns on their investment that it found itself in difficulties and had to develop a new strategic pathway. Cutting costs and developing new products, such as personal health plans, was a part of this process. Many dot com companies have been started in this way with the growth of internet access. They have been based on a 'good idea' and have been supported by investors anxious not to be left behind by the apparent boom in internet shopping. In the UK this activity was seen clearly at the turn of the century, with the boom occurring in the last year of the twentieth century and the bust (at least in the case of some companies) occurring in the first year of the new century.

A television programme in the year 2000 offered £1,000,000 to start up a new dot com company. Ideas were sought, heats were held and, in the final, two companies won £1,000,000 each. It was notable that they were both based on having a clearly defined market, providing clearly identifiable products and services, and on a well-written business plan scrutinised by experts (one was to provide information to disabled people and the other to provide a one-stop-shop for school supplies). This highlighted a more general situation where, following the initial euphoria of investment in the newly developed and rapidly expanding sector of dot com shopping and information, increasingly investors began to subject these companies to the same scrutiny as other companies by demanding a business plan, a clear strategic pathway and expectations of a return on the investment.

When 'The Communications Company' introduced its computer-based solution to the problem of company internal communications, its Business Plan had the mission and vision of introducing this service into every major company in the country. The managers made a strategic decision in deciding that they would position their product so that the price of their offer would
(Continued)

always be slightly lower than other, non-computer-based solutions to this problem, and that this would be a selling position which would help to provide a competitive advantage. The main selling point would be the innovative nature of the solution and its efficiency compared with other solutions.

The resources they needed to support this service included a sufficient knowledge of the companies they were targeting in order to prove to them that they could solve their communications' problems. In terms of access to these resources, the Company had the choice of carrying out all the selling and installation of the software with the existing members of the Company, or of employing more people or using external consultants. In order to pay for these resources, funds have to be obtained through the use of existing funds or taking out a loan. Based on a relatively modest forecast of sales, the Company expected to be in profit within eighteen months, while a more optimistic forecast suggested half this time.

ASSIGNMENT

Consider the elements of the Business Plan of 'The Communications Company' as they have been outlined so far.

Once a company is established with a portfolio of offers, its strategic choice is based on the present situation and its expectations for the future. It has a choice between staying with the present offers or reducing or extending these offers, maintaining or increasing market share, considering price and value options, altering costs, considering access to both financial and non-financial resources, and in all this it has to consider its external environment (Figure 2.3).

Offers:	reduce	–	maintain	–	extend
Positioning: (in terms of market share)	reduce	–	maintain	–	increase
Price:	reduce	–	maintain	–	increase
Value:	reduce	–	maintain	–	increase
Costs:	reduce	–	maintain	–	increase
Resources:	reduce	–	maintain	–	increase

Figure 2.3   Strategic choices for an established company.

The Assistant Managing Director of 'The Engineering Company' considers the choices open to the Company as he prepares his Strategy Report. The Company produces machinery for five different areas of industry; in some areas there are a number of different machines or adaptations of the same machine, so that it has a wide range of product offers. With the help of the Marketing Manager, he starts to investigate the market share of each of these products and their price, and to compare the market share and price with the other companies in each market segment. At the same time, he works with the Head of Finance to analyse the costs of each of the Company product offers, with the Divisional Product Managers on the resources applied to each product and with the Chief Personnel Officer on the Company labour force.

ASSIGNMENT

Has the AMD involved the correct people in the Company?

Customer needs and market considerations affect all of these choices so that this aspect of strategic management has to be fitted into the context of marketing, the needs of customers and maintaining competitive advantage (Chapters 5, 6 and 7). Offer extensions are an increasingly important aspect of companies who look for incremental developments building on past success. These offer extensions can be called 'food chains' or 'offer generations' and take the form either of extending the range of a product or brand name or of extending the market for a product. A company with a strong brand name may decide to extend its range in the expectation that the success of the brand will promote the sales of the new sections of the range. Examples are the move of Mercedes into producing smaller cars and of BMW into four wheel drive cars. When Ladbroke acquired Hilton International, the Hilton name was transplanted to an extended range of hotels. There was concern that this might devalue the name in customer perceptions and that this could have an effect on the whole range, including the original Hilton hotels.

Market extension occurs when an offer is introduced into a market segment other than the one where it is currently positioned. Many companies have opened websites on the internet in an attempt to extend their sales to a new segment of the market. For example, Tesco has developed an online shopping service for customers who for one reason or another do not want to do their shopping personally in the Tesco stores. Some of these may be existing customers who find this a convenient way of shopping, but others will be new customers. If a product or service is not selling sufficiently well, a company may consider changing the product, looking for different market segments or reducing the range and number of goods offered.

Market positioning is often considered in terms of market share seen as a precursor to profits, because the two are seen to be linked. There are different views of exactly how they are linked, and market segments may be exploited successfully even though they represent a small part of the overall market. Large market share may be the result of success rather than the cause of it, however there is felt to be a strong link between the return on investment and market share. A company may aim to consolidate its market share and this will still involve improving the product in one way or another in order to keep up with competitors. Market share can be increased by either reducing prices or by increasing perceived value or by doing both; or it can be reduced by not enhancing the product and saving or reinvesting the costs of doing this.

The value of a product or service consists of the price plus the consumer surplus. The concept of a consumer surplus is used by economists to distinguish between the price a consumer is prepared to pay for a product and the price they do pay. Provided the price of a product is below the value to the consumer, it likely to be sold; if it is not, then a sale is unlikely. On a cold day the value of an ice-cream will be lower to most consumers at a seaside resort than on a hot day, even though the price is the same on both days. The weather has a strong influence on the sale of ice-creams in these circumstances and, in order to maximise sales, the price could be lowered or raised in line with the temperature. Alternatively, the ice-creams could be made more attractive on cool days by enhancing the product, for example by offering one or more chocolate flakes with every ice-cream sold. So long as the value of the product to the customer is equal to or above the price level, a sale is possible.

Therefore a company can increase customer value either by reducing the price or by improving the product. Of course there are many other factors involved in the transaction so that the consumer surplus may depend on a range of factors and situations. The actual location of the ice-cream seller, for example, may play an important part in terms of perceived value, a factor recognised by ice-cream companies in having many mobile selling units. At the same time there are a range of other influences on consumer purchasing decisions, so that an actual purchase will depend on the economists' idea of marginal utility as well as social and economic factors.

In his discussions with the Chief Personnel Officer, the Assistant Managing Director of 'The Engineering Company' covers a wide range of issues. The Personnel Officer is able to supply him with information about the labour costs applied to each product, the age profile of the people working in different areas of the Company, the changes that have occurred in wages over recent years, and some industrial comparisons. The AMD asks the Personnel Officer to collect more detailed industrial comparisons by industrial sector and particularly of competing companies. He also wants details of the skills of everybody working in the company, development and training programmes in operation and those which are thought to be needed. The Chief Personnel Officer says that the information is available but not exactly in the form that the AMD wants. The AMD asks the Divisional Product Managers to review their pricing policies for each of their products and to suggest ways in which their products could be improved. He also asks them to look into ways of streamlining their manufacturing systems and reducing costs.

ASSIGNMENT

What is the purpose of the information that the Assistant Managing Director of 'The Engineering Company' has asked the Chief Personnel Officer and the Divisional Product Managers to obtain for him?

The problem with increasing the value of a product or reducing its price is that it may put pressure on the **company's costs and resources**. If the demand for a product is increased by this strategy, the company has to access the resources to meet this demand. It may be able to do this through the economies of scale, that is by reducing unit costs as the demand increases. As the cost for producing each item falls, the company is able to produce more goods without increasing all of its resources. For example, it may use a production line more extensively, or it may be able to buy raw materials more cheaply because it is now buying in greater bulk. Another approach may be to increase the productivity of its manpower so that it does not need to employ more people. If economies of scale do not arise or increased productivity cannot be obtained, then the company will have to employ more resources and pay for the cost of these.

Obtaining more resources involves employing more of them or accessing them through some other approach such as out-sourcing or by redeploying current resources within the company. Out-sourcing involves paying for other companies' capabilities and by this approach making use of their assets. For example, many companies out-source specialist functions such as the recruitment of staff, relying on another company to recruit their staff for them and to provide all the services that this process requires. Redeployment within the company, or in-sourcing, will mean moving resources away from other activities, so that, for example, people in the manufacturing section may be moved into distribution.

Whatever method is used to gain access to additional resources, **funding** will be required. This may be in the form of company savings, or through loans or by using a range of means such as mortgaging the firm's property, or factoring so that money owed to the company is available at an earlier stage than before, or by asset management. In terms of asset management, the company can reduce its holding of stocks by moving to a 'just-in-time' approach so that stocks are available only a very short time before they are needed, or tighten up on trade credits so that more credits are obtained from suppliers and fewer given to customers.

2.3 Testing a strategic pathway

The consideration of strategic options in order to arrive at a strategic pathway is more complicated as the company adds to its portfolio of offers. One of the reasons for 'sticking to the knitting', as Peters and Waterman described it in

In Search of Excellence (1982) is that a company that adds to its portfolio by using its present capabilities does not have to access unfamiliar resources. In order to assess the suitability of a potential strategic pathway, one test is in terms of strategic fit. **Strategic fit is concerned with the match between an organisation's vision and objectives and its resources, with its environment**. Questions have to be answered as to the feasibility of the intended strategy in terms of whether the resources can be obtained and whether the proposed strategic pathway can be supported within the expected time scales. The pathway also has to be acceptable to the organisational stakeholders, whether they are primary stakeholders in the form of shareholders and financial supporters, the customers and the labour force, or secondary stakeholders such as the local community or the government. Although stakeholders may be mainly concerned with results, they may also be concerned with how these are achieved.

Any new strategy will be judged on how well it fits with the company's existing strategic resources. If new and different resources are required, this puts pressure on the company. At the same time, the new pathway has to fit in with the mission and objectives of the organisation – to 'stick to the knitting' – and it will need to fit in with the other offerings of the organisation in terms of the support required in order to maintain the pathway. New products will require considerable support in terms of obtaining access to resources, and support in increasing market share. These needs can be balanced against those of more established products which have access to all the resources they need and may have established themselves in their markets. The new products will need cash while the established products are generating cash.

'The Communications Company' has experienced a downturn in demand for its single product portfolio. It has considered the various options such as reducing the price and increasing the value of its offering, but feels that it has carried these policies as far as it can. It decides to introduce new products based on its expertise and for the first time it carries out a SWOT analysis and a skills audit of the Company. The SWOT analysis highlights the internal strengths and weaknesses of the Company, as well as clarifying the threats to the Company and the opportunities for it. The skills audit identifies the capabilities within the Company. (SWOT analysis and skills audit are discussed in Chapter 5.)

The Boston Matrix (see Chapter 6) suggests that products and services can be characterised by their position in terms of competition or their share of the market and in terms of growth within their market. While a commodity with a low market share in a static market (a cash dog) may need financial support, another commodity with a high market share in a static, mature market (a cash cow) may generate a high level of funds. Over a period of time, the position of products and services within this framework will change under the pressure of competition and changing market conditions and as they move

Stakeholder perceptions

Existing resources

Sustainability
  durability
  imitability
  resource and skills ownership

Acceptability
  available resources
  workplace attitudes
  risk management

Figure 2.4 New offerings.

through their life-cycles (see Chapter 6). Many products will start as 'question marks' or 'problem children' with a low market share in a growth market, and the company will have to decide on the level of support it is going to provide because these products typically require a large investment of cash while they establish their position in the market.

A strategic manager has to decide not only which products to support and which to dispose of, but also how to provide the best level of support for all the organisation's offerings. This will depend to an extent on how well the new offering fits in with stakeholder perceptions and expectations (Figure 2.4), with the existing strategic resources of the company and with a judgement, based on market research (see Chapter 5), about the future success of the product. One aspect of this judgement is the question of the sustainability of the product or service.

2.4 Sustainability

A strategic manager will be aiming to achieve a sustainable competitive advantage (see also Chapter 7). **A competitive advantage arises when the company receives a return on investment that is greater than the norm for its competitors for a period long enough to alter the relative standing of the company among its rivals** (see Chapter 7). This will depend partly on the durability of the product. It has to have a competitive advantage for long enough to achieve the required return on investment and preferably to enhance the reputation of the company. In due course, competitors will succeed in imitating it and technological advances and social change can shorten product life, but reputation can lengthen this process in the way that the Hoover company was able to maintain its competitive advantage in vacuum cleaners, long after competitive products had been produced, as a result of its brand image and reputation.

Sustainable competitive advantage will also depend on how easy it is for rivals to imitate or emulate the company offerings. The harder it is for competitors to copy a product or service and understand the processes used by the company, the less confidence potential rivals will have that they know how to produce a similar or better product or attempt to do it. At the same time, a potential competitor will also have to acquire the resources necessary to replicate the processes in order to develop the offering.

Competitive advantage can only be sustained if the company receives the financial rewards of this advantage. Where the resources, skills and other assets required to produce the offering are owned by the company, this is less of a problem that when knowledge and skills are owned by the individual. The knowledge-based companies have difficulty in holding on to their knowledge because it is owned by individuals in the same way as the skills of footballers are owned by individuals. When these individuals leave a company or a team, they take their skills and knowledge with them.

2.5 Acceptability

The suitability of a strategic pathway can also be judged against its feasibility and acceptability. A new business pathway will need the acquisition of extra resources, either by obtaining new resources or by redeploying those that are currently available. If the changes that need to be made to resources are great, the new strategy is less feasible than if the changes are small. This will also depend on how easy it is to access resources and how well the proposed strategy can be accepted into the company's present culture (see Chapter 8). The strategic pathway also has to be financially feasible in terms of the amount of funding required and how easily such funding can be obtained.

The new pathway has to be acceptable to the organisation's workforce. For example, if the new strategy requires team work, whereas the working practices have previously encouraged individual competition, the members of the workforce may be concerned about their autonomy and their ability to work in a team. A further factor is the question of risk management. Any new development has risks attached to it which need to be identified and assessed. Strategic management is involved in assessing risks and reducing them or limiting their effects, and at the same time producing contingency plans by allowing for events that it is hoped will not happen. Even the best laid plans may go wrong, so that, for example, the new London Millennium Bridge was found to sway dangerously when it was used by pedestrians, even though it was designed as a pedestrian bridge.

Crisis management makes it necessary for strategic management to react fast and use public relations in an appropriate way. One approach is CRUNCH (Figure 2.5). The means that a strategic manager should have a contingency plan, should then react fast when matters go wrong, use experts to present a convincing message, nurture the media if it is important to convince the public, centralise control so that there is one person or team in charge of the crisis, and emphasise the concern of the organisation for the crisis and its results.

Contingency plan

React fast

Use experts

Nurture the media

Centralise control

Human interest and concern should be emphasised

Figure 2.5 Crisis control.

The Millennium Footbridge across the River Thames had to be closed soon after it opened as a result of it swaying when large numbers of pedestrians used it. There was a fast reaction to this from the engineering company responsible for it, declaring that the problem could be solved relatively easily. Engineering experts were used to talk to the media and there appeared to be central control over the issue. The importance of the safety of the public was emphasised in seeking a solution (some months later it was announced that it would be some time before the bridge reopened).

2.6   Strategic decisions

The actual decisions made by organisations have been analysed to produce a number of guidelines for strategic development. Michael Porter, for example, in his book on *Competitive Strategy* (1985) suggested that there were three basic or generic strategies open to a company:

- Cost leadership;
- Differentiation;
- Focus.

The first, cost leadership, occurs when an organisation places the emphasis on cost reduction at every point in its processes. This does not necessarily mean that the company charges a low price, because it may choose to sell its products at an average price and reinvest the extra profits generated in order to retain its advantage. The second basic strategy, differentiation, occurs when the products of an organisation meet the needs of some customers better than others. When a company is able to differentiate its products, it is able to charge a price that is higher than the average price. This depends on a segment of customers of the market who will pay more for a differentiated product that is targeted towards them. The main problem with this strategy is that there are likely to be extra costs incurred in providing the product which may be difficult to recover from customers. Examples are better levels of service.

Focus strategy occurs when an organisation focuses on a specific market niche and develops its competitive advantage by offering products especially developed for that niche. In a cost focus strategy, the objective is to obtain a cost advantage in the target segment only, while in a differentiation focus a company seeks to differentiate its product in the target segment only. The problem may be that the niche market or segment may be small and specialist in nature, so that it could disappear over time. At the same time, there are dangers if a company does not compete in any of these strategy areas because companies that are achieving one of these basic strategies will be in a better position to compete. There are dangers associated with being stuck in the middle.

2.7 Market-based strategic options

This is based on market options (summarised as the Ansoff Matrix in Chapter 6). This not only considers the possibility of launching new products and moving into new markets, but explores the possibility of withdrawing from markets and moving into unrelated markets. A company may withdraw from a market because a product is reaching the end of its life-cycle (see Chapter 6) and there is little chance of reviving it. Or it may withdraw because of an over-extension of its product range which can only be resolved by withdrawing some products, or it may want to raise funds for investment in another product and may be able to sell the asset that it is withdrawing. At the same time, holding companies often consider that their subsidiary companies can be sold if the price is attractive, particularly if the parent company is trying to consolidate its holdings.

Market penetration is another market-based strategy which enables a company to expand without moving outside its present range of products and services. It involves both existing customers in an attempt to encourage them to buy more of the product, and new customers in attempting to convert them into buying the company products. Companies will look for new segments of the market, new geographical areas and new uses for its products. Product development is a strategy which companies may adopt in order to exploit new technology, to counter competitors and to protect overall market share. This process can move companies into new markets and towards new customers.

A company may decide to diversify into existing or related markets. These may be markets in the existing value chain or value system. The value chain is the contribution that each part of an organisation makes to the added value of the whole organisation, while the value system is the contribution of each part of the process involved in supplying customers with goods and services. This system can include raw material suppliers, manufacturers, distributors and retailers. Company strategy can be directed at enhancing the value of the outputs of each part of its organisation, or it may be directed at raising the value and reducing the costs of each part of the value system.

Companies may become involved in the activities of suppliers in forms of 'backward integration' or of distributors in forms of 'forward integration' or into areas of related activities in forms of 'horizontal integration'. The control of its suppliers in terms of design, quality and costs by Marks & Spencer is an example of backward integration, the control by car companies of their distributors is a form of forward integration, while the acquisition by BMW of Rover in 1994 was a form of horizontal integration. These are all forms of market-based strategic options which may also be part of an expansion strategy. These are structured ways in which companies seek to develop in order to meet their objectives. Acquisitions, such as Rover by BMW, may be made in order to move into a new market, or to take advantage of perceived assets or opportunities for introducing more productive production methods.

2.8 Resources-based strategy

This is strategy which considers the opportunities available to a company to add value to its products and services or to cut costs. It may be possible to add value early in the value chain, in terms of the procurement of raw materials and adding value to the production processes. Buying in bulk, for example, may be one way of doing this, or making few changes to the production process. Standardising products helps here, but may not add value further down the business process. At later stages, value can be added through research and development, or through advertising and market positioning. Motor car companies, for example, may add value to their products by lengthening the life of their models so that they can standardise the production process. They often attempt to extend the life of particular models by adding extras to the model, many of which may be largely cosmetic, and then advertising them as a 'special edition' of the model.

Product branding is also an attempt to add value. This provides a specific name or symbol to distinguish a product or service so that either it can be sold at a higher price or the reputation of the producer will help to ensure demand. BMW has branded a range of car and motorcycle models, and used the brand name when it extended its range of models into compact cars, sports cars and off-road cars. BMW did not use the brand name when it took over the Rover car company, but attempted to enhance the reputation of the Rover brand. The brand is not only about reputation, but also provides continuity and reflects a distinct formula. Customers know what to expect in a McDonald's restaurant in any part of the world.

Each organisation is unique in terms of its resources, and this is particularly true in the range and depth of its core competencies. These are the skills and technologies that enable an organisation to provide particular benefit to its customers. Unless strategic options address the core competencies of an organisation, they are unlikely to be successful. An exploration of core competencies is an important element of strategy development. One way of generating options based on core competencies is to consider them as a hierarchy of competencies, starting with low-level individual skills and rising though the organisation to higher-level combined knowledge and skills.

2.9　Strategic analysis

Strategic decisions are concerned with achieving an advantage for an organisation in the long-term. They are concerned with the scope of an organisation's activities in terms of what products and services it provides and which markets it is in. The search for strategic fit is a search to match the activities of an organisation to the needs of its customers, at the same time as identifying the opportunities available to the organisation and arranging the future of the company to capitalise on these. Strategic decisions are also about creating or building on or stretching an organisation's resources and competencies to create opportunities or to capitalise on them.

Strategic choices may require major resource changes for an organisation and will affect operational decisions. A strategy will not succeed unless the operational aspects of the organisation are able to support it, and it is at the operational level that strategy is implemented and competitive advantage is achieved. These choices are affected by the values and expectations of those who have power in the organisation; these are the stakeholders, including the workforce, the shareholders, the funding agencies, the local community and the chief executive. Leadership in the organisation will have a strong influence on the strategic options actually chosen, whether this leadership is provided by an individual or by a team (see Chapter 9).

Strategic analysis is concerned with understanding the strategic position of the organisation in terms of its external environment, internal resources and competencies, and the expectations and influence of stakeholders; while strategy can be seen as the direction and scope of an organisation over the long-term which achieves a competitive advantage for the organisation through organising resources within a changing environment, to meet the needs of customers and to fulfil stakeholder expectations.

SUMMARY OF CONCEPTS

Strategic models — Strategic options — Strategic pathways — Strategic choices — Market extension/penetration — Product value — Consumer surplus — Testing a strategic pathway — Strategic fit — New offerings — Sustainability — Competitive advantage — Acceptability — Crisis management/control — CRUNCH — Strategic decisions — Cost leadership/differentiation/focus — Market-based strategic options — Penetration/ diversification — Resources-based strategy — Strategic analysis

ASSIGNMENTS

1. What part can strategic models play in the development of organisational strategy?
2. How does an organisation make important strategic decisions?
3. What are the considerations that an organisation takes into account in deciding on its strategic pathway?
4. What is the purpose of strategic analysis in an organisation?
5. What strategic decisions have been made recently by an organisation that is known to you?
6. What strategic decisions have been made so far by 'The Communications Company' as a result of its market analysis?

▪▾ **3** Strategic options

OBJECTIVES

To understand the operating environment of strategic management
To analyse the importance of value chains
To discuss strategic resources
To discuss critical success factors

The operating environment – Value chains – The intensity of rivalry – Strategic resources – Organisational forms and structures – The learning organisation – Risk management – Operational and strategic control – Stakeholders – Critical success factors – Selecting a strategy

3.1 The operating environment

Strategic management requires an assessment of the organisation's operating environment and the influences on its success. Operationally an organisation performs a conversion or transformation process whereby it is adding value to a commodity or service. This means that the value of the output of the organisation is greater than the cost of the inputs and the process involved; so that, whatever an organisation starts with in terms of 'raw materials', the processes it applies to these add value. For example, a bakery starts with raw materials consisting of ingredients such as flour and ends up with bread, buns and cakes. The baking process requires knowledge skills and other competencies, used so that the price obtained for the loaves of bread exceeds the cost of the materials and the baking process. In the service sector, a package holiday company for example, starts by putting together a package of airline flights, hotel room bookings, and excursions and events organised by its representative; it then arranges these elements into a package which it sells to holiday-makers at a price that exceeds the cost of the various elements and the process of organising them. In this process, a hotel room is transformed or converted from a 'raw material' for the holiday company into an important element in a holiday.

There is usually a linked set of conversion processes between the beginning of the process and the final product, which together constitute a **value chain**. For example, in the production of a motor car, at each link of the chain, value is added to the product in the sense that the raw materials, whether they consist of tons of iron ore, body panels or a complete car, have value added so that the value of the output is greater than the cost of the raw materials and the process of conversion.

Steel foundry → Panel makers → Car assemblers → Distributors → Retailers → Consumers

Figure 3.1   A value chain.

Figure 3.1 is an illustration of a very simple value chain. It is a simple chain because each link is feeding only one other link and is itself only fed by one link. The steel foundry adds value to the raw materials it uses and passes on sheets of steel to the panel makers whose value is greater than these raw materials, including such factors as labour costs, power costs and transport costs. The panel makers pass on completed panels to the car-assembly companies with a value added to the sheet steel they received, and the car assemblers pass on completed cars to the distributors which have added value compared to the components which went into them. The distributors provide nation-wide advertising and other services so that the retail car companies are able to sell the cars. Finally, the retailers add value by providing customer services for the final consumer.

In practice, each link may be fed by a number of suppliers and may feed a number of outlets at the next stage. For example, at the car-assembly stage a company will need to receive not only body panels, but also tyres, engine parts, electric components, window glass, upholstery and so on. Each of the companies that supplies these products is involved in its own value chain and the car-assembling company may be only one of the companies that they supply. This means that there may be many different value chains merging into or coming out of the competitive area in which a business is operating. All the relevant value chains are part of the operating environment of the business.

Each link of the value chain is a competitive area or 'arena' or 'market', in the sense that there will be a number of competing businesses in any one area all undertaking conversion processes that satisfy similar customer needs. This means that the concept of the value chain is in fact far more complicated than the simple one depicted in Figure 3.1. In each of the links there are competing firms receiving supplies from a range of firms that are also competing and themselves supplying firms who are in a competitive situation (Figure 3.2).

Figure 3.2 illustrates the situation of one company with a number of suppliers and a number of customers. This company is in competition with similar companies and each of its suppliers, and customers are also in competition in their own particular area of work. If all these value chains and competitive areas are considered together, they can be said to form an 'industry'. This is in the sense of 'the motor car industry', which consists of all the companies

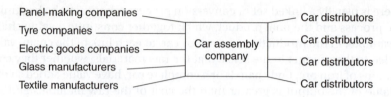

Figure 3.2   Example of a value chain.

responsible for converting raw materials into a finished motor car which is used by the final consumer. Companies may integrate in a vertical direction in order to control a number of stages or links in the value chain, or may integrate in a horizontal direction in order to control a number of links at the same stage of the value chain. An example of vertical integration is the control exerted by the Ford Motor Company over its distributors, while an example of horizontal integration is the merger of the Rover Car Company with Honda and (for a time) with BMW.

A motor car company will be in competition with other companies at the same stage in the motor car industry. In a wider sense it will also be in competition with other forms of transport, because the main purpose of a car can be described as 'providing a form of transport'. There are other aspects of the car which complicate this situation, such as describing it as a 'status symbol', which means that it may have other uses as well, but transport could be considered to be its main purpose. The direct competitors for any company are those that seek to satisfy similar customer needs, so that horizontal integration is a strategy to control a competitor. Companies may also introduce particular features into their product or into their pricing policy in order to attract particular customers, and by segmenting the market reduce competition. Some car companies, for example, target sales to businesses for their sales-people by providing discounts and cars with particular specifications. Competition will arise mainly from other companies with similar policies and not from the whole car industry or all companies in the competitive area.

In a similar way, a holiday company will be in direct competition with all the other companies selling holidays and will also compete in a less direct form with all the alternative uses for people's money, especially for the money they want to spend on recreation. Their particular competition will be with companies in the same segment of the holiday market, such as 'sunshine' holidays, or 'winter sports' holidays or 'long-haul' holidays. They may be in competition with other companies for selling holidays in a particular country or continent. Some companies specialise in organising holidays to, for example, South America, while others cover a whole range of holidays which they may segment by producing specialist brochures or by setting up subsidiary companies.

As in the example of the motor car industry, in the holiday 'industry' each link of the value chain illustrated in Figure 3.3 is a competitive area or arena.

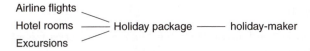

Figure 3.3   A service company value chain.

So that hotels are in competition with each other in particular places to find occupants for their rooms, airlines are in competition to sell seats on their flights and so on. They have their own 'raw materials' and will be supplying a wide range of people and companies.

The actual environment in which a strategic manager is working will depend on the nature of the value chain and the level of competition. It will depend on factors such as those described by Michael Porter in his five force model (see Chapters 6 and 10 for further discussion of these forces in different aspects of strategy) of the immediate operating environment of an organisation. **The intensity of the rivalry in the area** in which an organisation is working depends upon its positioning compared to its immediate competitors. If there are a few organisations of similar size in terms of market share, the rivalry will tend to be fierce; while if there is one dominant organisation, the smaller organisations will have to find methods of surviving which do not require direct competition with the dominant company.

At the same time, if it is relatively easy for a company to move to another market area when rivalry becomes too intense, then it will simply move away from the competitive area; but if the barriers to moving are high, the company will have to find ways of competing. For example, the channel tunnel and the ferry companies are in a competitive relationship which it is difficult for them to leave because there are no easy alternative uses for their main capital assets. Companies with wide interests, such as large corporations, may be able to move their assets from one area to another in order to take advantage of different levels of rivalry. Large corporations are in this position.

The Assistant Managing Director of 'The Engineering Company' asks each Divisional Product Manager to provide details of all their suppliers and all their customers. He also asks the DPMs to provide information on alternative suppliers and possible alternative markets for their products. The longest serving of the DPMs points out that they have used the same suppliers for many years and have been able to negotiate excellent terms with them over the years. He cannot understand why they should change now. The AMD asks him to collect the information and then they will discuss what might happen next. 'The Marketing Manager might be able to help you,' he says, 'he knows where to collect information like that and he has masses of contacts.'

(Continued)

Companies will try to differentiate their products in order to improve their competitive position, but some products are easier to differentiate than others. Car companies, for example, add features to their car models in order to make them different from their rivals, while with products such as bricks and electrical fittings there are standards and regulations which limit the degree of differentiation.

The power of customers and buyers is particularly strong where there is only one, or a very few, customer(s) and many suppliers. This is the case in the UK grocery industry where the top five or six food retailers control the majority of sales and are able to 'dictate' their demands to their suppliers. Companies such as Tesco and Safeway also purchase goods in large quantities so that they can demand discounts as well as require particular specifications in terms of size and quality.

The bargaining power of suppliers can be described as a mirror image of the bargaining power of buyers since they are part of the buyer/supplier equation. The suppliers will tend to be more powerful if there are few of them, since they supply in small quantities to many buyers and their products are differentiated. If there is one, or a few, dominant buyer(s) and the supplier's product is different from that of others and in demand, then the supplier will be in a strong bargaining position.

The threat from potential entrants into the competitive area will be greater if the returns appear to be high. If, on the other hand, the barriers to entry into competition are high, they may be deterred from attempting to compete in the particular area. New entrants may have to acquire new competencies which may be difficult to access, either because there are relatively few experienced staff, or because of the difficulty and cost of training existing staff. Established companies may have the advantage of experience in the area of competition, which new companies have to develop over a period of time. The new organisation also may have difficulty in accessing channels of distribution (see Chapters 6 and 7) because the present channels are well supplied and need very good reasons to alter their suppliers. There are also legal restraints on entry to markets in some cases, for example because particular companies hold the patents for some products or because of other factors. For example, the allocation of landing and take-off slots at airports is strictly controlled and it may prove difficult for a new company to obtain slots. Virgin Atlantic experienced this difficulty in attempting to obtain slots at Heathrow and at the same time British Airways has fiercely defended its position.

The threat of substitutes is an important factor for any competitive area because customers will usually be prepared to consider goods and services that provide better value for money than those available, provided the costs and risks involved in changing are not too great. For example, as computer games have become more sophisticated, users have been prepared to substitute one game for another. This is also true to some extent of computers, although here the cost of switching is greater. A prime example of this threat to established companies was the substitution of digital watches in place of the more traditional mechanical ones. The Swiss watch industry had great experience and competence in mechanical design and organising the production of high-quality mechanical watches. They were dramatically undercut in terms of both price and accuracy by the development of digital watches produced by electronics companies who were new entrants to the industry.

3.2 Strategic resources

The ability of an organisation to achieve a strong competitive position in its operational environment depends on how well its strategic resources support the products and services that are critical to its success within its competitive market. So-called **strategic resources of an organisation include structural assets, reputation, internal and external relationships** (Figure 3.4). **Structural assets** are whatever advantage a company may enjoy because of the structure of the competitive area in which it is involved. This is an advantage which has arisen in the past and is largely fortuitous. For example, it may arise because the company happens to be in the right location to obtain an advantage. **Location** has been important for example for government development grants, which have been paid from time to time to companies in some parts of the country rather than others. Other companies may move into the 'development' areas to take advantage of the grants but a company that happens to be already located in one of these areas may have an advantage.

Structural assets

Location

Reputation

Internal relationships –   process management

                              organisational culture

                              organisational structure

External relationships – clusters

                              information

                              alliances

Figure 3.4   Strategic resources.

The internet has altered the idea of 'location' for many companies as they have developed websites and been able to network between websites.

Dot com companies have used location in terms of the internet as a major advantage as a strategic resource, by moving the location of a product or service onto the nearest computer screen. Traditional companies have moved in the same direction, developing internet shopping sites and adding value to their traditional offerings.

The **reputation** of a company's products and services may have been established in the past and may provide an advantage with which it is difficult for others to compete. A reputation, for example, for reliability may carry over to new models or even new products. The reputation of BMW in motor cars has carried over to its production and sale of motorcycles. Where the customer is unable to see a product, reputation may be very important, as for example in the sale of canned fruit where the contents of the can cannot be viewed. Customers will often buy such goods on reputation, based on their experience of consuming products of the company in the past. Well-known car hire firms with a worldwide reputation may be able to charge more than local car hire firms because customers do not know how good the service provided by the local companies is.

Internal relationships between people and between the company processes and capabilities can provide a strategic resource. This is sometimes referred to as the internal 'architecture' of the organisation, although it is concerned with more than organisational or management structure. How the relationships between processes are managed is of vital importance, so that one of the main decisions that organisations have to make is how they structure and organise themselves. Companies organise themselves in different ways and have a variety of organisational cultures (see Chapter 8) and there have been a number of attempts to provide a classification of different forms of organisational structure. For example, Henry Mintzberg (1994) has identified a number of different organisational forms and other forms such as the J-form have been added to these (see Figure 3.5):

Entrepreneurial	J-shaped
Machine	Shamrock
Professional	Federal
Innovative	Triple I

Figure 3.5 Some organisational structures.

- **the entrepreneurial organisation** – typically with one or a few dominant managers directly controlling the operative labour force (such as sole traders);
- **the machine organisation** – usually a large middle-management controlling the organisation through standardised processes (such as car plants);
- **the professional organisation** – characterised by a large number of professionals and controlled by their knowledge and skills (such as universities);

- **the innovative organisation** – typically with specialist and highly trained staff, with control exercised through expertise and need (such as management consultants);
- **the J-shaped organization** – characterised by organisational knowledge and expertise, controlled by project-groups under a central hierarchy (such as Japanese industrial companies).

Mintzberg (1994) has argued that there are five basic parts of an organisation which have to be organised in one way or another (Figure 3.6). These are: the operating core which contains the people and equipment carrying out the basic work of the business; the strategic apex which provides leadership and the overall direction of the business; middle managers linking the strategic apex and the operating core; a support group providing indirect support in the form of security, building maintenance and catering; and a technical group providing support in the form of information technology, market analysis and product development (Figure 3.6).

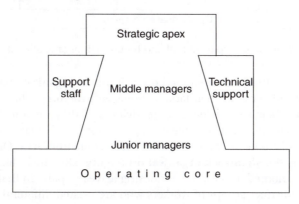

Figure 3.6   Mintzberg's basic parts of an organisation.

The entrepreneurial type of organisation is typical of the small firm where control is informal and strategy is based on the vision and drive of the entrepreneur. As the organisation grows and becomes more complex, it becomes more difficult for the dominant individual to act in this way. The machine organisation arises typically in mass-production situations where the environment does not change rapidly and there tends to be centralised, bureaucratic management. The professional organisation has few middle managers and a large core of professionals, so that while it has a bureaucratic management style it is not centralised. The innovative organisation is appropriate where there is a need to face new situations frequently and where the organisations is based on task forces and a flexible matrix structure. The J-shaped structure is based on organisational knowledge rather than individual expertise, and along with a strong central control the structure is based on project teams consisting of people from different functions.

The traditional organisational structure (Figure 3.7) is hierarchical with operational employees reporting to junior managers and supervisors, who report to senior managers. The structure is usually based on departments and divisions with an emphasis on line management.

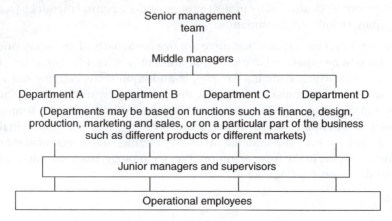

Figure 3.7 Traditional (departmental and functional) organisational structure.

Charles Handy (1990) has identified other forms of organisational structure based on knowledge rather than labour-intensive structures. They are able to add value from their knowledge and creativity, and they need to be flexible, learning organisations which are able through their internal organisation to face the challenges of frequent change in their external environment. One of these organisations is the **shamrock organisation** (Figure 3.8) which, like the plant after which it is named, has three interlocking leaves or parts in that it is composed of three distinct groups of workers who are treated differently and have different expectations. There is a small groups of 'core' workers who are the nerve centre of the organisation, running it and controlling the technology which has replaced, to a large extent, much of the labour force. There is then a contractual fringe of workers who are contracted to carry out certain tasks for the organisation. The third part of the organisation is a pool of part-time workers who have skills relevant to the organisation but who are prepared to work part-time. This structure enables the organisation to have a flexible response to changes in demand for its product or service while controlling labour costs by only paying for what it is receiving. Developments such as those in information technology, the increased popularity of 'home-working' and the demand for part-time work by housewives have all enabled this form of organisation to flourish.

The **federal organisation** (Figure 3.8) consists of a variety of individual organisations or groups of organisations which are allied together by a common approach and mutual interest in order to obtain some of the advantages of large companies. The **triple-I organisation** (Figure 3.9) is based on Intelligence, Information and Ideas, which form the intellectual capital represented by the core workers. Such a 'learning organisation' serves its customers as a result of its employees remaining at the leading edge of knowledge and skills. Management control is concerned with performance rather than formalities, and managers act as coaches, advisors and facilitators.

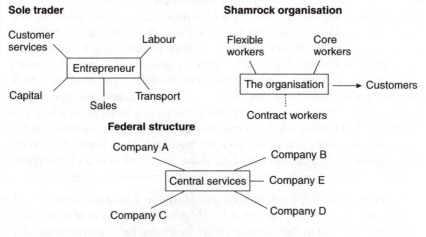

Figure 3.8 Organisational structures.

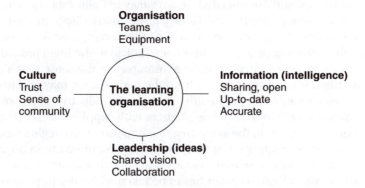

Figure 3.9 The learning/innovative, triple-I organisation.

The development of telephone and internet business has lead to new forms of organisation being developed which do not necessarily fit neatly into any of these categories but can be illuminated by comparing them with these forms of classification. Many of these companies have a central core of specialists and a large number of workers carrying out relatively mundane tasks such as telesales and distribution. The dot com e-commerce internet companies have seen a huge increase in entrepreneurial organisations taking advantage of new technology, while the demand for market information and research has lead to professional organisations and shamrock-type structures.

'The Communications Company' started as an entrepreneurial organisation managed and controlled by the founders who had the original idea (see Figure 3.8). As it expanded into a wider business-solutions company, it took on some of the characteristics of a professional organisation including technological experts and business consultants. Further expansion has required the Company to take on people on a contractual basis and as part-time workers. As new business has come into the Company, it has been able to call on the contracted experts to help in providing business solutions, while it has used part-time workers (mainly housewives working from home) to carry out market research on the telephone. While the company is developing some of the characteristics of a shamrock-type organisation, it has been approached by other companies to form an alliance or federation, but the founders are concerned about their autonomy and feel that they can compete on their own because they have begun to develop into a learning organisation based on ideas, information and intelligence.

External relationships can also be considered as a strategic resource. This includes the relationships that exist in 'clusters' in the sense of a number of companies all based in the same location. In towns, for example, banks have traditionally been clustered together in one area – the City of London is full of finance companies, and the so-called silicon valley in California is a centre for information technology companies. These clusters help to facilitate the flow of information between organisations as well as the development of subsidiary organisations providing products and services linked to the main industry.

These are examples of external strategic resources in the sense that a company established some distance away from the main cluster may find itself at a disadvantage. It may find it more difficult to obtain industrial and commercial information and to form strategic alliances with suppliers and customers, and also with companies in the same area of competition. Strategic managers need to consider developing the strategic resources required for an organisation's future development, so that a decision to relocate into an area which is well away from its industrial cluster has to be taken with care. Improvements in communication through information technology have reduced the importance of external strategic resources to some extent.

3.3   Risk management

In management terms, 'risk' means the same as 'uncertainty', in that a particular course of action can lead to a number of possible outcomes. To put it another way, risk is the situation where there are several possible outcomes and the probability of their occurrence is unknown. In deciding on a course of action in strategic management there is an attempt to assess the risks involved, that is the outcomes of the alternatives. All courses of action carry risks, even doing nothing. If a company decides to carry on working in the same way that it always has, the risk it takes is that other companies will innovate and overtake it. It could be argued that this is what happened to Marks & Spencer in the last years of the twentieth century, so that while it relied on its past reputation and continued in much the same mould as it had for many years, other companies in the retail clothing industry introduced new strategies in terms of such factors as price, design and the supply chain. Figure 3.10 provides a checklist of factors which may need to be considered in risk management.

'The Communications Company' was initially successful because companies wanted its product and services. When competitors began to improve on these, the founders of 'The Communications Company' were faced with two clear choices. One strategy was to attempt to build on its present success, and the other was to attempt to alter its product so that it would compete with the newer products. In terms of risk management, the company had a tried and tested product and it was confident about its capability to provide the services which satisfied its customers; while if it changed its product it would have to repackage and re-sell, and it would have to retrain employees or employ new people. It would also need more funding in order to bring about the necessary changes.

In assessing the risks, it decided that its strategy would be to stress the reliability of its product because it was tried and tested, and to find ways of encouraging customer loyalty.

Life-cycle – questions of growth and decline in terms of products, and product and service sectors

Substitutes – to the product and service offerings

Environmental factors – such as changing legal, social or economic pressures

Operational issues – in terms of capital resources, staff competencies and management skills

Critical success factors – identifying exactly what is required for the success of the organisation

Evaluation of 'worst-case' situations, contingency plans and consequences of strategic decisions

Ethical and pollution issues – and their effect on the organisation

Figure 3.10   Risk analysis checklist.

The financial aspects of alternative strategies are particularly important in risk management. Innovation and change involve investment in terms of such factors as design, testing and training, while 'doing nothing' may cost very little. The need for increased funding increases the company's 'gearing' and can be seen to increase the risk it faces because it has to consistently generate the cash to cover the interest payments of the loan. The gearing ratio of a company is the ratio of debt finance to the total shareholders' funds, so that any increase in borrowing increases the gearing of a company. At the same time, a company has to consider its liquidity in the sense that it has to cover its operational costs before payment is received from its customers, and these costs include interest payments on loans. If its operational costs are increased in one way or another, the company will have to finance these in some way and this has to be a consideration in risk management.

'The Communications Company' finds that its 'loyal' customers are increasingly moving to newer products or thinking of doing so, and realises that the strategy of 'doing nothing very much' (apart from re-emphasising the reliability of its product and service) has not worked. The founders of the Company decide that they have to turn to their stakeholders to provide fresh funds in order to develop its products and services. Although this will be a risky strategy in that the Company will have to generate extra income to cover the increased operational costs, it has now become clear that the present strategy, although it involves relatively low gearing, will lead to the generation of less income than before so that operational costs will be increasingly difficult to cover. The alternative option is to reduce the Company costs but, because it is a small Company based on the skills of its employees, there are few opportunities to do this. A cheaper location is considered, but the costs of moving and then of travelling once the move has been made do not make this attractive. Another alternative is to seek an alliance or even a merger with another company to take advantage of the economies of scale, but the founders reject this because they established the Company in the first place in order to manage their own business.

3.4   Operational control

The purpose of strategic control is to identify whether the organisation should continue with its present strategy or modify it in the light of changed circumstances. Operational control should assist the organisation to be both efficient and effective, and in this way help the chosen strategy to work successfully. The basic forms of control are concerned with physical systems, so that for example a wall thermostat may control the central heating system of a house. If the room temperature falls below the desired temperature set on the thermostat, the boiler is started so that water in the radiators is heated and the temperature rises to the desired level.

Many of the quality control processes within companies are physical control mechanisms designed to indicate whether or not a particular physical process is operating at a desired level of efficiency. At the end of a manufacturing process, for example, a commodity can be checked to see if it operates as it should. If it is rejected, it can be scrapped or reworked. It is obviously better to discover any faults at an earlier stage, and the usual method is to sample units of the product in order to check that they conform to the agreed specifications. Modern control techniques are based on an 'error-free' or 'zero-defect' approach and 'doing it right first time'. At a strategic level, quality can be built into the planning of the product or service, so that it conforms to design specifications and processes are introduced to get it right first time.

These process controls are also applied to people in attempting to assess those parts of their work which can be measured. For example, salesmen are subject to sales targets which may be in terms of the number of sales or their value. Double-glazing sales are often based on this system, so that the people employed to make the initial approach to households may be rewarded according to the number of sales interviews they arrange. The salesmen are then paid according to the value of the sales they make. In a similar way, the work of people in tele-sales can be monitored by a central control system so that the number of calls per hour or per day and the number of successes can be measured precisely.

More general control methods used in organisations to encourage a high level of efficiency and effectiveness in employees include quality assur-ance (QA) and QUEST (QUality in Every Single Task). QA supports teams of employees with systems and resources to help them understand the quality characteristics of their products and services and to undertake quality control. QUEST is based on the idea that every individual or group in an organisation is both a customer and a supplier to other people in the organisation; and con-siders how best they can meet the needs of their 'customers' and 'suppliers'. Key Result Areas (KRA) is a technique aimed at focusing on realistic outcomes for each team or individual by identifying a range of quality characteristics for the team which are consistent with the company's strategy, and then agreeing realistic standards for each of these quality characteristics and devising a system which can be measured and monitored.

Total Quality Management (TQM) is based on the idea that managers are so sure of their objectives, within a broad vision, that all employees in the organisa-tion have both a clear focus on their aims and goals and an understanding of the context in which they are working, as well as taking responsibility for work over which they have control. Quality improvement and accountability then become a question of peer pressure within the 'internal customer' framework, and qual-ity improvement is a responsibility in which everyone actively participates.

When it was founded, 'The Communications Company' brought together a number of enthusiasts who did not need systems or structures to monitor their work or to motivate them. They all wanted the Company to succeed, so that the only measurement that made sense to them was the degree of success of the Company. As the Company grew in size and more people were employed, the original team found that such levels of motivation could not
(*Continued*)

be taken for granted, and the importance of meeting customer needs when and where they wanted was not necessarily the top priority for the new members of the Company. The importance of meeting objectives had to be emphasised to new employees, and a Company culture encouraged to develop that ensured attempts were made to meet customer needs before all other considerations.

Strategic control can be described as 'the continuous critical evaluation of plans, inputs, processes and outputs to provide information for future action'. Controls are concerned with what has happened, but are also aimed at anticipating what may happen. The control of manufacturing processes by sampling and testing the products occurs after the processes have taken place. Control applied through the company culture and by quality assurance systems are attempts to provide a situation where problems are anticipated. For example, public relations is both about the quality of the relationships with customers and others, and is also about the way of achieving favourable relationships. Publicity and public relations attempt to maintain the reputation of an organisation and to enhance it, so that it is not just concerned with reacting to problems but also with encouraging an environment that enables the organisation to work through problems without losing its good reputation. For example, some motor cars have a strong reputation for being reliable, and when a particular car proves to be unreliable this is the 'example that proves the rule' in the sense that it is seen to be very unusual and therefore does not dent the reputation of the company.

3.5 Stakeholders

Stakeholders (see also Chapter 10) are involved in the effects of strategic management because the actions and the development of the organisation will result in change in their circumstances in one way or another. **Stakeholders can be described as individuals and groups who are affected by the activities of the organisation.** It can be argued that the most important stakeholders are those who have the most to lose from the organisation's actions. It is also important for an organisation to be able to assess the power of these groups to influence events and the attitudes of the most powerful groups and individuals.

Stakeholders include a range of people involved with a company:

- **the shareholders** – who own the company and receive dividends;
- **financial bodies such as banks** – who fund organisations in one way or another, and receive added value through interest or by other means;
- **the employees** – who receive some of the added value through their pay;
- **the management** – who receive added value through their pay and other benefits;

- **the government** – which receives part of the added value in the form of taxes;
- **the customers** – who consume the results of the value added to a commodity or service through the value chain.

The mission and the objectives of an organisation have to be developed taking into account the interests of the organisation's stakeholders. There are those who have to meet the objectives, such as the managers and the employees, and there are those who are interested in the outcomes, such as the shareholders, banks, the government, customers, suppliers and other interested parties. All these stakeholders are interested in the company and may want to influence its future direction (Figure 3.11). Some of these interests may be in conflict, and strategic management is concerned with attempts to resolve these different interests. For example, while shareholders are looking for large dividends and a rise in the value of their shares which may be achieved by maximising profit rather than long-term development and growth, managers may be more interested in the size of their organisation so that they can claim larger pay and benefits. Customers may be mainly concerned with the supply and distribution of the company's goods and services and their quality and price, while the employees are concerned with maximising their pay and the stability of their jobs.

Stakeholders	Expectations
Shareholders	Financial return
Creditors	Interest, creditworthiness, prompt payment
Suppliers	Payment, long-term orders
Employees	Pay, stability, job satisfaction
Managers	Pay, benefits, power and control
Customers	Supply of goods and services, quality
Government	Taxes, employment, economic growth

Figure 3.11 Stakeholders and their expectations.

In terms of strategic management the major issue is to identify the relative power of the various stakeholders so that it is clear which of them is the most important to satisfy. On the one hand, it can be said that for any organisation the customer comes first, second and third because without the customer the purpose of the organisation will not exist; on the other hand, there may be other stakeholders who if not satisfied have the power to bring the organisation to an end. For example, creditors have the power to close an organisation if they are not paid, and employees can bring a company to its knees by withdrawing their labour. Every organisation has to decide which are its most influential stakeholders and balance out their interests.

'The Communications Company' was started on funds from a variety of sources. The two largest cores of funding were a bank loan secured against the small terraced houses owned (although heavily mortgaged) by the founders, a government 'start-up' grant, with added funding for a variety of small amounts from individual friends and relations. The start-up grant was based on the original business plan of the Company with established criteria for success based on a six-monthly review. The Company knew that it had to meet the agreed targets if this grant was to continue, so this is a high priority in its operational thinking. However, it has discovered that these targets are negotiable and that, provided the Company is clearly developing and has a continued chance of success, the grant is unlikely to be withdrawn. On the other hand, the bank loan is not negotiable and the repayments including the interest on the loan have to be made on time. When a payment was not made on the due date, the Company received an immediate reminder from the bank and an attempt to renegotiate the debt was rebuffed by the bank. The loans from individual friends and family are each too small to threaten the future of the Company and by talking to the people involved there is little pressure for repayment. The Company concluded that its most powerful stakeholder and the one it needed most to satisfy was the bank. It was only when the Company began to find that it was harder and harder to sell its products and services that it realised that its customers were also powerful stakeholders. As it expanded, the Company also discovered that it was increasingly reliant on the expertise of its employees and that they were also important stakeholders. The employees are not unionised, but the most expert of the employees 'own' their skills and they are not easy to replace.

This analysis of stakeholder influence can be described as 'stakeholder mapping'. This process has to take into account the formal structure of an organisation and the informal stakeholder groups. The formal structure will show who are the large shareholders, what the union structure is, and whether or not there are some particularly important suppliers or customers. Informal groupings may arise because individuals may be in more than one group – they may be shareholders as well as employees for example – and because on specific issues different alliances of groups of stakeholders may be formed. For example, marketing and production departments may both be in favour of introducing market extension for an established product, but may be on opposite sides when a new product is proposed.

In terms of strategic issues, stakeholder mapping is concerned with how interested each stakeholder group is to impress expectations on the organisation's choice of strategies, and whether they have the means to do so. Strategies have to be considered in the light of these factors. Stakeholders will have more or less power to impress their expectations on particular choices of strategy and more or less interest in doing so. Their interest will depend largely on their expectations, so that employees will be very interested in anything which affects their pay or long-term employment, and creditors will be interested in anything which affects the company's ability to repay them. The power will mainly be concerned with how far they can affect the overall viability of the company. If creditors are a small part of the financial structure of the company, their power will be more limited than if they are a major part of it. Employees will be in a stronger position if they have a well-organised union and where the company is dependent on their skills.

The sources of stakeholder power include such factors as the structure and hierarchy of the organisation, how decisions are reached, the control of strategic resources and the possession of knowledge and skills. Shareholders may not be particularly powerful because there are large numbers of them and they have little knowledge of how the organisation is performing. Provided they are reasonably satisfied with the value of their shares and the dividend they receive, they may not seek to be involved in any other aspects of the company. A few large shareholders may play a more active part in a company and may want and be able to exert much more influence on its strategy.

Managers may control decision-making in a company through the possession of knowledge and skills or because of the established hierarchy, and therefore play a major part in establishing strategy; or they may have to consult major shareholders, or the main suppliers, or powerful unions before they can make any strategic decisions. Strategic management involves assessing the strengths and weaknesses of stakeholders and deciding how to negotiate with each group in relation to any proposed strategy. Some stakeholders can be brought in to support a policy, while others can be easily persuaded, and with others there may have to be a negotiation.

3.6   Critical success factors

Whatever the agreed strategic purposes of an organisation, strategic implementation requires the identification of those factors which are critical to achieving these strategic objectives, and the resources and competencies which will ensure success. **Critical success factors are those components of strategy where the organisation must excel to outperform competition**. Managers have to assess the resources and competencies which have been built up through the delivery of the organisation's current and previous strategy. There is a problem that managers will favour new strategies that use these resources and competencies, and not see any of the threats and opportunities which may arise as a result. This can lead to **strategic drift where the actual strategy of an organisation drifts further and further away from the strategy needed for success**.

In practice, it is essential for managers to analyse the strategic capability of a organisation in order to understand whether the resources and competencies fit the environment in which the organisation is operating and the opportunities and threats that exist.The organisation may be able to exploit its unique resources and competencies by taking advantage of opportunities and stretching these resources in ways which rivals find difficult to match. For example, an e-commerce company may have the expert and innovative employees to develop its offerings and to move into new areas. Although there will need to be a reasonable level of competence in areas such as office control and personnel management, these may not be critical to the success of the company, while information technology expertise and innovation may be critical and therefore they can be described as core competencies.

The Assistant Managing Director of 'The Engineering Company' discusses the structure of the Company with the Managing Director. 'What's wrong with the present organisation?' the MD asks. 'It has developed over many years, everybody understands it, they know where they are, who they have to report to and it seems to work.' 'I am not suggesting that we have to change it,' the AMD replies, 'it is just that as part of the Strategy Report you asked me to produce I am looking at all our methods and systems to see if they can be improved.' 'If it works, why change it?' 'Well, there is the question of communication up and down the Company and across functions and divisions. For example there is very little cross-over between the five Divisions. Even though the DPMs meet every so often, not much action arises from these meetings except to pass on grumbles to us.' 'Well what action do you expect?' the MD queries, 'we set them up as separate business units, as cost and profit centres, so what do you expect?' 'Some of the components of different products are in fact the same, yet they are produced separately by each Division or ordered by each Division in some cases from different suppliers. We could gain economies of scale ...'

ASSIGNMENT

Is the Assistant Managing Director of 'The Engineering Company' correct to raise the question of organisational structure as a strategic issue? What reasons does he have for doing so?

Strategic management is concerned with ensuring that there are sufficient core competencies to provide a competitive advantage, to identify performance standards which are needed to be achieved to outperform competition and how far competitors can imitate the organisation's core competencies. An organisation also has to decide how it will counteract competitive moves or potential competitive moves by its rivals. Strategic plans and operational plans can set out the resources which are needed or need to be acquired in order to be competitive. These plans can be in the form of strategic plans, budgetary plans and action plans. Strategic plans are usually medium or long-term while action plans are more short-term, but they will both include performance targets.

A critical path plan or flowchart is a technique sometimes applied to this process. **It is a technique for planning projects by breaking them down into their component activities and showing these activities and their interrelationships in the form of a network** (Figure 3.12). This process considers the resources and the times required to complete each of the activities involved in a project or policy and locating the critical path of activities which determines the minimum time for it. This technique is particularly useful where there is a clear start and end to a project, but the process can be applied to some extent to most plans.

Figure 3.12 is a simple example of critical path analysis showing possible solutions to the problem of an organisation with a restricted and expensive

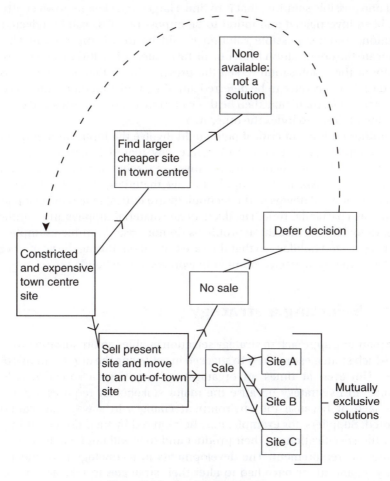

Figure 3.12   A critical path plan.

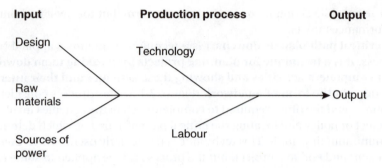

Input	Production process	Output
Design	Technology	
Raw materials		Output
Sources of power	Labour	

Figure 3.13   A critical path plan for a production process.

town centre site which has become too small and too costly. The chart shows that one possible solution, that is to find a larger and cheaper town centre site, has been investigated and found to be impossible. This can be rejected as a solution. Another possible solution would be to sell the present site and re-locate the organisation to an out-of-town site. This solution depends on the ability of the organisation to sell the present site. If this proves impossible, the decision may have to be deferred and the problem remains unsolved. If a sale is possible, there may then be three or more alternative sites and choosing any one of these excludes the other two.

Another example of critical path could involve the inputs and outputs in a production process (Figure 3.13). Here raw materials and labour are the inputs, there is a production process involving technology and people, and an output. Any break in the supply of raw materials, or staff illnesses and absences or breakdowns in the technology are critical in achieving a planned output in a particular time. The detail of raw material supplies and staffing can help to make sure that these problems do not arise. A simple example is the charting of staff holidays so that they are evened out during the year, or casual staff are employed when a number of workers are on holiday.

3.7   Selecting a strategy

The planning approach to strategy selection enables an organisation to evaluate which strategies are likely to succeed in achieving the organisation's objectives. However, at times an organisation may have a so-called enforced 'choice' in its strategy because the major stakeholder requires a particular approach or because the environment changes in a way that cannot be ignored. Suppliers, for example, may be required by their dominant buyer to alter the specifications of their product and they will not be able to afford to ignore this requirement. The developments in technology have meant that many organisations have had to alter their strategies to take account of the new technology in their environment. In large corporations, the strategy of subsidiary companies may be established by the 'parent' company, without any choices being offered.

Some strategies are incremental in form, adding a step at a time to previous experience. There is a danger in this approach that it becomes a 'do nothing' approach, which leads to strategic drift. **Gap analysis** can be used to identify the extent to which existing strategies will fail to meet performance targets and company objectives. Other ways of evaluating strategies include **ranking**, whereby options are assessed against key factors in the environment, resources, core competencies and stakeholder expectations. A score or rank is established for each option. This may show clearly that an incremental approach has a low score and will not easily achieve the organisational objectives, while other approaches involving various levels of investment in re-training, new technology and market choices achieve higher scores.

Decision trees rank strategic options by progressively eliminating others. For example, choices for the current business are looked at and some eliminated. One choice may be between growth and no growth; if growth is chosen as the essential strategy, then there may be a choice between high investment or low investment; if high investment has been chosen, there may then be choices between investment in technology or in re-training employees, and so on. The main criticism of this approach is that it is over-simplistic in looking for answers one way or another.

Another approach is through **scenario planning** where choices can be screened by matching them to possible scenarios. This is a 'what if?' approach based on possible changes in the organisation's environment. This leads to the formation of contingency plans in order to meet the requirements of each of these possible scenarios. For this approach to be useful, the strategic manager has to recognise the onset of the elements of a particular scenario so that the appropriate contingency plan can be introduced.

The acceptability of a strategy may be an important feature of selection. This can be assessed by analysing the likely returns of choosing a particular strategy, analysing the risks involved and considering stakeholder reactions. The returns on a strategy can be considered in terms of a profitability analysis in which there is an assessment on the financial return on investments. This considers such factors as how long it will take to receive a return or 'payback' on extra investment. Cost–benefit analysis considers the costs of a particular strategy, including both tangible and intangible costs set against the benefits received from it. Shareholder-value analysis considers the impact of new strategies on shareholder value. This is particularly the case when there are mergers and take-overs.

The risks involved can be tested by financial ratio projections in which the impact on gearing and liquidity is assessed and break-even analysis may be used to consider the robustness of the strategy. The assumptions behind a strategy may be tested to assess their strength, and simulation modelling may be used to consider the impact of a range of factors and the risks involved.

Stakeholder reactions may be crucial to the overall choice, particularly the reaction of the most powerful stakeholders. Stakeholder mapping encourages managers to predict the degree of interest of particular stakeholders in the choice of a strategy and whether they have the power to help or hinder the adoption of a strategy. At the same time, the organisation has to consider the feasibility of a strategy. This includes the assessment of the funds required for a particular strategy and the resources and core competencies needed. Any strategy that is chosen will have an impact on the operational aspects of the organisation, on all those involved in the value chain, its strategic resources, the organisational structure and its operational control.

SUMMARY OF CONCEPTS

The operating environment – Value chains – Intensity of rivalry – Benchmarking – Strategic resources – Organisational forms and structures – Learning organisations – Risk management – Risk analysis – Operational control – QUEST – Strategic control – Stakeholders – Critical success factors – Selecting a strategy – Gap analysis – Ranking/decision trees/scenario planning – Strategic options/choices

---

ASSIGNMENTS

1. What is the importance of a value chain in strategic management?
2. Describe strategic resources and discuss the importance of organisational structure as a strategic resource.
3. Analyse the role of stakeholders in strategic management.
4. Discuss the importance of critical success factors for organisations.
5. What strategic options face an organisation that is known to you?
6. What options face 'The Communications Company' at this stage of its development?

◧ ▼ 4 Strategic action planning

OBJECTIVES

To define strategic planning and to consider its purpose
To analyse aspects of strategic planning
To consider organisational mission, vision, objectives and goals
To outline the process of strategic planning

The differences between strategy and strategic planning – Purpose of strategic planning – Passive and active plans – The development of strategy – Types of strategy – Incremental strategy – Deliberate and emergent strategy – Mission and vision – Goals, aims and objectives – Structure of a strategic plan – The allocation of resources – The action plan – Monitoring the strategic plan

4.1 Strategy and strategic planning

In practice, strategic management is the implementation of a plan of action to move an organisation from where it is now to where it wants to be at a future date. However, in Chapter 1 a distinction was made between strategy and planning, in which **strategy can be seen as an on-going 'positioning' process for an organisation and strategic planning can be seen as a separate activity reviewed at periodic well-defined intervals**. Strategy involves achieving a competitive advantage for an organisation in meeting the needs of customers and fulfilling the expectations of stakeholders. A strategic plan may be 'an intended method' or a 'scheme for accomplishing a purpose' as the dictionary states, rather than 'a representation projected on a flat surface'.

In fact, corporate strategic plans are often 'representations projected on a flat surface' in that they are written documents, with diagrams and charts, and in some cases videos and computer disks. In large companies there may be special teams whose role is to produce a corporate strategic plan in conjunction with senior management, and then to make sure that it is implemented through a monitoring process. These corporate plans do, of course, attempt to reflect the strategy of the organisation and may be a very useful tool in the implementation of this strategy.

> Do you have a strategic vision, a sound knowledge of the market, business planning experience and the ability to work as part of a team? We wish to appoint a Director of Strategic Planning at our head office. The Strategic Planning function supports 800 staff in the achievement of the main aim of the organisation. As a member of the Management Team, reporting to the Chief Executive, the postholder will be responsible for taking forward the organisation's market strategy and delivering its business planning, including production of the annual Corporate Plan and Annual Report. We are looking for a highly motivated individual who can think clearly and strategically. You must be an effective senior manager with a proven track record in motivating staff and have a thorough understanding of corporate business planning procedures. Strong interpersonal skills are prerequisites for the post. We are offering a salary and benefits package which is commensurate with the senior level of the post.
>
> (Adapted from a UK national newspaper, 2001)

The question is: how close to or far away from the actual behaviour of people in an organisation is its 'ideal' strategy? Strategic management can be seen as implementing a pattern of behaviour, a way of doing things and a 'plan' of action. It is about decision-making and it is about planning in the sense of 'bringing together a series of decisions so that they relate to each other to establish the action to be taken'. The written strategic plan of the organisation may represent this 'ideal' strategy (but is not in itself the strategy) and may also indicate ways in which it will be monitored.

Managers may have a 'passive' strategy whereby they simply continue to do what they are doing now. They work on the basis of 'if it's not broken, why fix it?'. The problem with this approach is that an organisation, whether it is a company, a public institution or a charity, is working within an environment which is changing – and to cope with this the organisation does need constant 'fixing'. This is because other factors such as economic considerations, political policies and technological developments are not fixed, in fact they are constantly changing, while competitor organisations will also constantly be searching for ways to expand their share of the market and take customers away from rivals. Historically, with relatively poor communications and distribution systems, changes such as these were slow to develop and organisations were able to follow a reasonably 'passive' plan.

The Ford Motor Company in the 1930s continued to produce the Model T in 'any colour the customer wanted, provided it was black', while their competitors were producing more varied models. These met customer requirement more closely and the Model T lost its share of the market. Of course, the Ford Motor Company has flourished since those days and is still one of the world's major car companies. It can be argued that the 1930s policy was a 'strategic error' from which the company recovered. It was a relatively passive policy at a time when active strategy was becoming increasingly important. The Ford Motor Company has obviously been able to overcome this hitch in its successful progress and now follows an active strategy where its car models are often replaced well before they have reached a downward turn in their life-cycle.

An organisation with an 'active' strategy will have a 'plan' on which to base its decisions. This plan may be in the form of a written document, or it may be a way of approaching matters as they arise. For example, if a company decides that its strategy is to have a customer focus, this may be written into the strategic planning document and followed up by a training programme to encourage all employees to think in terms of providing customer satisfaction, or it may be implemented largely through the example of managers and encouragement to all staff. Whichever way it is implemented, the progress of this strategy may then be monitored by customer satisfaction surveys where customers are asked to rate the company on a scale of whether they are more or less satisfied. These surveys may be taken at monthly intervals and the results are analysed to see how far the strategy is working.

The problem with this process is that it may be too slow and too reactive, in the sense that the company should be anticipating customer requirements, not simply waiting for survey results to show a two or three month drop in satisfaction before any action is taken. Another problem with this approach is that the survey may not show exactly why customers are not being satisfied, or on the other hand exactly why they are satisfied. Even if the survey asks questions in this area, there may be a combination of factors involved which is difficult to discover as the result of a survey. These factors may include the product range, the price, the services provided, or many other factors which are found to give more or less satisfaction.

In the case of Marks & Spencer in the late 1990s, its surveys showed that customer satisfaction did fall over a period of months, but there were a combination of factors causing problems, including a general recession in High Street shops in 1998. Other possible problems for M&S that were reported were that the company did not accept major credit cards, carried out limited TV advertising, its supply lines were relatively expensive, and it had difficulties with its product range and with the presentation of its clothes. Although the company recorded profits of over £1 billion in 1997 and 1998, there was a 23 per cent drop in profits in November 1998. The CEO left the company in 1999 and there were further changes in senior management in the following two years. Major credit cards became accepted, product ranges were altered, product presentation was reviewed and a TV advertising campaign was undertaken under the slogan 'Exclusively for Everyone'.

4.2　The development of strategy

Strategy may be 'intended' so that it does indicate the desired strategic direction of the organisation which is deliberately formulated and planned by strategic managers. This **'deliberate' strategy is a systematic process of development and implementation**, but it does not necessarily explain how strategies are actually formed. Strategy may also be 'unintended' in the sense that the organisation has not planned this approach. When Honda entered the motorcycle market in the United States, it intended to sell its larger more powerful range. It was not very successful in doing this, but the small and much less powerful motorcycles that Honda company employees used themselves did become popular and a new and successful strategy 'emerged'. This is also an example of an 'unplanned' strategy succeeding where a 'planned' one had not.

Planned strategy – an organisation creates a strategic plan

Intended strategy – patterns of decisions that an organisation plans to execute

Deliberate strategy – the strategy that had been accomplished was intended

Imposed strategy – strategy imposed by an outside body

Realised strategy – patterns of action that have been accomplished

Unrealised strategy – when intended or deliberate strategies are not accomplished

Emergent strategy – where a strategy was not intended but emerges over time

Figure 4.1　Types of strategy.

'Realised' strategy is the strategy that an organisation is actually following in practice. There may be a difference between this and the intended or deliberate strategy (Figure 4.1) because although it has been planned it may not be implemented. However good the plan might have been, it may be decided by managers that it should not be put into effect, or there might be opposition to the strategy in the organisational culture which can mean that the plan is not in practice put into effect. Strategic managers have to take into account the cultural and political aspects of working in an organisation. The 'way of doing things' in any organisation is built up over a period of years and develops into a company 'culture'. This has to be taken into account in the implementation of strategy otherwise it will remain unrealised. The same is true of the 'political' aspects of an organisation. These are the power bases within the structure held, or felt to be held, by individuals and groups. If these are felt to be undermined by a new strategy, this strategy will be opposed (Figure 4.2).

　Strategy can also be 'imposed' on an organisation, for example government legislation or regulation may limit a company in one way or another. Monopoly legislation may limit the ability of a company to merge with another one; the competitive environmental conditions in the industry may limit managers' choice of strategy so that they have to follow similar strategies to competing companies. For example, a recession in the industry may cause all companies to cut prices in an attempt to maintain their share of the declining market. Public sector organisations are particularly affected by legislation, whether they are government funded corporations like universities and colleges, or representative bodies such as local authorities.

The development of strategy is most clearly seen in the distinction between deliberate and emergent strategy. One view of strategic management is that strategy should be developed by formulating complicated plans in a deliberate manner, and only then implementing them. Another view is that in reality strategy emerges over time and that organisations should make this process as easy as possible. The first view can be described as planning, while the second is incremental, that is one step at a time. Figure 4.2 illustrates the link between these perspectives.

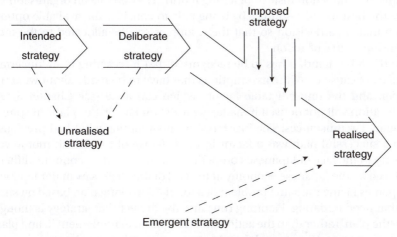

Figure 4.2   Forms of strategy (based on Mintzberg, 1994).

4.3   The purpose of strategic planning

Planning helps to make sure that the efforts of an organisation are deliberately co-ordinated and that managers and staff are not heading in different directions. It also helps to ensure that the future is taken into account, which may help the organisation to control the situation it finds itself in as far as possible and to prepare for unexpected eventualities. The daily routines and 'noise' of working may lead to medium or long-term problems being forgotten. Also, the process involved in planning can promote a rational form of management which can enable an organisation to acquire greater control over its development.

'So long as management is overwhelmed by the details of task performance, planning and policy will not occur ... that is, until what is routine is systematised and performance replicable without extensive management attention, management attention will necessarily focus on the routine. By the time of Du Pont and General Motors, the specification of task had moved from codifying workers' routine activities, to codifying managers' routine activities.'

(Mariann Jelinek, 1979)

The arguments in favour of planning (see Figure 4.3) are based on the view that it is the key to the formulation of strategy. At an extreme it can be said that anything that is not planned is not really strategy, so that a successful pattern of action that was not intended would be seen as a brilliant improvisation or a lucky chance. This view suggests that strategic managers cannot afford to rely on good fortune or skills at muddling through a situation. They should put effort into formulating a plan on the best information that is available and making whatever decisions have to be made. Plans, of one kind or another, give an organisation direction instead of letting it drift. They enable an organisation to make the best use of resources by being able to consider the available options before making a decision so that the resources can be allocated to the most promising course of action.

On the other hand, it has to be recognised that forecasting is an 'uncertain science', because of all the assumptions that have to be made about what will happen and the unpredictable factors which can arise (see Chapter 5). An organisation will not do well if managers insist on keeping to plans in spite of changing circumstances. The insistence on maintaining what had previously been a successful plan was a factor in the collapse of the British motorcycle industry in the face of Japanese competition. Ironically, the economic difficulties faced by the Japanese economy at the end of the 1990s saw major Japanese companies facing the same problem of a too rigid working plan based on strategy that need updating. Planning runs into the danger that strategy is thought of as 'the plan' rather than the action that is required to implement it, and plans may become so well accepted that they create opposition to change.

Advantages of planning	Disadvantages of planning
Co-ordination of work	Uncertainty of forecasting
Long-term thinking	Assumptions
Control	Rigidity
Rational management	Creates opposition to change
Commitment	Internal and external reactions
Key to strategic formulation	May be confused with strategic action

Figure 4.3 Advantages and disadvantages of planning.

4.4 Incremental strategy

It can be argued that the formation of strategy should not occur ahead of time, but arise from actively discovering it through action. **The formation of**

strategy by increments is a process of doing things and gradually blending together initiatives into a coherent pattern of actions. The process is one which involves sense-making, reflecting, learning, envisioning, experimenting and changing the organisation; it can be described as messy, fragmented and piecemeal. It is much more like the unstructured and unpredictable processes of exploration and invention, than like the orderly processes of design and production.

One of the Divisional Product Managers asks the Assistant Managing Director of 'The Engineering Company' about the progress of the strategic plan for the Company. 'It is not a strategic plan,' the AMD explains, 'it is an analysis of our present position and a look at possible alternatives in order to help us decide what strategy we should follow in the future.' 'So it will be a plan?' 'There will be a plan of action, once it is decided what to do.' 'I suppose we will be told about it?' the DPM asks. 'You have already been asked for information and any conclusions will be discussed with you. It is not as if we can afford to do nothing, we have to change some things otherwise we won't survive.' 'That's true.'

ASSIGNMENT

Consider the organisational structure of 'The Engineering Company' as far as it has been revealed.

This view of strategy sees planning as useful for routine tasks that need to be efficiently organised, but is less suitable for non-routine activities, such as doing new things. Innovation requires tinkering, experimenting, testing and patience as new idea grow and take shape. Throughout the innovation process it remains unclear which ideas might be successful and which will be disappointing. Therefore, strategic managers must move towards new strategies step-by-step or incrementally.

The idea that strategic management is about innovation suggests that it is a challenging process which questions the current state of affairs in the organisation, because creating new strategies involves confronting people's current interests and the organisational culture. In this sense, the formation of strategy becomes a disruptive process of organisational change as incremental, step-by-step changes are introduced. Strategic managers have to be 'organisation developers' supporting change and gradually moulding the organisation into a satisfactory form.

There are arguments against an incremental approach. One is that problems have not only to be analysed but also have to be interpreted, and they are linked to other problems. It can be argued that planning leads to 'paralysis by analysis' – by over-analysing problems before they occur rather than learning about them as they are worked through. This assumes a rigid, 'grand' plan which stands or falls as a complete whole. In practice, solving one problem will raise another one, so that for example costs may be lowered by reducing staff numbers but this will raise problems with the unions and with levels of production. In the same way it can be argued that planners cannot forecast other people's reaction to their plans, so that plans become outdated as soon as implementation begins.

4.5 The differences between the planning and the incremental approach

The differences between a planning and an incremental approach to strategic management are based on whether strategy formation is to be mainly a 'deliberate' process or more of an 'emergent' one (Figure 4.4). There is no single factor that can decide this, because the circumstances of every organisation vary to some extent. Many organisations do in fact produce strategic plans as a guide to their actions while at the same time not treating these as 'written in stone' but as a guide which can be altered if circumstances change. It is also possible that 'emergent' strategy can exist at the same time as 'deliberate' strategy to become 'realised' strategy, and provided that managers are not too rigid they can manage this situation. The implementation of a strategic plan is usually a step-by-step process with frequent reviews to make sure that the organisation is on course.

Planning approach	Incremental approach
Control	Interpretation problem by problem
Commitment	Muddling through
Long-term	Short-term
Grand plan	Step-by-step
Forecasting	Innovation and change
Organisation of activities in advance	Fire-fighting
Top-down control	Flexibility
Co-ordination of initiatives	Encourages initiatives

Figure 4.4 Planning and incremental approaches.

A plan is an intended course of action and it can be argued that without a plan of one kind or another, an organisation does not have a sense of direction and will simply drift, pushed this way or that way by the latest influence. So that while a step-by-step approach may be applied in practice, this is likely to be against the background of a plan of one kind or another. It may be a written strategic, corporate or business plan which is published and communicated both inside and outside the organisation, or it may be a general approach to problems which either emanates from the chief executive or is agreed by senior managers and may appear in written form only in the minutes of meetings.

Plans can provide a sense of commitment although, at the same time, this can reduce flexibility: they enable the co-ordination of strategic initiatives although they can also stifle innovation, and they enable optimum resource allocation and the organisation of activities in advance rather than 'fire-fighting'. Plans can also be seen very much as 'top-down' control, with ideas imposed on the rest of the organisation.

In the end it can be argued that the advantage of a particular approach depends on how it is implemented. If the application of a plan does in fact stifle initiative, promote bureaucratic central control, and reduce the ability of parts of the organisation to learn from their experiences and to make decisions, this is because it is being used in the wrong way. As a framework or a point of reference for the work of an organisation, a plan can be invaluable. A mission statement, for example, can be looked at from time to time to see if the organisation is drifting from its central purpose and the position can then be adjusted either by returning to it or by altering the mission.

4.6 Mission and vision

A mission or vision statement written by a company represents 'what it is about', it describes an organisation's basic purpose. It should encapsulate the purpose of the company and provide a clear idea of the business of the company, while being sufficiently vague to include all aspects of the activities of the company.

> Original mission statement: *The purpose of 'The Communications Company' is to develop and sell its software package*
> Revised mission statement: *The purpose of 'The Communications Company' is to provide technological solutions to business problems for the retail industry*

In the example above, the revised mission statement makes it clear that the company is not primarily involved with manufacturing products or selling products such as clothes or cars. It is about providing a service to business, the service of solving their problems, and it is narrowed down further by mentioning 'technological solutions' which are for the 'retail industry'.

In practice, mission statements are changed from time to time by organisations to reflect adjustments to markets and to competition. For example, 'The Communications Company' may find that mentioning the retail trade is not a true reflection of its work because it has expanded into other areas such as the public sector, or the leisure industry. The characteristics of mission statements are that they are brief, distinctive and wide in scope; they are 'short in numbers and long in rhetoric' in that they identify the purpose of the organisation without too many limitations. A mission statement answers the question: **'what business are we in?'**, and this requires the managers of the company to decide its basic purpose. For example, a company selling motor cars could describe its purpose in terms of 'providing solutions to transport problems', but this may be too vague for a company which sees itself as selling cars. It does not sell motorcycles, bicycles, lorries, buses or anything else except cars, and it may sell only one make of car. In these circumstances its mission statement will be more like: 'we are (or we aim to be) the best car dealer in the area (or country)'.

Mission statements can also be **aspirational**, in the sense that they are about what the company hopes to achieve. The description by British Airways of itself as 'the world's favourite airline' could be described as an aspiration rather than an established fact. The company hopes to become the favourite airline of people who book flights and shows the importance of its customers to this company. All companies have to decide who they are serving, what benefits they are delivering and how the consumers of their products or services are to be satisfied.

'The Communications Company' provides a service to its customers by solving business problems. It specifies in its mission statement that it will find 'technological' solutions in order to indicate the type of business it is in. Its customers are seeking the benefit of a solution to their problems and for them whether or not the solution is a technological one is not important; so if a customer decides that the problem cannot be solved by technology it will not seek the help of this company.

4.7   Goals, aims and objectives

Once an organisation has decided what business it is in, it can focus on its goals, aims and objectives. In contrast to a mission statement, **corporate or business objectives are precise statements of intent which emphasise the aims and goals of an organisation**. They must be capable of measurement, in one way or another, so that it can be shown whether or not they have been achieved. It is possible to distinguish between objectives, which fill out the mission statement, and goals and aims, which provide operational details, but there is often little difference made between the way the three terms are used. The objectives should be capable of translation into operational details that can lead to an action plan. They should answer the question: **'where do we want to go and how do we get there?'** Objectives are often expressed in terms of profit, market share, growth, the value of shares, customer benefits, company culture or a combination of these.

The business objectives of 'The Communications Company' are:

- to provide the best possible service to its customers;
- to continually improve the quality of its products;

- to be profitable by a focus on customer needs and providing better products and services than competitors;
- to promote teamwork by employees.

In order to make the objectives of 'The Communications Company' measurable, these overall objectives may be supported by more detailed aims. For example, customer service may be measured by the number of complaints or the speed of response to customer orders. The quality of the products may be measured in terms of competing products.

The aims of 'The Communications Company' are:

- 'The Communications Company' will deal with company complaints within 24 hours of receiving them;
- the aim is to eradicate customer complaints, and all complaints will be reviewed and analysed in order to achieve this aim;
- the company products will remain the leading products on the market;
- the profitability of the company will grow by 7 per cent a year;
- all employees will receive three days of training annually in order to encourage teamwork.

The aims and goals of an organisation have to be SMART (Figure 4.5). They must be specific and clearly and precisely expressed so that everybody can understand them. The aims of 'The Communications Company' are clearly about customer service, the quality of its products, company profits and company culture. The aims must be measurable so that it is possible to decide whether or not they have been achieved. The aims of 'The Communications Company' include an annual percentage growth rate, the aim to eradicate complaints and deal with those that exist promptly, the aim to keep the company products superior to those of competitors and a certain number of days for training. The last aim is difficult to measure and only by constant monitoring and review will it be at all clear that teamwork has improved. Aims should be agreed with those responsible for achieving them, sufficiently realistic for them to be achieved and timed with a deadline for achievement.

Specific	– precise and understandable
Measurable	– in order to confirm achievement
Agreed	– with those responsible
Realistic	– achievable
Times	– deadline

Figure 4.5   SMART objectives.

4.8　The strategic plan

The strategic plan of an organisation involves matching its business objectives and its available resources. The objectives, aims and goals of the organisation have to be translated into an operational plan and into action. The use of resources has to support the goals agreed in the organisation and these agreements will determine the priorities in the use of resources.

Figure 4.6 outlines the questions every organisations has to ask itself in order to carry on a successful operation. In a large organisation there may be a specialist corporate planning department which answers these questions in consultation with other departments. Corporate planners may create a system for ensuring that this process is put into action. In smaller organisations the senior managers are likely to be responsible for this function. Different companies and different management styles will mean that the way these questions are answered and who is responsible for answering them will vary considerably.

Mission statements may be created and written by the chief executive of a company, or may be the result of discussions throughout the organisation. Corporate objectives may be the responsibility of the senior management team, while the market research and the SWOT are the responsibility of the marketing department.

> 'I don't believe top management should be in the business of strategy setting at all, except as creators of a general business mission. Strategies must be set from below. (No, not 'from' below. Set 'in' below i.e. by the autonomous business units, for the autonomous business units.)'
>
> (Tom Peters, 1992)

Mission	What business are we in?
Business objectives	Where do we want to go?
Strategy	How do we get there?
Market research	Who are our customers?
	What are their needs?
SWOT	What are our strengths and weaknesses?
STEP	What are the threats we face?
	What are our opportunities?
Marketing objectives	How do we achieve our objectives?
Strategic plan	How do we match our objectives with our resources?
Action plan	What do we have to do to achieve our objectives?
Monitoring and review	How well have we done?

Figure 4.6　The structure of a strategic plan.

The senior managers will usually establish the overall purpose of the organisation and the corporate objectives, but this needs to be based on feedback from the monitoring process which reviews the results of the action plan. It is not impossible for a company to alter its overall purpose or its objectives. 'The Communications Company', for example, changed its purpose from a concentration on its one unique product to providing a service solving business problems. A real company, Fretwell-Downing, was originally a catering company that developed an expertise in information technology and shifted its main objectives into this area.

The strategic plan outlines the process of allocating resources in an organisation in order to achieve its strategic objectives. This allocation will be carried out at different levels, according to the detail of the action plan and based on the priorities determined by the strategic plan. Decisions in an organisation will depend on some level of market research, on an audit of the external environment and an analysis of resources, which are all aspects of an organisational audit and the marketing function (see Chapter 5).

4.9 The action plan

Action plans are concerned with turning objectives and priorities into reality; they can also be seen as **providing a mechanism by which senior managers can satisfy themselves that what is being implemented is consistent with the intentions of the strategic plan** (Figure 4.7). Action plans will indicate how resources are to be used, both physical resources such as money, buildings and equipment, and the deployment of people, including how many people are to be involved in a particular activity. Action plans can be as simple as a list of actions to be carried out by particular managers or other members of staff in order to achieve the objectives of their particular area of the organisation.

A telesales operative, for example, may have a list of telephone numbers to work through in a day, while the telesales manager has a similar, although larger, list to divide up between all the operatives. In addition to the telephone numbers, the list is likely to include targets for the telesales unit as a whole and for each individual operative. These targets may be in the form of a certain number of 'hits' in a day or in a given number of telephone calls. 'Hits' may mean different things in different circumstances, but will include favourable responses from the people being telephoned. Returning to double-glazing (!), a 'hit' or successful outcome from a particular number of telephone calls could be agreement to a salesman visiting the home of the people being telephoned for a 'free estimate, without obligation'.

Even this apparently 'simple' action plan includes a means of control in the form of targets. A telesales operative who falls well below the target that has been set may not last very long in the job, while the one who achieves above target may be rewarded in some way.

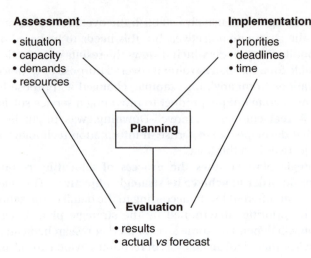

Figure 4.7 The planning process.

More complex action plans may be produced for a whole function in an organisation, such as for finance production or marketing. Long-term plans, policies or procedures may be produced to establish guidelines for recurring activities. Project plans can also be described as action plans produced on a one-off basis in order to control specific programmes of work. It is possible to look at the work situation as a series of projects, each planned in order to control specific programmes of work and operating within policy guidelines. These project plans can be imposed on individuals or on teams or groups, or agreed with them, and contain actions that keep within the functional plans and policies established by corporate managers in order to achieve corporate objectives.

4.10   Monitoring the strategic plan

Strategic management is not about producing a strategic plan although it may involve producing one, and when this is the case it also involves making sure that the plan works. In order to do this, there has to be a monitoring system. **The monitoring process provides the loop back to all stages of the strategic plan and prompts constant reminders that change and improvement are constant features of organisational life**.

The looping-back process can be seen as promoting an upward spiral as a result of improved market information, better systems for competitor analysis, and increasingly efficient and effective use of resources. Detailed monitoring is carried out by establishing targets, for individuals, teams, departments, functional areas and for the whole organisation, which can be measured. In the 1950s and 1960s there was a view that everything worthwhile could be measured:

> 'When I first started in industry in the fifties, attractions of work measurement and method study as a means of improving productivity seemed almost like a philosopher's stone.'
>
> (John Harvey-Jones, 1993)

In the setting of targets and measured incentive programmes in business and the introduction of league tables in schools and universities, measurement has become popular again over the last decade. In certain areas of work, establishing targets which can be measured is relatively easily, while in others it is more difficult and targets have to be less precise. In all circumstances, measurement has to be applied with care. It is relatively easy to establish targets in a telesales office, but if measurement is applied too crudely it can be counter-productive. For example, the number of telephone calls may be taken as the main measure of an operative's efficiency, while the number of 'hits' could be a better test. An operative who makes relatively few calls but ends up with more successful ones may in fact be the most productive. The use of league tables for schools has been criticised on the grounds that they are mainly about results in the form of examination passes and do not take sufficient account of the achievements of pupils when they start at the school compared with their achievements when they leave. A school whose pupils at entry have a very low level of achievement may do more to improve that achievement than a school whose entry has a high achievement level, but where examination results are better.

In some areas, measurement of any direct kind may be difficult. For example, direct measurement of the design department's work may only be possible over a long time-period when the sales figures for the products are available. Even then it may be difficult to know how much of the success or failure of a product to attribute to design, and how much to other factors such as the skills of the marketing or sales departments, or changes in competition. The management of quality, through quality control and total quality management, is an important aspect of the monitoring process, and measurement can be a mixture of precise quantities and less precise quality factors.

The strategic plan can be monitored by reviewing it in terms of the match between what has actually happened and what was planned. It can then be revised and altered in response to this match and to the changing environment in which the organisation is working. In a successful organisation this should be an upward spiral, with rising aspirations for success. Strategic managers will have to consider business objectives and goals in response to changes as market research identifies new customers or new needs for existing as well as potential customers, while marketing objectives will be considered in response to the clarification of threats and opportunities. As strategy develops the strategic plan will have to be revised and altered to keep up with it.

ASSIGNMENTS

1. Discuss the differences between strategy and strategic planning and the purpose of strategic planning.
2. What are the differences between active and passive plans?
3. Analyse the development of strategy.
4. Collect and comment on the mission statements of different companies.
5. What are the organisational objectives of an organisation that is known to you?
6. What are the objectives of 'The Communications Company'?
7. Consider the strategic development of 'The Engineering Company' in relation to the different types of strategy.

▼ 5 Strategic marketing

OBJECTIVES

To define and explain strategic marketing
To understand the differences between marketing and selling
To consider the concept of 'customer benefits'
To analyse the nature of customers and the process of satisfying customer needs
To discuss the use of market research in developing strategy

Definition of marketing – Comparison between marketing and selling – Customer satisfaction – Customer benefits – Identifying the customer – Knowing the customer – Identifying customer needs – Marketing research – Forecasting – The marketing process – Strategic marketing

5.1 What is marketing?

Marketing is now defined in terms of satisfying the needs of customers, whereas at one time there was more of a concentration on technical excellence, costs and prices. This was **a product-orientated** view of marketing in which companies thought that if they produced an excellent product at an affordable price, it would sell. This worked well when competition was limited, when the product was well known to customers and they wanted it. At that time, marketing was hardly recognised as a separate function to production in these circumstances, because the focus was on producing a commodity for which there was an obvious demand.

As the range of manufactured products increased and competition both for a share of people's expenditure and between similar products became an important feature of the economy, **a sales-orientation** became more important. This was based on the need to interest potential customers in existing products and in particular examples of these products. Today, although quality and sales play an important part in the process, **a customer-orientation** has taken over in terms of marketing, based on determining the needs of customers and satisfying them.

'Marketing is the whole business seen from the point of view of its final results, that is from the customer's point of view.'

(Peter Drucker, 1992)

This shift of orientation has been combined with the much greater importance marketing has assumed in companies, from a situation where it was barely recognised as a separate activity, to becoming a second-tier activity below finance and production, to being the integrating force represented at the top of organisational structures.

Some organisations are very **market-orientated**, with the marketing function at the centre of their structures integrating the work of all the other functions. Other organisations treat marketing as a less important function, perhaps as a part of the sales department. This is partly related to the industry that the organisation is in, its position in this industry and to its leadership and management style. An innovative company with a product that 'sells itself' will have little need of marketing, while a company in a highly competitive situation will tend to place marketing at the centre of its structure if it is to survive. Companies (such as 'The Communications Company') may move from a situation where marketing is not very important when they are new and innovative, to a situation where marketing becomes essential because of the growth of competition.

'Marketing is the management process responsible for identifying, anticipating and satisfying customer requirements profitably.'

(The Chartered Institute of Marketing)

The importance of the customer is emphasised in this definition and it amplifies Drucker's definition in recognising that customer wants are not only identified in marketing but also anticipated and satisfied. In fact there are few organisations that are able to ignore the needs of their 'customers'. Even in the public sector and the non-profit sector, particularly in recent years, many organisations have developed a marketing function in order to improve their effectiveness.

There is evidence that the UK National Lottery has drawn money away from donations to charities. A proportion of the lottery money is passed on to good causes and this encourages potential donors to feel that charities are well funded from this source. As a result, charities have had to increase their efforts in raising money and to find new sources of funds. This has involved using marketing techniques common in the private sector, such as newspaper and television advertising, mailing lists and sponsorship.

The Assistant Managing Director of 'The Engineering Company' arranges a meeting with the Marketing Manager. 'As you know,' he says, 'I am analysing the strategy of the Company, looking into all aspects of how we function. When I ask anybody who has been here a few years about improvements to the way we work, they tend to reply by asking what is wrong and they are doing the best they can. I think that "the devil is in the detail" in that nobody can see any problems because they have not unpicked the whole operation to see how it works and whether it could work better.' 'You know that I have had difficulty in persuading people that marketing is part of everybody's job,' the Marketing Manager observes. 'Yes, and we must change that,' the AMD agrees, 'what I want you to do is to provide me with the information I need. I know you are having difficulty keeping up with my demands so I have agreed with the MD that you should employ someone to help you.' 'That would be a great help. I simply have not been able to collect and put into a useful form the data you want; not only the competitor analysis and other external information, but also data about our customer care and customer service.'

In the public sector, government legislation has altered the position of organisations so that there are increased levels of competition. This has happened, for example, in the health service to some extent and through the funding mechanisms in education in universities and colleges, and even charities are in competition with each other for donations. Charities are also in a wider sense in competition for people's money, in that there are a whole range of calls on people's spending, and charities have to compete for the attention of the consumer with other goods and services. **Strategic marketing is about moving the organisation from its present position to a more competitive one where it has a competitive advantage.**

5.2 What is selling?

While marketing can be seen as the whole process involved in satisfying the needs and wants of people, selling can be seen as the culmination of this process. At the point of sale, customers move from a situation where they want a product or service to actually purchasing it (Figure 5.1). There will be some products and services which customers will actively seek out with very little prompting, but usually this is not the case.

The nearer goods and services are to this ideal position, the easier they will sell. So the more closely they match customer needs, the more likely they are to 'sell themselves'. The further away goods and services are from this 'ideal', the more skill is required in selling them. 'Selling snow to Eskimos' is a difficult process, equalled by the difficulty of 'selling sand in the Sahara'! If a company produces the right goods, at the right price and they are available at the right time and place, selling them is unlikely to be a problem. If customers are not sure that the goods are right, or that their price is right, or that they are available at the right time and place, selling these goods will be a problem.

Marketing	**Selling**
Who are the customers?	How can customers be persuaded to exchange their money for the organisation's products and services?
What do they want?	
Does the organisation produce the commodities or services to satisfy their wants?	How can agreement be reached on this exchange?
If not, what changes need to be made?	
What price will meet the requirements of the customers and the organisation?	

Figure 5.1   Marketing and selling.

Double-glazing window salesmen are notorious for their 'hard sell', perhaps because they have products which are hard to sell. The double-glazing market is highly competitive, and there are differences in the products, but it may be difficult to convince potential customers that these differences are important. At the same time, double-glazing may be desirable for the customer but usually it is not essential and customers can put off buying it. It is seldom bought because a customer's present windows are falling out.

The salesman's task, in an example like double-glazing, is to convince the customer that the product in front of them is the best available, that the price is a bargain which the customer can afford and that the product has a range of benefits.

5.3   How are customers satisfied?

Customer benefits are at the root of marketing and selling because, in order to satisfy their needs, customers are not so much looking for particular products and services, they are looking for the benefits that these may be able to provide. For example, customers may be looking for the benefits of a warm house which is cheaper to heat than at present. Double-glazing will provide these benefits, but if there was some other method of providing these benefits that was more attractive and cheaper, double-glazing would be even more difficult to sell.

Double-glazing salesmen will outline a range of benefits to customers, hoping that one of them will 'make the sale' or 'clinch the deal'. As well as reducing draughts and providing greater comfort levels, double-glazing can be said to reduce noise levels, reduce the need for maintenance, increase security and improve the appearance of the house. The last thing the salesman will mention is the price, because in no way can this be considered to be a benefit. The price from the customer's viewpoint is a cost to be weighed against the benefits conferred by the product. The salesman will attempt to reinforce the importance of the benefits to the customer and obtain the agreement of the customer about the quality of the product and the benefits it will confer, before mentioning the price.

When the salesman does eventually come to the price, there will be an attempt to mention a price that the customer can afford, such as the monthly repayment on a finance agreement. The total price for all the windows and doors in a house may have to be dragged from the salesman as though a tooth is being extracted.

Putting the satisfaction of customer needs at the root of the marketing process emphasises that companies should be producing what can be sold, not selling what they can make. In order to survive and prosper a company has to produce what people want to buy, rather than producing goods and then attempting to sell them. This does not stop managers attempting to anticipate customer demands, but they need first of all to determine the demands and wants of their target market, and the benefits people want or will want to satisfy. **The marketing approach starts with the needs of the target customers, while the selling approach starts with the existing product and searches for ways of promoting it to achieve profitable sales**.

5.4 Who is the customer?

The obvious answer to this question is that the customer is the person who pays for the product or service, and it is possible to define the customer in these terms. The customer of any organisation can also be described as the 'end user' of its products or services, the person who receives benefits from them. This is often the person who pays. However this is not always the case, because someone who is not the end user may pay.

For example, children's products tend to be bought by adults and then given to children, so that even though the adult pays for the toys or clothes or sweets, the child is still the end user, the person who makes use of the product and 'consumes' it. The same position is of course true of any situation where a commodity or service is bought by one person and given to another, that is where there is a difference between the person who pays and the person who consumes.

In these circumstances, from the viewpoint of strategic marketing, both of these people are customers; so that, for example, the adult buying a toy for a child is a customer in the sense of wanting to buy the toy and obtaining satisfaction from buying it even though, or even because, it will then be given to a child. In order to be successful the toy will have to satisfy the needs of both the adult and the child, and confer benefits on both of them. This illustrates the fact that there are different types or levels of customer. For example, if a commodity is manufactured by one company, sold to another wholesale company, and then to a retailer before being sold to a consumer, each of these (the wholesaler, retailer and consumer) are consumers. They all use the product after it has been produced, although for different purposes, and they all receive benefits from it.

This view of the customer as the people who receive benefits from a product or service is the other side of the coin to the view that a product or service should satisfy customer needs if it is to be successful. In some cases there is not a direct payment involved in a transaction. In the public sector, for example, payment may be indirect through the taxation or national insurance system. In the National Health Service, there are many services for which a direct payment is not made and in these circumstances the 'customer' is the person who benefits from the service. This is true also of other public sector areas such as education and local government services. Schools, for example, have two types of 'customer' – the school children and their parents. Both of these groups receive benefits from the services provided by the school and although they may not be called customers, from a marketing point of view that is what they are.

The public sector is not necessarily comfortable with such commercial terms as 'customer' and would prefer to call parents and pupils 'stakeholders' or 'people with interests in the development of the school', or simply 'parents' and 'pupils'. Other terms used instead of 'customer' are client, consumer, patients (in hospitals) and so on. Where marketing exists in the public sector, there is a growing tendency to use the term customer even if it is only in the marketing department.

Voluntary sector organisations, such as charities, also have to identify their customers, or the people who receive benefits from their activities. Again there are at least two groups of people in this category – the people who receive the services of the charity and also the people who donate to the charity. The first group receive benefits from the service, while the donors receive less tangible benefits in the form of the satisfaction they have from contributing to a good cause. In the public and voluntary sectors, terms are used such as 'patient care programmes', 'student services' and 'information and support services', and these services are part of the process of satisfying needs and can be considered to be part of a marketing strategy.

In all organisations, public or private, there is a 'circular' or 'spiral type' relationship between the organisation and its customers (Figure 5.2). The organisation produces products and services which are bought by customers and the money obtained from these sales is recycled into the provision of more products and services. In the private sector, payment for goods and services is direct and a proportion of the sales revenue is siphoned off into profits for the owners and shareholders. In the public sector, income is obtained directly or indirectly from central or local government through grants, fees and subsidies. Instead of profits, public sector organisations may have surpluses which may be added to their budgets.

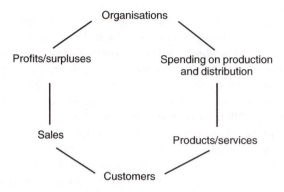

Figure 5.2 Organisations and customers.

5.5 Knowing the customer

In order to understand the 'end users' of their products and services, organisations need to be clear about what business they are in. This may appear, and in fact be, obvious in some organisations. A car showroom is in the business of selling cars, but even though this is obvious the question still arises: to whom are they selling? Is the company hoping to sell to anybody who wants to buy a car, or is it selling to a particular group of car buyers? Groups of buyers may be determined by their income levels, or by whether they want new or second hand cars, or by family as against business buyers and so on.

Unless the company identifies which of these groups it wants to serve, it will not be able to concentrate its efforts on this group's needs. Once it has established its target group, it is able to find out about their needs and meet them. It can stock the cars which are likely to appeal to target customers because they meet their needs, it can establish financial services to support that particular group, and support services and customer care services for that group. The company can find out what influences its customers' purchasing decisions, the amount of money they have to spend, their style of living and their aspirations. This is the process of becoming 'customer-centred'. Once the company knows what business it is in, it is beginning to identify marketing as an essential element of strategy because **the company is viewing its business from the position of its final customer**.

5.6 What do customers want?

In order to find out what customers want, companies carry out market research. This may be of a very limited kind with the company more or less guessing what its customers want or leaving it to trial and error. Small firms may have little choice other than to try out goods or services and wait to see if there is a demand for them.

The Marketing Manager of 'The Engineering Company' uses his new Assistant to carry out a customer survey. First the Assistant talks to people in the Product Division about their customers, asking how long they have been supplying them, how the customer demands have changed over this period and how satisfied the customer appears to be. Then the Assistant visits the customers and asks them about the products they have received, their relationship with the Company, how they find the Company as a supplier and the quality of after-sales service. The most experienced Divisional Product Manager complains to the Marketing Manager and then to the Assistant Managing Director that the Marketing Assistant is interfering with the work of the Division, 'making waves' and 'treading on toes.' 'The Marketing Assistant is simply collecting information,' the AMD tells the DPM, 'apparently the Marketing Manager talked to you about the information he needed and you told him that you did not have time to provide it and you asked him what it had to do with marketing. He came to you because you and your staff are the experts in this area of industry and only you can talk in detail about what our customers want. What we have to do is to make sure that we provide what they actually need, not just think they want. We have to be ahead of the field.' 'We work to specifications that they set, what more can we do?'

ASSIGNMENT

Consider why a customer survey is being carried out and the form it might take.

Small shops may introduce new lines to see if they sell or not. Newsagents may stock flowers as a new offering to customers alongside the newspapers and confectionery that they normally sell and wait to see what happens. Larger companies can afford to be more systematic in their approach and in fact may not be able to afford not to be well organised, because this is the only way they can find out their customers' needs and if they do not understand these they will have difficulty meeting them.

Market research is the planned, systematic collection, collation and analysis of data designed to help the management of an organisation to reach decisions about its operation and to monitor the results of these decisions. The British Market Research Society has described market research as being able to provide **information on people's preferences, attitudes, likes and needs, to help companies understand what consumers want**.

Strictly speaking, **market research** is concerned with the analysis of markets (such as the market for car sales), while **marketing research** is concerned with the marketing process (how goods and services are marketed), but in practice distinctions between the two terms are often vague and they are used synonymously. **The market for any commodity or service is the group of actual or potential customers who are ready, willing and able to purchase.** The market for motor cars consists of the customers who want to buy one, have the money to do so and are ready to do so in the near future. Strategic managers want to know:

- the size of their markets in terms of volume and value, that is the number of people in it and the amount of money they are willing and able to spend;
- the pattern of demand in their market, including such factors as economic and social influences on demand;
- the market structure in terms of the size and number of companies with which they are competing, the geographical distribution of the people who make up the market, and their income, age and sex distribution;
- the market share of their company, past and future trends that will influence this share, and the size of the total market and any other opportunities that exist.

Market research is essential in strategic management in providing the information required to make decisions based on evidence, rather than trying to decide with very few facts available. In the end, a decision is based on a judgement of the situation or the problem with which the organisation is faced. The information produced by the process of market research helps to reduce the range of possible conclusions or solutions.

Definition of problem
Objectives of the research
Information required
Sources of information
Research process
Sample process
Results
Analysis and interpretation
Presentation
Monitoring and evaluation

Figure 5.3 The market research process.

The process involved in market research includes a number of stages of more or less importance depending on the subject of the research (Figure 5.3). The situation or problem has to be defined, then the objectives of the research can be decided. This will lead to a clarification of the information required and help point to the sources of this information. The research process can then be decided, sample surveys carried out, and the results analysed, interpreted and presented. The results and the whole process can be monitored and evaluated, and information can be updated.

'The Communications Company' is expanding so it wants to develop its offices on to an area of the company car park. It wants to know what
(Continued)

problems this will cause for its customers, visitors, staff and suppliers. It decides to carry out a survey of the use of the car park. It does this by selecting a 'typical' week and observing the number of parked vehicles at intervals through the working days. The results are analysed, interpreted and presented to the company management. As a result of this report, the company is able to make a decision about expanding its office building.

5.7   Market research methods

The market research process may be concerned with a problem which is as relatively simple to investigate as in the example above of 'The Communications Company', or it may be much more complicated. It may involve discovering people's opinions or their behaviour, or technical aspects of products, and there are a range of research methods available as detailed in Figure 5.4.

Document searches
Observations
Interviews
Questionnaires
Samples
Experiments

Figure 5.4   Market research methods.

Document searches may prove to be the easiest form of market research, with documents ranging from the company's own records, to reports available in the industry, to government publications. Many of these will be readily available and easily accessed, and with the development of computer records and the expansion of the internet the amount of information and the ease of access have greatly expanded. The company's own records, which are collected for administrative purposes, may provide information which is useful to the company. Sales figures may indicate clear trends that demand for the products is seasonal or is closely linked to promotional campaigns. Personnel and human resources records may show patterns of absenteeism among staff linked to the timing of school holidays or other local events. Some of this information is obvious and much of it will not be what the company requires to make strategic marketing decisions.

Observation tends to be used for information about people's actions and behaviour, for example to see where and when they park their cars, or the route they take through a supermarket when they are shopping for food. Direct and systematic observation is the classic method of scientific enquiry, and applied to market research it is a relatively objective way of collecting information. Observation may be carried out by trained observers or by mechanical and electronic means, such as cameras. The main problem is that while observation can show what people are doing, it cannot provide information on why they are doing it.

A CCTV camera may show that people usually start shopping for food by going to the fresh fruit and vegetable area, and then on to the bakery and to packaged food. It does not show why they do this, while a survey will. **Surveys** consist of interviews or questionnaires which do ask people for their opinions as well as for facts about events or actions. **A full survey means that everybody in a 'population' is surveyed. The 'population' is the group of people or items about which information is being collected. A sample survey is anything less than a full survey of a 'population'.**

Interviews can be described as conversations with a purpose. In an informal sense, everybody uses interviewing to obtain information, whether it is to find out the latest football score or where a commodity is in a supermarket. An interview is likely to be more structured than an ordinary conversation and it will be initiated by the interviewer in order to obtain information. This information may be about people's attitudes or motives, or about events and actions. Interviews may be relatively formal and structured, in which set questions are asked, or semi-structured or informal, in which questions follow a pattern, but will vary in order and content between interviews.

The success of interviews will depend on the skills of the interviewer and the way questions are asked, as well as the ability of the respondent to 'make a success' of the interview. The respondent needs to be able to answer the questions and needs to want to answer them. Even though 'street-corner' and 'door-to-door' interviewers may be well trained and experienced, unless the respondents are willing and able to answer the questions being asked then the process will not be successful. However, if interviews are carried out with due care and attention, they can be an excellent method of collecting quite complicated information.

A questionnaire is a list of questions aimed at discovering particular information. Everybody fills in forms from time to time, whether they are for the Inland Revenue, VAT, to register a car, to join a club or as part of a survey. When these forms are well designed the questions are easily understood, appropriate spaces are left for replies and the form can be completed in a reasonable length of time. Every ten years, in the first year of each decade (1991, 2001, 2011) the government distributes the Population Census to every household in the UK. The return of this questionnaire is compulsory, while the return of most postal survey forms is not, so response rates can be low.

Experiments are the classical research methods used in the physical sciences. In these terms, **an experiment involves the manipulation of the independent variable to see the effect this may have on the independent variable**. This means that one factor is changed, such as the temperature, to see what effect this has on the subject being studied, such as the behaviour of rats in a box. In market research the same approach can be used, so that something can be changed and the effects observed. For example, the location of the fruit and vegetable counters can be moved in a supermarket and the behaviour of shoppers can be observed.

In market research it is not possible to have fully controlled experiments as is possible in the physical sciences, because people are unpredictable in their behaviour and are not amenable to laboratory observation. However, aspects of the experimental method can be applied to market research. Attempts can be made to choose people to be surveyed on a **'random'** basis, **where each unit of the population being studied has the same chance as any other unit of being included**. Lottery numbers are chosen on a random basis, but it is more difficult to do this with large numbers of people. There can also be attempts to **'match'** groups of people being surveyed, **so that the characteristics of one group, in terms of say sex or age, are matched with the same characteristics in another group**.

A sample is anything less than a full survey of a 'population'. It is a small part of the population of people or items about which information is being collected. The UK Census of Population is a full survey, sending questionnaires to 100 per cent of households. This is unusual in that the vast majority of surveys are samples. On the basis of the theory of probability it is possible to be confident that a reasonably large sample of a population will be, on average, representative of the characteristics of the population. This does depend on the sample being large enough to include any variability in the population, that there is an accurate sample frame, that bias is removed and that the sample is chosen on a random basis. Bias can be removed by making sure that the sample frame covers all the people or units in the population to be surveyed, that questions are not ambiguous, that selection of the sample units (people or items to be sampled) is on a random basis, and that non-response to the survey is taken into account in case some groups of people or of items are under-represented.

'The Communications Company' wants to find out what the opinions of its staff are on changing the timing of the working day, so that everybody starts work earlier and finishes earlier. Managers distribute a questionnaire to 10 per cent of its staff in order to obtain a quick indication of views in the company as a whole. The managers believe that 10 per cent is a large enough sample to include all the various opinions that are likely to exist among the staff. The questionnaire is kept very short, with clear questions, and it is distributed directly to each person in the sample and collected from them. The people sampled are chosen on a random basis by picking names out of a box which includes everybody who works for the company.

The only way of being certain that the sample chosen by 'The Communications Company' is an accurate representation of staff views would be to carry out a survey of all the staff in the company. It could be that the sample was too small to allow for all the various views of the staff, or it could be that even by chance a larger number of managers were picked than the actual proportion of managers on the staff.

The reasons for carrying out a sample is that it is cheaper and quicker than a full survey; it is also an advantage that greater care can be taken when surveying a relatively few people or units in a sample than the whole population. The reliability of the results will depend on it being a sufficiently large size and with a good design. Whether a sample is the best method for a survey depends on the importance of accuracy. Many surveys are carried out in order to obtain a good indication of a situation rather than absolute accuracy. If greater accuracy is required, the sample taken can be made larger. The size of a sample is independent of the population size, but it does depend on the resources available and the accuracy required. Other things being equal, a large sample will be more reliable than a small sample taken from the same population.

Sampling errors may arise because of poor design in the sense of the list of people or units chosen, or the survey methods used. Errors may also arise because the sample cannot be an exact representation of the population from which it is chosen. Provided the sampling method used is based on random selection, it is possible to measure the probability of errors of any given size. The further away a sample is from the random selection of people or items in the population, the more difficult it is to measure this type of error. There are a range of sampling methods (Figure 5.5), some of which are random; others are quasi-random because each unit in the population does not have the same chance of being included in the sample.

Random sampling: simple random sampling – this uses 'lottery' type selection

Quasi-random sampling: systematic sampling – this involves a system whereby the first unit is chosen at random and then names or units are chosen at regular intervals

Stratified random sampling – people or items are divided into groups, categories or strata, and within each of these a simple random sample or systematic sample is selected

Non-random sampling: quota sampling – interviews are carried out with a certain number of people with specific characteristics

Figure 5.5   Some sampling methods.

5.8   Forecasting

Strategic management involves making predictions and decisions about what an organisation should do to be successful. It relies on a focus on the customer and finding out what customers want so that the organisation can supply it. A marketing orientation means that a company does not just produce a commodity or service and then try to sell it; it decides what business it is in, and who its customers are, and then finds out what they want and attempts to provide it. Market research supplies information which helps in making decisions on these matter; it is a process of finding out about the market that the company is operating in, the organisations and people in this market and what actions are required to make the company a success. The market research process cannot, of course, provide all the answers. The company has to have an excellent product, there has to be a degree of leadership and 'flair' or 'hunch' in making some difficult decisions, and timing may be a vital factor in success.

Forecasting is a way of considering the future, while market research and the methods applied to it are considering the present or the past. They are ways of discovering what customers want now, but this is not necessarily what they want in the future. **Forecasting can be seen as a systematic way of combining managerial judgement with market research data to say something useful about the future**. In forecasting it has to be assumed that the behavioural patterns that have been traced in the past will continue in the future for a reasonable time.

What a reasonable time is will depend on what is being measured. For example, national economic trends change over years, while the sale of ice-cream changes weekly or even daily. Yet even with ice-creams there are seasonal trends which can be measured over months and years. These seasonal trends can be charted and can help to indicate the demand for ice-creams at different periods of the year. This process of taking present and past trends and carrying them forward to the future is extrapolation, and it can provide an indication of what is likely to happen. Of course, various events can affect this extrapolation, so that a particularly hot summer may increase the demand for ice-creams more than any of the past trends predicted.

One method of forecasting is by the use of time series, which consist of numerical data recorded at regular intervals of time and then extended into the future. For example, share prices can be measured on a daily basis, and rises and falls can be measured and extended into the future. Although share prices rise and fall, the general trend has been for prices to rise over a matter of years. The long-term rise has cyclical and short-term fluctuations. These trends can be shown by calculating moving averages which even-out the more frequent fluctuations and can show a general trend by allowing for seasonal variations (Figure 5.6). Trends can be shown by a straight line to show a linear relationship between the variables through the use of such statistical methods as the least-squares method and regression analysis.

Analysing the various types of trends can indicate a pattern in the data which can be repeated in the future, but this is not a substitute for the use of judgement in analysing the available data. For example, it may be possible to identify cause-and-effect relationships in the data, so that, for example, the cause of the increased sale of ice-creams can be seen to be due to hot weather. However, weather is unpredictable and difficult to forecast some way ahead, while other cause-and-effect relationships are easier to predict. For example, if it is known that there is to be an increase in the building of new houses in an area, then there is very likely to be an increased demand for carpets, furniture and other

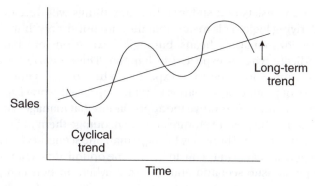

Figure 5.6 Long-term and cyclical trends.

consumer goods. For instance, the County Town of Buckinghamshire, Aylesbury, is predicted to increase its population by a third between the years 2000 and 2010 as a consequence of the building of new houses and office blocks.

Forecasting by time series and by cause-and-effect relationships are both concerned with quantitative data rather than qualitative information, and thus judgement is required. In practice, forecasting is often a combination of factors, based on market research, the analysis of statistical trends, considering cause and effect, and above all using judgement to decide what in fact is going to happen and how the organisation should react. Strategic managers have to use whatever methods they have available to make decisions about the marketing strategy they should follow. For example, the fact that a certain number of houses are to be built can be combined with information about the quality and price of the houses, the type of jobs that are likely to be created in the area, and statistical information about the level of disposable income that is predicted to be available to the people who might move into these houses. Even if all this information is available, judgement is needed to decide what to do with it in terms of the goods and services that can be offered profitably.

Of course, all the information about the increased housing and the quality and price may prove to be inaccurate for one reason or another. Forecasting methods attempt to predict what is 'most likely' and may also include an estimate of the confidence that the forecaster has in the forecast. Political opinion polls, for example, may give a percentage forecast of the results of an election with a 2–3 per cent level of error. In a close election this level of uncertainty may make the result of the election difficult to predict, as for example the polls produced before the American Presidential election opinion polls in November 2000.

Forecasting is based on the belief that the future can be predicted, but the difficulty of doing this in rapidly changing times has lead to the development in strategic thinking on processes which assume that the future is hard to predict. Strategic managers can consider the likely developments in the future and decide what strategies to follow to cope with them. These considerations can be called 'scenarios' or narratives of how the future might plausibly turn out. A scenario consists of a statement of how things will develop, together with an underlying logic. This means that they are not simply 'hunches' or 'off the top' of senior managers' heads, but logical extensions of what is already known to indicate what is expected to happen. The scenario for a film, for example, is a framework of how it is expected to turn out, it is not a blueprint.

The purpose of producing scenarios is not to improve the precision of strategic planning, but rather to improve the appreciation that managers in an organisation have about the possible future and to encourage them to face up to the uncertainty of the future. There may be more than one scenario at any one time, so that strategic managers may consider, say, one optimistic scenario about the future, one pessimistic scenario and one somewhere in between. Managers may talk about 'the worst-case scenario' in order to consider what strategy should be introduced to deal with the most pessimistic view of the future.

'The Communications Company' senior managers develop two main scenarios for the future of its products. One scenario is based on the assumption that economic growth is likely to continue at least at its present level and therefore that the demand for its information technology services will continue. The worst-case scenario is that economic growth may slow down so that there is a fall in demand for its services in the retail trade in which it has specialised. They decide that if the first scenario proves to be correct then they will continue with their present strategy; on the other hand, if the second scenario proves to be correct they will have to adopt a strategy of expanding its services into industrial and commercial areas with which they are not familiar.

5.9 The marketing process

Market research emphasises a market-orientation for a company where selling will become as superfluous as possible by understanding the customer and adopting a strategy which meets customer needs. In this way the product or service 'sells itself'. **A fully integrated marketing-orientation will permeate the whole structure of an organisation and will influence the actions of every manager, because while profits are fundamental to business survival, they depend on the organisation satisfying the customer**.

'The Communications Company' started with a good idea – a computer package that 'sold itself'. Once this product was overtaken by cheaper and more powerful products, the company found that it had to develop a strategy for survival which involved it in market research and in producing a marketing plan.

The starting point for a strategic marketing plan is to chart the environment in which the company is working in a **marketing audit**, and to understand the company itself in a **SWOT analysis**. The first step is to audit an organisation's environment. **An organisation's marketing environment consists of all the**

Social	Political	Social
Technological	Economic	Political
Economic	Social	Economic
Political	Technological	Cultural
	Legal	Technological
	Environmental	Aesthetic
		Customers
		Legal
		Environmental
		Sectoral

Figure 5.7 STEP, PESTLE and SPECTACLES.

factors that are external to it and that influence its successful operation. These factors can be collected into categories which can be referred to as the STEP (or PEST, PESTLE or even SPECTACLES) factors (Figure 5.7).

Social factors include the size and composition of the potential market, age and sex distribution of the population, income and education levels. As the composition of the population changes and it becomes wealthier and better educated, the range and quality of the goods and services demanded change, and companies have to keep up with these changes. Changes in **technology** have become particularly rapid, both in the way goods and services are produced and distributed, and also in the way they are demanded. The growth of internet shopping is a good example of this.

Strategic managers have to keep up to date with **economic** changes that affect their organisation, such as alterations to interest rates and the strength of Sterling in relation to other currencies. A 'strong' pound may make exports relatively expensive compared with competing products from countries with weaker currencies. **Political** factors such as government legislation may also affect organisations and they will need to take account of such factors as taxation regulations or health and safety legislation. This may be so important that STEP or PEST can be changed to PESTLE, to include **legal** matters and **environmental** issues. The environment in this sense includes questions of pollution and the conservation of resources.

These factors can be extended even further to arrive at SPECTACLES, which adds **cultural, aesthetic, customers and sectoral** to political, economic, technological, legal and environmental factors, which together make up the context in which organisations work. This approach suggests that it is important to include a detailed consideration of the culture within which an organisation operates, the customer base, competition within the sector, and the aesthetic implications, both physical and behavioural, of the organisation on its external operating environment. **Cultural** factors are usually defined as 'the way things are done around here', or 'the way we do things around here' whether it is within an organisation, a particular society or country. The importance of the culture within organisations for strategic management is analysed in Chapter 8, but organisations also have to consider the culture of the region and country within which they operate. They cannot operate in exactly the same way in the UK as they do in the United States or Japan, for example, because people's customs, expectations and behaviour are different from the UK in these countries.

Although **aesthetics** is concerned with 'beauty', it can also be thought of in terms of an image that an organisation projects. There may be a difference between the image it wants to project and the one it actually does project and, although promotional campaigns are designed to affect the image of an organisation, they do not always produce the expected results. As a clothes retailer, Marks & Spencer has had an image among many consumers of providing good-quality products, which are middle-of-the-road in terms of style and of price. It has attempted to alter this image in order to compete with firms offering trendy and relatively cheap products. It has experienced difficulty in doing this because its previous image was well established and was a fundamental part of its past success.

The importance of an organisation understanding **customer** requirements is analysed in Chapter 6. The twentieth century saw a rise in 'consumerism' where the 'consumer is king (or queen)' and customers are aware of the choices open to them and expect these to expand. The 'power' of consumers has increased in the twenty-first century so that a focus on the customer is essential if a company is to survive – without customers, an organisation will not last long. **Sectoral** factors are important in an organisation's external considerations in order to analyse its position in the sectors in which it operates, and also the position of any actual and potential competitors. The importance of maintaining a competitive advantage is examined in Chapter 7.

In the previous twenty or thirty years, there has been a growing interest in **environmental** matters and worldwide damage to the environment. The effects of different industrial sectors on the environment vary considerably. For example, it has been argued that the oil companies very business is environmentally damaging, while the service sector has a less direct impact. The demand for consumer goods has placed huge pressures on resources and as a result on the environment. Organisations face the challenge of meeting customer needs on the one hand, and integrating environmental considerations into their production and marketing plans on the other. Legislation has placed some responsibilities on companies and has, for example, made car companies produce more environmentally friendly vehicles. Customers may also put pressure on companies to produce less environmentally harmful goods and this is an element, for example, in the debate about organic food.

The organisation needs to understand all these external influences on its market, as well as the size of the market, its likely growth or contraction and its potential customers. At the same time as carrying out an audit of the environment of their organisations, managers need also to carry out **a SWOT analysis in order to understand the organisation itself**. This analysis helps them to

Strengths

Weaknesses

Opportunities

Threats

Figure 5.8   SWOT analysis.

focus their attention on the key areas that need to be taken into account in producing a strategic marketing plan (Figure 5.8).

The SWOT analysis highlights the internal strengths and weaknesses of a company from the customers' point of view, as they relate to external opportunities and threats. In drawing up a marketing plan, strategic managers will start by looking at each of these areas in turn and then considering how they interact. The strengths of an organisation may include the expertise and experience of its staff and its ability to produce high-quality goods. Weaknesses may be a poor distribution system and a reputation for delivering goods late. There may also be weaknesses which are the opposite of the strengths or even arise out of them. For example, it may be that because the staff in a company are highly skilled and have long experience, they are slow to change their working methods and resist moving into new areas in which they are not as confident in their abilities.

The strategic manager's role is to exploit the strengths of the company and to correct and compensate for the weaknesses. For example, a new production and distribution system may be introduced with improved control and delivery of the company products. At the same time, staff training and development may help to overcome a reluctance to change. The weaknesses of an organisation can also give rise to opportunities, in the sense that the exposure of a weakness may be seen as a opportunity to improve company performance. If a company has managed to survive with a poor delivery system, when it is improved the company should do even better.

Opportunities may also arise out of company strengths; so that if the staff are experts in their field and the company is a market leader, customers or other people who develop new needs may turn to it to provide these.

'The Communications Company' is the expert in providing information technology solutions for the retail industry, so other service industries may turn to it to solve their problems in this area. Originally the company had staff who were experts in a narrow area of IT, and the company had to introduce a staff development programme in order to enable the staff to adapt their skills to other areas. This strength enables it to take advantage of the new opportunities.

Threats to an organisation may include competition from other companies or institutions, a fall in demand for products or services, or changes in government policy or regulations. The ability to meet and overcome these threats successfully is one of the strengths that distinguishes companies that are able to survive from those that cannot. Once managers have a good idea of what their customers need, know the position of their organisation in relation to its market, and understand its internal and external situation, they can develop a marketing strategy. In order to produce this strategy, managers have four main variables which they can control. These are the **product** or **service** produced by the organisation, its **price**, the way it is **promoted**, and the **place** or places through which it is made available to consumers. The four 'Ps' constitute the **marketing mix:**

Product

Price

Place

Promotion

The marketing mix is the appropriate combination, in a particular set of circumstances, of the four Ps. These summarise everything that an organisation can do to influence the demand for its products and services. An effective marketing strategy will bring together these four variables in a combination which satisfies customer needs. If the balance of a successful marketing mix is upset, the whole marketing strategy may fail. For example, if the price of a commodity is raised by a company, demand for the product may fall unless the company can promote it better or show that the quality has improved in a way that more closely satisfies customer needs.

Other factors can be added to these four, making seven, in summarising the marketing mix:

People

Process

Physical evidence

These factors are particularly important in the supply of services. For example, when a holiday is bought through a travel agent, the people who sell it and supply it are important, as well as the **process** involved in taking the holiday, and physical elements such as aeroplane tickets. The customers are also important because they will have certain expectations and unless these are met, the service will not be a complete success. Holiday-makers may have their expectations raised by exaggerated descriptions in the travel company's brochure and be disappointed by the reality. The process of marketing is the interaction between all the people involved in the transaction, whether it is selling a car or arranging a holiday. If this interaction is successful, selling the holiday will be more straightforward. **Physical evidence** can range from the location in which the service takes place, to a ticket or voucher with which the customer is provided. A voucher may be evidence that the holiday-maker has purchased a place on a guided tour.

Including **people** as a factor in the marketing mix emphasises the importance of all those involved in the transaction. The success of a holiday will depend on the customer as well as all the people providing the service. Customers will have certain expectations and these need to be met in one way or another. The obvious example of marketing problems in this area is when holiday brochures appear to, or actually do, promise smart hotels and glorious beaches when the reality is half-built accommodation and dirty sand. With the rapid expansion of internet access, people can easily carry out their own research into holiday resorts, airline flights and so on, and travel agents can not rely on a high level of ignorance among their customers.

5.10 Marketing strategy

The marketing mix also depends on the customers who are the target consumers of the company, its particular product and its marketing promotion. Chapter 6 considers consumers in more detail, together with their decisions which depend on the choices they are offered, the convenience of making a purchase and the cost. The 'four Cs' can play an important part in marketing strategy and can form an element of that strategy:

> **Customers**
> **Convenience**
> **Choice**
> **Cost**

Marketing strategy has to be developed with a clear understanding of the customers for a product or service and their behaviour (see Chapter 6). The approach to established and loyal customers will need to be different from the approach to new customers who may show a resistance to the product. Market research will help to identify the customer base for a product or service, and the expected customer behaviour. Convenience will also play an important part in marketing strategy. What customers will actually buy will be affected by the convenience of making a purchase. For example, where local shops have survived the competition from supermarkets and superstores, an important factor in this survival is the very fact that they are local and therefore convenient for customers in their area. The same factor is important in the growth of shopping by telephone and through the use of the internet, because customers are able to purchase goods from the comfort of their own homes.

Marketing strategy will also depend on the choice of goods or services available in a particular market. A company will have to take into account the nature of the offerings, in terms of products and services, that compete with its own and their price. In highly competitive markets this is a major factor in the approach to marketing, so that for example motor car companies try to provide extra features in their cars in order to compete or emphasise the excellent value for money that they offer. The cost to a consumer of making a purchase is also important in marketing, and this may be more complicated than simply comparing prices. Local shops, for example, can sometimes charge higher prices for their goods than competing 'out-of-town' competitors, because transport costs for consumers shopping in their immediate area will be less and there may also be a saving in time. Marketing strategy will depend on the particular customers to be targeted; it will take into account the importance of convenience for consumers, the choices open to them and all the costs with which they are faced.

Strategic management includes marketing at every stage and in every area. Unless customers are satisfied and there is a demand (in the sense that consumers are prepared and able to make a purchase) for the products and services of an organisation, it will not be successful. Managers may have a sense of direction for a company but, unless this is a direction for which there is a demand, the company will eventually collapse. Companies may be able to create a demand through advertising a service, which clearly provides customer benefits even if the needs that are satisfied have not been fully realised by people.

Many of the 'dot com', e-commerce companies have spent large amounts of their start-up finance on advertising and marketing their services, and they have taken a long time moving into profit. Meanwhile their shares have moved through spectacular rises and falls. In the long run, the successful companies are likely to be those that have carried out market research, and that are well organised and well marketed. It also helps if they are the first in the field and are able to maintain this position. The amount of investment required to market their services and to provide a reliable and efficient service is a deterrent to new businesses entering their market segment, however easy it is to establish a website. The same requirements apply in this area of business as they do in others. A company needs to understand its own strengths and weaknesses, the environmental pressures of its market and how it can provide benefits for its customers.

The business strategy of an organisation will include a marketing strategy which is concerned with the position of a company in its market, the strengths and weaknesses of that company, an understanding of its customers and potential customers, and the ways in which their needs can be satisfied. These are all the 'nuts and bolts' of strategic marketing which have to be brought together in organisational strategy in order to enable a company to navigate its way through the uncharted waters it faces in attempting to achieve it business objectives.

ASSIGNMENTS

1. Discuss the role of strategic marketing in the development of a company.
2. What is the difference between marketing and selling?
3. Who is the 'customer' and what benefits are customers seeking?
4. Analyse the processes by which a business can understand itself as well as its external environment.
5. What forecasting is carried out by an organisation that you know?
6. How does 'The Communications Company' use market research?
7. Discuss ways in which 'The Engineering Company' could apply some marketing techniques in order to support the strategic analysis being carried out by the Assistant Managing Director.

ⓥ 6 Strategy for meeting the needs of customers

OBJECTIVES

To analyse how to meet customer needs
To consider the characteristics of products and services
To consider customer strategy
To analyse the strategic importance of the product life-cycle
To discuss the product/service portfolio

How to meet customer needs – Market segmentation – Target markets for products and services – Competitive advantage – Niche marketing – Customer strategy – Life-cycle analysis – Critical success factors

6.1 The customer comes first

Meeting customer needs is the foundation of any successful organisation: without customers, the organisation is without purpose, so that the customer come first, second and third in terms of the organisation's priorities and its strategic management. Customers have always been important to companies but, with the increases in competition created by world trade, the priority given to them has changed and so has the urgency with which their needs are considered. It can be argued that customer service is the main factor which distinguishes one organisation from another in the same business. At the same time, customers have changed – they have become more demanding and they have more choice, and this in its turn has changed the strategic role of managers.

The change was heralded by the so called 'death of bureaucracy' identified by Warren Bennis (among others) in 1966. He argued that every age develops the organisational form appropriate to its time and that bureaucracy was appropriate to the first two-thirds of the twentieth century but not beyond that. His view was that the order, precision and impersonal nature of bureaucracy were a reaction against the personal and capricious nature of management in the nineteenth century, remnants of which survived into the twentieth century.

Bennis recognised that there were new conditions developing in the last third of the twentieth century which had major implications for management. There was rapid and unexpected change in the position of most organisations, with increasing diversity which created a need for flexibility and new and specialised skills.

'The Communications Company' was founded on the basis of information technology solutions to business problems. It was immediately successful because companies wanted the service that the Company offered. As a result of the small size of the Company and the small number of employees, customers were put on a waiting-list and were dealt with on a first-come first-served schedule. The Company did not take into account the urgency of the problem that the customer was experiencing and it did not have a customer service unit of any kind. When rival companies began to offer similar services, 'The Communications Company' altered its policy so that it attempted to deal with customers according the urgency of their problems, and it introduced a rapid response unit to deal with immediate problems.

Most organisations have become increasingly influenced by outside factors such as competition, government legislation, the state of the economy and the internet. Regional and international influences have also increased, so that UK organisations are affected by the state of the European economy and the Euro, and by European Community legislation as well as by world trade. Organisations are increasingly 'open' in the sense that they are characterised by uncertainty over the actions of others, such as customers, which leads them to constantly monitor these actions. At the same time, there are wide variations in the use of technology within organisations even by those producing similar products or services, and in the speed of change and innovation.

Strategic management has become more and more involved with producing contingency plans to deal with the uncertainties of outside influences. Management needs to be flexible and to apply the appropriate techniques to factors such as the size and situation of an organisation. In particular, managers need to understand their customers in order to meet their needs better. Organisations need to know the specific requirements of each customer and whether these requirements can be segmented.

6.2   Market segmentation

Customer segmentation is the identification of specific parts of a market and the development of different market offerings that will be attractive to these segments. It is possible to distinguish between broad target segments that involve large numbers of customers (Figure 6.1), and narrow market segments that involve small niches in the marketplace. At their broadest, market segments can include differences between products for women, for men and for children. Clothes and shoe manufacturers and shops make this distinction.

Geography and location
Demography (age, sex, education etc.)
Socio-economic groupings and income
Benefits sought
Usage rate and brand loyalty
Lifestyle

Figure 6.1   The basis for market segmentation.

Further segmentation may be into sports wear, formal wear and so on. Narrow segments may include sports clothes for golfers, or children's clothes for a particular age group. **Market segmentation analysis seeks to identify similarities and differences between groups of customers or users**.

Market segmentation is important for strategic management because some segments may be more profitable and attractive than others. Large segments may have low profit margins but their size make them attractive, while small segments may have high profit margins and loyal customers. Some segments may have more competition than others, so that for example a specialised segment may have only a limited number of competitors. Also some segments may grow faster and offer more opportunities than others.

Market segmentation is useful in strategic terms only if customers can be distinguished. Not all users of a product or service are the same; each can have different characteristics and needs, behave differently and so on. Customers must be distinguishable so that they can be isolated in some way. At the same time, the distinguishing criteria must relate to the differences in market demand, so that for example some customers may be prepared to pay higher prices for better quality goods. The segment has to be sufficiently large, even if it can be described as a niche, to justify the resources needed to reach it. It must also be possible to access the segment.

Motor car manufacturers use market segmentation in their strategic planning. The large manufacturers, such as Ford and General Motors, produce a range of cars to match various customer markets. These include small, economical cars, family cars, company fleet cars, executive cars and sports cars. Small manufacturers, such as Morgan, produce cars for a particular niche market in which customers are prepared to pay and wait for a car that looks different and is largely 'hand-made'.

6.3   Products and services

Products and services are anything that can be offered to a market for consumption that satisfy a want or need, however they cannot be treated in exactly the same way in marketing. Whereas **a product is tangible and its sale involves a change of ownership, a service is essentially intangible and does not result in a change of ownership**. When a book or a computer is bought or sold, there is a change of ownership; while when a packaged holiday is bought and sold, ownerships of the travel company, the airline and the hotel remain unchanged.

At the most fundamental level, every product or service can be seen as the packaging of a problem-solving service. The Chief Executive of the Revlon Company has argued that 'in the factory we make cosmetics, in the store we sell hope'. In buying a coat-hanger in order to hang up a coat, the consumer is not so much buying the hanger as solving the problem of how to hang up the coat. When ordering a portion of chips in a restaurant, the customers are satisfying their hunger. They have chosen to do it in this way out of a variety of alternatives. Buying a holiday package is with the hope of satisfying the need for rest, enjoyment and leisure. If the holiday is a disaster, it will not have satisfied any of these needs. Products and services satisfy, or are expected to satisfy, basic or subsidiary needs. These needs include the necessity for food, clothing, shelter, security and 'happiness', and there is a range of products which may be aimed at one or more of these. The manager's role is to provide the best possible products and services to solve consumer problems and provide consumer benefits.

Every car that is road-worthy will possess the benefit of providing transport. Cars may also have other features which provide further benefits. The size of the car, its relative power or economy, the colour, air-conditioning and so on are all benefits. Car salesmen may concentrate their efforts on persuading customers of the particular benefits of cars they are selling over the makes or brands of other cars, while taking for granted the fact that they all provide the benefit of transport.

The marketing of products or services and selling them may concentrate less on the basic need that they satisfy as on the value added by a range of features which provide consumer benefits. At the same time, managers need to take account of all aspects of the target market. These aspects can be summarised in **'the six Os'**:

> **Occupants** – which individuals make up the market?
> **Object** – what do they want to buy?
> **Occasions** – when do they make their purchases?
> **Organisations** – who decides what to buy?
> **Objectives** – why do they buy particular goods and services?
> **Operations** – how do they buy products and services?

The sales management in a car showroom will want to know who in its area have the disposable income to buy its cars and the need to buy a car, what price they are prepared to pay, and the size of car and the features for which they are looking. It will also want to know when potential customers will want to buy a car, who in fact will make the decision to buy, for what purpose they want the motor car and what process they are prepared to go through in order to make their purchase.

A family may decide to buy a car which is reasonably priced, sufficiently large to carry the whole family and is also economical. They may decide to buy the car in preparation for their summer holiday, with different members of the family emphasising different features that they would like. One of them may be more concerned with the colour or the overall 'image' that driving the car or being in the car is thought to impart. There may be agreement on size and price and it may be that the parents, or even just one of them, will in the end decide what to buy. In order to keep the process as simple as possible the car may be bought from a local showroom where it can easily be returned if there are any problems.

Image can be an important aspect of buying some goods, such as motor cars. It can be described as a set of beliefs, ideas and impressions that a person holds of a product or service. Image can be created by word of mouth, through an advertising and promotion campaign, or it may be the result of particular prejudice or fashion. A particular make of car may have a poor reputation for reliability among some people which may not have arisen because of any facts about the number of breakdowns but is based on their own experiences or that of people they know. Strategic marketing is about creating a good image or reputation for a company's goods and services.

6.4 Competition

Strategic management is concerned with creating **a sustainable competitive advantage for an organisation compared with its rivals**. This arises when an organisation has an advantage in competing with its rivals which enables it to earn returns on investment which are higher than the average for the sector (see Chapter 7). This involves every aspect of the way that the organisation competes in the marketplace, including product range, price, manufacturing quality, service levels and so on. However, some of these factors are easily imitated. Price, for example, can be changed very rapidly so that a price which provides an advantage for a company at one time may last a very short time. In order to be sustainable, competitive advantage needs to be difficult to imitate and it needs to be deeply embedded in the organisation.

A product or service which is difficult to imitate will have an advantage in terms of its design, its quality and its after-sales service, and it will also have a price which customers consider to be good value for money. These factors can be deeply embedded in an organisation through the skills of its workforce, its overall culture or its investment in resources. Sustainable advantage can take many forms as organisations look for something which is unique and different from the competition, and it can be said to be a vital aspect of strategic management (Figure 6.2).

Service providers will attempt to provide a high-quality service which is both reliable and prompt. They will want to employ high-quality staff and provide them with training to prepare them for their jobs. Customer service will be a top priority for service companies that want to remain ahead of their competitors, and the whole company and the way it works will need to be customer-orientated. Manufacturing companies will want to provide good value for money, by producing high-quality products at low cost. A good distribution system will help to provide their products to their customers and strong branding will help to market their products. Again, customer-orientation is essential for a manufacturing company that wants to maintain a lead over competitors.

Service providers	Manufacturers
Reputation for quality service	Low costs
High-quality staff	Strong branding
Customer service	Good distribution
Well-known name	Quality product
Customer orientated	Good value for money

Figure 6.2 Possible ways of maintaining a sustainable competitive advantage.

Even public sector and non-profit organisations need to consider competitive advantage because although they do not have the same level of competition as organisations in the private sector, they still have to compete for funding and they are accountable for their performance to funding agencies. Increasingly, public sector organisations, such as National Health Service trust hospitals, universities and colleges, are in a competitive situation where they are judged as service providers against other organisations in their part of the sector.

One aspect of developing competitive advantage is through product differentiation (see also Porter's generic strategy in Chapter 2). **Product differentiation is the development of unique features or attributes in a product or service that position it to appeal especially to a part of the total market**. One method of doing this is by **branding**. Companies will attempt to develop a brand image for their products or services so that customers will develop loyalty to them, recognise them when they see them and perhaps ask for them by name. A famous example is the 'Hoover', a brand name for a vacuum cleaner. People will ask for 'Coca-Cola' or 'Pepsi-Cola' but they will not ask for lemonade by a brand name. People develop customer loyalty for particular makes of car, so they 'always buy a ...', or for television sets, or cameras and so on. Companies will also try to develop unique features for their services, by providing extras as part of the overall package or some other distinctive feature. Holiday companies try to differentiate their holidays from those provided by other companies by offering children's clubs, extra luxuries, or upgraded car hire, and by dressing their couriers in distinctive uniforms.

'The Communications Company' carried out little marketing in its early development and relied on 'word-of-mouth' recommendations. Once rivals appeared offering similar services, the senior managers of the Company decided they needed to find out about marketing. So they sent one of their employees on a marketing course. As a result of this, the Company introduced changes to the way it dealt with customers and it began to look at market segmentation and a niche market. This lead the senior managers of the Company into concentrating their effort on retailers and then into expanding their services within this particular niche.

Competitive advantage can be obtained through the development of **low-cost** production (Figure 6.3), which enables a company to compete either on the basis of lower prices than rival companies, or by charging the same prices but adding more services. In the 1990s production of many products moved to South-East Asian countries where labour costs were lower than in Western countries. In 1999 Marks & Spencer announced that they were changing their traditional policy of buying from British manufacturers in order to take advantage of lower costs in other countries.

Product or service differentiation

Low cost

Value for money

Niche marketing

High technology

Quality

Style, vertical integration

Special factors

Figure 6.3 Factors creating competitive advantage.

Companies will often offer a level of **quality** that their competitors may find difficult to match. Some car companies, for example, emphasise the high quality of their products or service. Quality may mean that prices are higher for these products, although this will not always be the case. So while customers may think in terms of high quality/high price and low price/low quality, what they are really looking for tends to be 'value for money'. Japanese car manufacturers made inroads into many Western country car markets by offering reliability and a large range of 'extras' at a relatively low price. Special levels of technology or service can be developed by a company which others cannot match. Management and financial consultants, for example, work on this bases.

Niche marketing provides differentiation by a company selection of a small market segment and concentrating on satisfying the customers in this market. Holiday companies may concentrate on providing travel facilities for one region of the world, adventure holidays, or low-cost budget holidays. Fashion goods are frequently targeted towards specialist niches. The **style** of an organisation may make it different from competitors in customers' minds: **vertical integration** may provide advantages in terms of control over suppliers and/or distributors, location may provide an advantage, and **special or exceptional factors** may differentiate organisations, for example many countries have national airlines which offer particular advantages.

There has tended to be an emphasis in terms of strategic management on differentiation, low costs and niche marketing as the most important factors in creating competitive advantage, although stability and continuity within an organisation can be considered to be just as or more important. These involve the long-term development of the culture and style of an organisation.

Michael Porter (1985), in a book called *Competitive Strategy*, identified five basic industry forces that act on an organisation (see Chapter 10). These are the bargaining power of suppliers, the bargaining power of buyers, the threat of potential new entrants, the threat of substitutes and the extent of competitive rivalry. These 'forces' are concerned with the main factors that an organisation needs to take into account in order to develop opportunities in its environment and protect itself against competition (Figure 6.4).

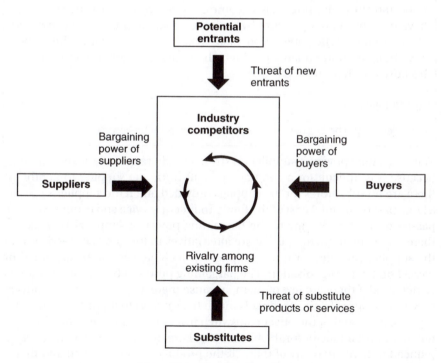

Figure 6.4   Five forces analysis.

The Assistant Managing Director and the Marketing Manager of 'The Engineering Company' are discussing the contents of the Strategy Report. 'In marketing terms,' the Marketing Manager observes, 'we have segmented the market for machinery and precision equipment into five sectors and we are making product offers in each of these sectors. In the past there has been a clear need for our products but with developments in technology some of these segments have developed different needs, with the result that competing companies have felt it is worth their while coming into those markets.' 'Yes,' agrees the AMD, 'but we seemed to keep our customers even after the technology had changed. We adapted our products to the new technology, because after all product design is one of our strengths. So why have we seen a recent fall in demand, what has changed?' 'We had built up a brand loyalty among our customers simply by being around a long time and with a reputation for being dependable and producing high-quality products.' 'There has not been anything simple about it, its required hard work and an emphasis on quality.' 'What I meant,' the Marketing Manager explains, 'is that we have not done anything special to nurture loyalty among our customers. We have provided good products, but we have not promoted ourselves to them or gone out of our way to find out exactly what they need. We have not noticed that while quality is still important to them, price has become a more prominent feature as they have been put under pressure by their customers to produce cheaper and cheaper goods. The squeeze on their costs has meant that at times they have bought poorer quality products than ours from other manufacturers because they have been cheaper.'

ASSIGNMENT

Consider what 'The Engineering Company' can do about its problems.

The bargaining power of suppliers is stronger if there are only a few suppliers, because it is difficult for a company to shift from one supplier to another if there are no substitutes for the supplies provided and if the supplier's price is a large part of the total cost of the final product or service and cannot easily be passed on to the consumer. The bargaining power of suppliers is weaker if there are many of them, if there are alternatives to the goods or services that the supplier provides, or if the supplier's price-changes can be absorbed or passed on by the organisation. The bargaining power of buyers or consumers is increased if there are few of them, because there are few alternative buyers to whom to appeal if the product is much the same as that produced by other organisations so that the buyer can switch from one to another, and if price is not an important factor for the buyers. The bargaining power of consumers is reduced if there are many of them, if the product is differentiated and therefore it is special, and if the price is important.

The threat of potential new entrants into the marketplace that the organisation is in, is important in terms of increasing competition. The stronger the barriers are to entry, the weaker the threat will be of increasing competition; whereas if the barriers are low, competition can increase at any time. Barriers to entry include economies of scale in that existing companies are sufficiently large to achieve low costs, and new entrants would have to enter the market with similar economies of scale. Product differentiation will create barriers to entry with strong brands and specialist products. Requirements for high capital investment will restrict entry to those organisations able to raise the required finances and prepared to accept the risks involved. Engineering companies, for example, have usually invested in expensive machinery, and it is expensive for other companies to set up sufficient plant to compete successfully.

New entrants may find it difficult to access distribution channels which have been largely controlled by existing companies. They may have to spend more money on marketing and sales than existing companies in order to break into a market and to persuade buyers to switch from a supplier with whom they are satisfied. Entry into a market can be easier if the company produces a substitute for existing products which is lower in cost or uses new technology, or has other benefits. At the same time, some markets are much more competitive than others.

'The Communications Company' discovered that it was in an industry where entry was extremely easy as new companies began to offer similar services. The cost of entry was relatively small, without high barriers in terms of investment, and the Company services were not very difficult to copy. At the same time, these services were better quality and more robust than the services provided by the Company. The senior managers realised that they needed to develop their services, to integrate marketing into the work of every employee, to carry out some market research into their customers, and potential customers, and also to carry out a competitor analysis.

In order to maintain a strong position in a market, strategic managers in a company will attempt to maximise factors which provide a competitive advantage over competitors and potential competitors. This competitive advantage may be through product differentiation, cost and price levels, niche marketing as well as raising barriers to new entrants to the market. As part of the development of competitive strategy, a company may carry out competitor profiling. **Competitor analysis is the profiling of leading competitors in terms of their objectives, resources, market strength and current strategies**. Usually only the leading competitors are analysed in this way, that is the ones that represent the most direct threat. This threat may be for customers, which is typically the case for private sector companies, or for resources, which is typically the case for public sector organisations.

Competitor analysis usually includes consideration of the objectives of the competitor. These may include sales growth, an increase in market share or control over resources. The nature of a competing company's resources may be important in terms of size and scale, as well as of levels of technology and financial strength or weakness. Past records of achievement may be taken into account, the competitor's reputation and its future strategy. Competing companies, products and services are tested to 'destruction' by taking the products apart and by trying out services. This process enables an organisation to know what it is up against and to decide on its own strategy so that it can maintain its competitive advantage.

6.5 Customer strategy

In order to develop a strategy to satisfy their customers, managers need to fully understand their customers and their customer needs. Companies will attempt to segment customer requirements in an attempt both to satisfy as many people as possible, and also avoid the need to tailor-make every item for each individual. 'Getting to know the customer' involves being aware of how many different people are involved in the purchasing decision and the different kinds of requirements they may have. In buying a family car there may be a number of opinions within the family about what they need, with some members of the family looking for performance and style while others are looking for comfort and economy. In a company, the accountant may be largely concerned with the cost of raw materials, while the marketing manager may be more concerned with their quality.

People have different priorities in terms of the qualities they require in a product or service. These will include design, technical preferences, reliability and availability, as well as price. The producers and retailers of goods and services need to know the priorities of customers before they can decide which aspects to concentrate on improving. They need to understand why customers buy goods and services so that they can meet these requirements better than their competitors.

'The Communications Company' integrated marketing into the work of all its employees by providing training to them on how to deal with customers. This involved finding out the exact needs of the customers so that these needs could be satisfied in the best possible way. At the same time, the Company introduced an upgraded service in order to try to compete with newer rivals, and it introduced service-quality monitoring in the form of insisting on a rapid response to customer requests. It placed its employees into groups dealing with a number of accounts, so that employees could begin to understand customer problems and form a relationship with them.

The interaction of customer needs with competitor offering will determine who will make the sale, and it is the company which meets customer needs better than its competitors that is likely to grow and succeed. A fundamental advantage is likely to be in terms of costs or skills. The skills available to a company will depend heavily on its structure and organisation, its recruitment and retention policy, and on staff training and development. Cost differences arise because of the costs of production including wage costs and raw material costs, investment in equipment, and the skill and productivity of employees. Any structural skill or cost differences which are difficult for a competitor to keep up with can be the basis of a competitive advantage if they result in an organisation being able to provide for customer needs better and at a lower price. It can be argued that the Rover car company ran into difficulties at the beginning of the 21st century because, for one reason or another, it did not establish a competitive advantage over other car companies in terms of providing customers with what they wanted at the right price.

In keeping close to their customers, organisations need a sense of urgency and have to become customer driven, so that they not only meet customer expectations but exceed them. The customer can be seen as the driving force behind corporate strategy and it is customers, through their purchasing decisions, who define quality in products and services. The structure of a company or institution can help to monitor feedback from customers and inform all parts of an organisation.

The concentration on the division of labour in manufacturing in the past has led to the expansion of separate functional departments to specialise in production, marketing, sales and finance. At the same time a structure of senior, middle and junior managers developed in every department, and new departments, such as 'Human Resources' and 'Management Information', were formed in order to help in this managerial process. In these situations, employees could see themselves as working for a department as much as working for a company or for their customers. It can be argued that this structure has encouraged companies to divert time and energy into internal matters rather than to concentrate on the external customer. The re-organisations of the 1980s and 1990s and into the twenty-first century have helped to change organisational structure from a vertical and hierarchical structure into a collection of horizontal processes, each of which takes orders for products and services and delivers them (Figure 6.5).

The horizontal structure has helped to shift the focus of attention on to activities necessary to meet customer needs rather than on efforts to develop co-operation between internal departments. It can lead to employees working in integrated teams which are 'empowered' to make a range of decisions about the way they work. The teams will have responsibility for customer satisfaction through account managers who are accountable for levels of sales and satisfaction. This responsibility can stretch back to the design, production and supply of the product or service. They will be alongside, or even in competition,

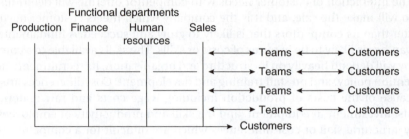

Figure 6.5 Vertical and horizontal structures.

with other teams, also in turn trying to satisfy their own customers. Employees will feel loyalty towards their team as much as their company, but the difference between this and loyalty to the old-fashioned departments is that the team is dependent on its success in meeting customer needs.

At the same time, it is important for teams and companies to recognise the variety of consumers whose needs they are attempting to meet. One way of considering groups of purchasers is in terms of their approach to new products and services (Figure 6.6). Consumers may be innovators, early adopters, early majority, late majority or laggards (see also Chapter 10).

Innovators – prepared to try something new, perhaps because it is new and innovative, whether it is a product or a concept

Early adopters – prepared to lead the way in terms of new products or services and to be among the first to try something

Early majority – not wanting to break new ground but following the innovators and early adopters once the product or service has been tested

Late majority – cautious imitators entering the market once the product or service has been established

Laggards – resistant to change and lacking in imagination in terms of new products and services

Figure 6.6 Product and service adoption patterns.

Research has shown that there are likely to be approximately the same proportion of innovators and early adopters as laggards, and with approximately 70 per cent of consumers divided between the two majority groups. These proportions vary for different products and may be influenced by the state of the economy in general and consumers' particular levels of disposable income. Innovators will tend to be found in the higher income groups for example, and there will tend to be more of them and early adopters if the economy is booming and income levels are high. At the same time, people may fall into different categories for different products and services. One family may be an innovator in terms of taking holidays, always prepared to travel to a new destination, while being laggards in terms information technology.

Another approach is to consider customer types and their behaviour. Six types of customer behaviour have been identified in dramatic terms:

Apostles
Loyalists
Mercenaries
Hostages
Defectors
Terrorists

'Apostles' are extremely loyal customers who are delighted with a product or service to the extent that they may personally identify with the organisation or its product. They are valuable to an organisation because they will spread the word about how satisfied they are with the product and the organisation responsible for it. The main problems arise just because of their fierce loyalty. They may demand special treatment or, because they begin to feel that they are part of the organisation they so admire, they may become a nuisance by involving themselves in areas which do not and should not concern them. Above all, the danger is that if they become dissatisfied with the product for any reason, they may become disillusioned to the point that they become the opposite of an 'apostle', they become a 'terrorist'.

'Loyalists' form the most important group of customers because they can be compared with the 'cash cows' of the Boston Matrix (see below) in forming the basis for organisational success. They are loyal customers who are less volatile than the 'apostles' and more critical of the organisation and its products, but they are the bedrock of support for a product or service and they need to be nurtured by the organisation so that their needs are met. On the other hand, 'mercenaries' are not loyal to any one product or organisation and they will go for the cheapest or most convenient without regard to the product brand or the organisation behind it. Some loyal shoppers buying, for example, cans of beer will always buy a particular brand irrespective of price or special offers. Mercenaries will buy their beer on the basis of price or alcoholic content without regard to brand. Strategic managers will have to decide how worthwhile it is to spend time and money on trying to convert 'mercenaries' into 'loyalists'.

'Hostages' are customers who appear to be very loyal but this may be because they do not have a choice. A supermarket may introduce lower prices and a wider product range than these in local shops so that all these products can be bought in one store, and the vast majority of local trade is diverted to it. The organisation will find it hard to distinguish between 'loyal' customers and 'hostages' until a competitor arrives, when it may become all too obvious. While some customers are hostages, the organisation has an opportunity to convert them into loyal consumers by satisfying their needs, but once a competitor arrives this could be too late. Dissatisfied 'hostages' will become 'defectors' as soon as the opportunity arises, and even 'loyalists' may defect if they feel that their needs are not being satisfied over a long enough period.

Once a customer has defected and given their custom to another organisation and to another product it may be very difficult to recover their loyalty.

The final group of customers are identified as 'terrorists', who are not just dissatisfied with an organisation and its products but want to attack it. These customers may have been apostles or loyalists until they felt let down by an organisation to such an extent that they are prepared to do something about it. They may start by complaining strongly to the organisation, then they may write to newspapers or appear on consumer affairs television programmes. Packaged holidays are an example of this escalation of dissatisfaction, where customers may feel that the company has not provided what they promised in their brochure. The splendidly equipped hotel in a quiet, convenient location may, in practice, prove to have a swimming pool in need of repair, be next to a building site and a 40-minute walk to the beach. A complaint to the local representative of the company may not lead to any action, stronger complaints to the company may 'fall on deaf ears' or produce a letter of apology which a 'terrorist' may feel is not sufficient to correct the situation, and the complaint is then taken to the trade association, newspapers, television or followed by even more direct action. A company can only hope to retrieve this situation by immediate, on-the-spot action, that is moving the customers to a hotel which fits the original description. After that point has been passed, the customers will have become 'terrorists' and the company can only hope to control the damage to its reputation by giving the customers what they want. They cannot hope to retain these customers as consumers of their products and services.

Strategic marketing in an organisation involves attempting to establish a strong base of loyal customers who are prejudiced in favour of buying goods and services from this organisation rather than from another one. Holiday companies want to encourage as many people as possible to look for their next holiday in the company's brochures – people who 'always go with X' who do not even bother to look at any other companies' brochures. These loyalists will be on the first posting list when brochures are distributed, and they may be offered discounts for early booking, or coupons for loyalty and 'long service'. At the same time, the company will want to encourage mercenaries, hostages and defectors to become loyalists. The company will usually want to rid itself of terrorists with the least possible damage, and apostles will decide for themselves when they have moved from being loyalists to becoming super-loyalists, and possibly a mixed blessing for the company.

6.6   The product life-cycle analysis

All products and services have a life-cycle in the sense that after they are introduced, they will tend to pass through periods of growth, relative stability and decline. In developing a strategy to market these goods and services, organisations need to consider the point in the life-cycle that they are at.

Introduction – a period of slow growth when the product/service is introduced

Growth – a period of relatively rapid expansion as the market accepts the product/service

Maturity – a period of slow but relatively steady growth as the product/service is accepted by most of the potential purchasers

Saturation – a period when a number of competitors have entered the market, which itself may not be growing, so that the demand for the product/service starts to fall

Decline – a period when performance starts a strong downward drift so that the demand for the product/service is in relatively fast decline

Figure 6.7 Life-cycle stages.

If a product or service is no longer 'solving a problem' in the best possible way for a sufficient number of people, the demand for it will decline. The performance of new products and services typically follows a pattern that includes four or five identifiable stages (Figure 6.7).

Of course, not all products and services follow this exact pattern, and time scales can vary considerably. Some products may be accepted very quickly, pass through a rapid growth period, followed by an almost telescoped maturity, saturation and decline. This is typical of sudden fashions or 'fads' such as the hula-hoop or the latest video film. Other products may take a long time to be accepted and have an introductory period of relatively slow growth before there is a sudden surge forward in demand. In the UK, the use of personal computers and logging into the internet have shown something of this pattern.

A careful analysis of the life-cycle helps strategic managers to focus on the appropriate marketing strategy for a particular stage in the life-cycle of their products and services. At the **introductory stage** a new product or service may be a substitute for an existing one, either directly or indirectly. A new car model may substitute directly for an existing one, while a new holiday destination may be an indirect substitute for existing destinations. Consumers may resist the new product for a time because they think that the old one still meets their needs. While the new product becomes known in the market, the demand will be slow, except in the case of a sudden fad or fashion which is able to make an immediate impact. Marketing strategy will often target previous customers because they have shown an interest in the past, and also people who are innovators who want to try new products.

'Did you realise,' the Assistant Managing Director of 'The Engineering Company' asks one of the Divisional Product Managers, 'that the main product produced in your Division is in the decline stage of its life-cycle?' 'Sales have fallen off recently, the DPM replies, 'but I'm sure its just short term.' 'If the analysis is correct and it is in the decline phase, this is a long-term

(Continued)

trend. Not only have sales declined, but so have future orders and it is difficult to see where new orders are coming from.' 'Something always turns up.' 'What!' the AMD exclaims, 'we cannot wait "for something to turn up", this is serious. What are you going to do about it?' 'It's a good product, we updated it a year ago.' 'Where are new customers coming from?' 'I don't know what Marketing and Sales are doing about that…' 'What are you doing about it? You know the product better than anybody, you have more contact with that area of industry than anybody.' 'I'm a product manager.' 'You may not have a product to manage soon! I want you to consider urgently ways of prolonging the life of this product, add features, make it more computer compatible and at the same time find out what your customers want in the future.'

ASSIGNMENT

What can the Divisional Product Manager do to satisfy the AMD?

At the **growth stage**, the benefit of the new product/service will have become accepted, production difficulties will have been overcome and development costs covered so that prices can be reduced. Marketing strategy will usually involve a wider promotion to target new customers. Competitors will start to enter the market and will promote their own product so that the awareness of the product in general will increase, thus helping to encourage further growth in the market.

At **maturity**, the product or service will have become widely accepted and competition will become the most important element for managers, so that strategy will be directed at attempting to retain market position or assume market leadership by emphasising the advantages of the company's products. **Saturation** will arrive when all the potential users of a product or service have satisfied their demand for it. Demand will be based on relatively few new customers and on existing customers buying additional items of the product or replacing products as they wear out. There will be strong competition in the market, which may lead to price wars. At the same time, managers will search for new products and services to replace the old ones.

A **decline** in the demand for a product or service will occur as new items are introduced, or as technology advances and fashion and taste alter. Marketing budgets may decline as companies decide that it is not worth spending money on an old product and feel it is better to invest in new products. One marketing strategy is to provide a commodity or service with a final boost by repackaging and reducing the price, perhaps in order to sell the last items.

A **recovery stage** may be possible with an item having a 'second life' as a result of a new surge of demand, perhaps because new products or services are not found to work well, or because of a new marketing and sales strategy. This occurs with companies, who also experience a life-cycle by going through a development period followed by rapid growth – a period of maturity followed by decline. This may be turned around by introducing new products, by internal restructuring, or by formulating a fresh strategy. In the early 1990s IBM experienced a fall in the demand for its products and a rise in the demand for new products in the information technology industry. This may have been due to a misjudgement of the point on their life-cycles of its established products.

IBM was a leader in terms of technology in the 1980s and saw tremendous growth, however the company was slow to move into the personal computer market and when it did competition was already considerable. The company went into decline, losing $16 billion between 1991 and 1993. However, IBM then appointed a new chief executive, altered its strategy and by 1997 had recovered to a point where its market value topped $100 billion and its shares were trading at record levels. The new chief executive had reduced the number of employees, in order to reduce costs, and brought about a fundamental change in corporate strategy by encouraging the company sales force to find out what consumers wanted, rather than believing that it knew best, and then giving that to them.

Strategic managers in the automobile industry certainly apply life-cycle considerations to the development and promotion of their cars. When a new car, or model, is introduced, the marketing strategy is likely to include heavy advertising to encourage an early demand. This will usually include a well-publicised launch of the new car, often in an exotic location, with a co-ordinated promotion campaign. As the growth of sales develops, this promotion of the new car will be designed to establish a market share and the reputation of the product will become more important. In the introductory stage, most of the purchasers will be innovators and 'risk-takers' who are prepared to buy the car before it has been tried and tested by other consumers.

In maturity, the attempt will be to maintain market share against the competition, and the emphasis in marketing and sales may be on the quality of the product and the features available in the car. After a period of wide acceptance, everybody who wants to buy a particular model will have bought it and new features or 'face-lifts' of the model will see only a small increase in demand while competition will increase as other manufacturers introduce newer models. After the saturation stage, the particular car or model will become relatively out of date compared with new models being introduced, and sales will start to decline as demand declines. At this point, manufacturers will have to decide when to phase out the present model and when to introduce the new one. Some producers have followed a policy of manufacturing models long after their popularity has declined but while there are still 'laggards' or 'loyal customers' willing to buy the model even if it is out of date. The cars may become cheaper in order to encourage a continued demand and as costs fall because development, tooling up, marketing and other costs have all been absorbed.

Most car manufacturers will stop producing a car model at a point on its life-cycle either when the demand for it has started to fall, or just before this point at a time when it is anticipated that the demand will fall. In the past,

British Leyland kept some of its models, such as the Mini, in production long after demand had started to decline. On the other hand, Ford has tended to follow a policy of replacing a model, such as the replacement of the Cortina by the Sierra and then by the Mondeo, directly saturation point has been reached. Another strategy used by many companies has been to sell off the end of a line by marketing the cars as 'special editions', often with extra features or in new colours.

6.7 The product/service portfolio

In developing a strategy, an organisation has to make decisions about the products and services it will produce, that is its portfolio (see also Chapter 3). Managers will want to be sure that their portfolio of products and services leads to profits. As well as profit, managers are concerned with market share, because this is an indication of the extent to which a product can generate cash. In general terms, the larger the share of the market that a product obtains, the more cash it can generate. On the other hand, there has to be a flow of cash to support the product and maintain its share of the market, in terms of product development and promotion. As a market expands, more will tend to be spent on a product in order to maintain its share or increase it and, in general, the greater the growth in the market, the more cash is used to support the expansion.

As the package-holiday market has expanded, for example, competition has increased, and for a company to maintain the market share of any of its products it has to spend more money on advertising and promotion. Maintaining this share may be important in order to retain the cash flow from the product to the company and therefore the company profits and share price. In strategic management it is useful to classify products in terms of those that generate cash for an organisation, those that require more money to support them than they generate, and those where the flow of cash in support and the flow of cash generated is about the same. New products, for example, will tend to need more cash support than they generate, and a company will need to have other products which are comparatively 'cash rich' in order to provide this support.

One classification used in strategic management is the **Boston Matrix, which is a classification of products/services within a portfolio linked to their cash usage based on relative market share and market growth rate**. The larger the share, the more cash can be generated from the production and sale of a product; while in growing markets, products will tend to be high users of cash in order to support the expansion. The Matrix provides the main categories of products or services with distinctive names to indicate their prospects (Figure 6.8).

A product or service that is a **star** has a high market share and a high market growth rate. It will also tend to generate as much cash as it uses and will be

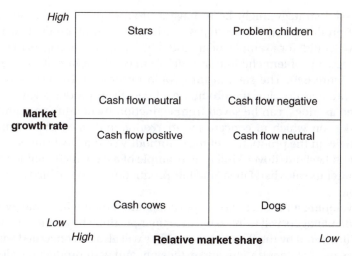

Figure 6.8　The Boston Matrix.

self-financing. In periods of economic expansion there will be a large number of star products which will normally be in a growing market and have a relatively large share of that market. Popular holidays, particular models of motor car, television sets and so on may fall into this category.

A product that is a **problem child** has a low market share but a high growth rate in a market that is itself growing. In order to increase market share, it may require investment and promotion and it will therefore use cash even though it is not generating very much. These products and services represent a problem because managers must decide whether to stop producing them or whether their potential growth makes an investment worthwhile. For example, a computer firm may decide that it is worth spending money on developing and promoting one of its software packages because, even though the sales are relatively small at the moment, there is considerable scope for expansion. It may be felt that the low sales are due to limited promotion and product development.

A product that is a **cash cow** has a high market share and a low market growth in a reasonably stable market. As a result of its established position, this type of product or service does not require developing or promoting and therefore cash is generated. A well-known brand of processed food may need little advertising for example, and may still hold a large share of the market. A product that can be described as a **dog** has a low market share and a low market growth, and in fact this type of product or service is likely to be a prime target for consideration for ending production. For example, a car model with poor and declining sales may cease to be manufactured, because the cost of the people and equipment employed in producing it may be considered a poor use of resources compared with the alternatives.

This Boston Matrix analysis can provide strategic managers with an indication of the type of policy they should follow for different products and services.

A successful strategy might be to have a product portfolio that included a range of products at different stages. Cash generated by products which are cash cows could, for example, be invested by company managers in the stars or in selected problem children in order to make them into stars (the 'rising stars') (Figure 6.8). The stars in turn could become cash cows as the need to promote and develop the product declines. Even products which can be described as 'dogs' can be saved from extinction by identifying segments of the market on which to concentrate marketing and sales, or by improving productivity in the production of the commodity so that cost can be reduced. The British Leyland/Rover Mini is an example of a car which retained a niche market after its sales had fallen, and low production costs enabled it to remain profitable.

In developing a product/service portfolio and a marketing strategy for this portfolio, managers will want to balance their portfolio by taking into account factors illustrated by the Boston Matrix. They will also be concerned with such factors as market penetration, and extension, and with product development and diversification.

Another matrix has been developed to summarise these strategies. **The Ansoff Matrix illustrates major business strategies which have a strong impact on marketing strategy**:

- **market penetration**, which involves either increasing sales to existing users or finding new customers in the same market;
- **product development**, which involves modifying the product/service in terms of such factors as quality and performance;
- **market extension**, which involves either finding new uses for the product/service and thus opening new markets, or taking the product/service into entirely new markets;
- **diversification**, which involves both product development and market extension.

Internet shopping has developed through market extension by companies using the service to open new markets. The internet also provides examples of market penetration by companies both increasing sales to existing customers and finding new customers. Motor car companies often follow a policy of product development in order to maintain or extend their share of the market. Particular models are provided with new features as well as being upgraded in terms of quality and performance. They also produce different models with different specifications in order to appeal to different segments of the market. This diversification includes more or less 'sporty' models, different sizes of engines, more or less economical models and so on, in order to produce market extension.

Figure 6.9 illustrates the Ansoff Matrix in terms of new and existing products/services and new and existing markets. Managers can develop strategy to place their products in different segments of the matrix, so that for

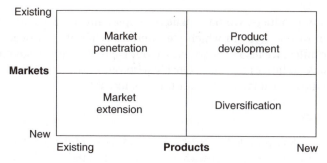

Figure 6.9 The Ansoff Matrix.

existing products they may attempt to achieve increased market penetration in existing markets while also attempting to find new markets. The market for four-wheel drive, off-the-road vehicles has been increased as a result of upgrading the luxury features of these vehicles to sell them as a fashionable vehicle for consumers who want to enjoy an outdoor image, while at the same time stressing their image as safe family vehicles.

In developing a product/service portfolio, management strategy will be to attempt to produce a range of products which are at different stages of their life-cycle, which are stars and cash cows or potential stars and cash cows, and which can be developed to further penetrate the market and extend it.

6.8　Critical success factors

Critical success factors are those elements of strategy in which the organisation must excel to outperform competition. Companies have to identify these factors for particular products/services and for specific strategies. A car manufacturer may decide that critical factors are the reliability of the motor car that the company produces and, as petrol prices rise, its economy. However, for a different model, economy may not be a critical factor whereas style and power may be.

'We are going to have to review our whole product portfolio,' the Assistant Managing Director of 'The Engineering Company' tells the Managing Director, 'I have started the process in every Division and Marketing have been analysing the data we have collected already.' 'So employing a Marketing Assistant has been useful?' 'We already had much of the information, but we had not used it very creatively. We hadn't properly analysed things like product life-cycle or cash flows, and at the same time we did not know our customers as well as we should.' 'So the Strategic Review is having an effect?' the MD asks. 'It's causing waves, but at least we are getting to grips with our strengths as well as our problems. We do make
(Continued)

high-quality products, we have skilled people, and we have an excellent reputation in the areas in which we operate. While it is critical we keep these attributes, we also have to reduce our costs so that we can cut prices and we have to link much more closely with our customers.' 'So you think those are the critical factors for our future success?'

ASSIGNMENT

Discuss the analysis provided by the Marketing Manager of the way the Company has operated in the past, and consider the importance of the critical success factors identified by the Assistant Managing Director.

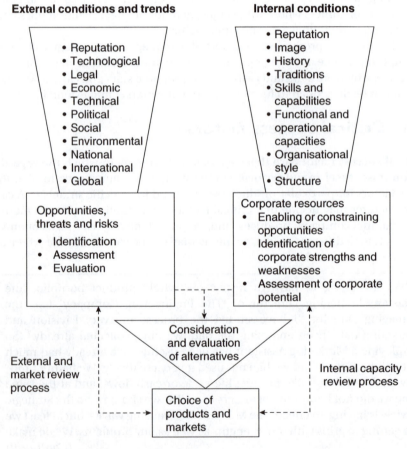

Figure 6.10 The development of organisation strategy.

The critical success factors have to be sufficient to provide a competitive advantage so that it is difficult for competitors to imitate these factors, while underpinning them are performance standards throughout the company which need to be achieved in order to outperform competing firms. These standards will depend on core competencies and the extent to which competitors are able to imitate them, so that a company will be in a stronger position if its core competencies are robust, difficult to imitate, and underpin high performance standards so providing a competitive advantage.

Strategic managers' plans of action will have to include a customer strategy which becomes a core competence for the company, so that the whole company is focused on the customer needs and on supplying them. Product development, product design, manufacture, marketing and sales have to be organised by managers in order to provide customers with what they want more successfully than other companies. Customer strategy and competitor advantage are at the core of this process. The external conditions and trends are one side of the equation in the development of organisation strategy, conditions internal to the organisation are the other, which are summarised in Figure 6.10. The PESTLE (or SPECTACLES) factors have to be considered along with the organisation's skills and capabilities, its reputation and image, its management and its structure. At the same time, the opportunities and threats to the organisation need to be balanced against its resources in a consideration of its offering of goods and services and the markets in which it operates. For long-term success, an organisation has to create the capability to enable it to identify and excel in the critical success factors for it to manage strategic change.

SUMMARY OF CONCEPTS

The customer comes first – Market segmentation – Products and services – The six target markets – The six Os – Competitive advantage – Niche marketing – Customer strategy – Vertical and horizontal structures – Life-cycle analysis – Stages of adoption – Product/service portfolio – Boston Matrix – Ansoff Matrix – Critical success factors

---

ASSIGNMENTS

1. What is the strategic importance of market segmentation?
2. What is the importance of competitive advantage for a company?
3. Discuss the part played by the product life-cycle in strategic marketing.
4. Why do companies need to have 'cash cows'?
5. How well does an organisation that you know provide customer service?
6. How has 'The Communications Company' attempted to improve its service to customers?

▼ **7** Strategy for maintaining a competitive advantage

OBJECTIVES

To discuss the importance of competitive advantage
To analyse distribution strategy
To describe channels of distribution
To analyse pricing policy
To provide an understanding of promotional strategy

Definition of competitive advantage – Transforming resources – Distribution policy – Channels of distribution – Pricing strategy – Influences of the market, consumers, the environment – Promotional strategy – Advertising – Maintaining a competitive advantage

7.1 **Competitive advantage**

Competitive advantage arises when an organisation has an advantage in competing with its rivals which enables it to earn returns on investment which are higher than the average for the sector. This means that a company which has a competitive advantage is able to compete successfully with other companies in its market. The objective of strategic management is to create a situation where the company has a sustainable competitive advantage. In order to maintain a competitive advantage, a strategic manager must have a clear view of an organisation's resources and how these can be used in the best possible way to achieve its corporate objectives.

The resources of an organisation include the skills of everybody who works for it, physical resources in terms of property, plant, vehicles and raw materials, and financial resources including cash and credit. **The management process is concerned, one way or another, with organising these resources so that there is a productive outcome.** This outcome is the production and development of products and services which provide benefits to consumers and are offered in such a way that the organisation is able to succeed. **Products and services have to be offered which customers want, are prepared to buy and** ·

able to buy, while the organisation has to make a profit or to receive sufficient revenue in one way or another to survive and flourish.

This process can be described as operations management. **Operations management can be seen as the process of transforming an organisation's resources from one state, such as raw materials, to another, such as a finished product**. This involves the management of a system which provides goods or services for a customer.

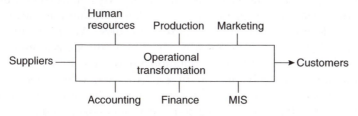

Figure 7.1   Transforming resources.

This transforming process (Figure 7.1) takes place in one way or another in all areas of the economy. In manufacturing, decisions have to be made about products, raw materials, machinery and equipment, employee skills, design and so on. In service industries, similar decisions have to be made. A fast food outlet has to decide what food to provide, where the supplies are to come from, how the food is to be cooked and how it is to be served. Holiday companies bring together airline flights, hotel rooms, rental cars, and couriers and guides in order to provide a package which will meet customer needs. **Whatever the process involved in transforming commodities and services to meet customer expectations, the final offering has to be distributed at the right time, in the right place and at the right price, and with sufficient information for customers to know what is available**.

In attempting to achieve a competitive advantage, resources are a foundation for an organisational strategy. One strategic option is to select a strategy that best exploits the organisation's resources and capabilities relative to external opportunities. To do this requires an analysis of the organisation's resources and capabilities, and their relative strengths and weaknesses compared to competitors, and then the identification of opportunities for a better use for them. Gaps in the resources or the capabilities of the organisation can be identified so that investment can be directed at filling the gaps and replenishing and upgrading resources and capabilities.

One aspect of competitive advantage is strategy aimed at positioning the organisation in its market, but fundamental to this process are the resources of the organisation and their availability. For example, the ability to establish a cost advantage requires: an efficient size of operating plant, whether it is a product unit such as a factory or an office-based operation; the excellent use of resources; and access to relatively low-cost inputs such as raw materials or labour. Low-cost labour has effectively been utilised by many companies in obtaining their goods from countries that pay low wages, such as China, or in obtaining high levels of productivity in the employment of people which can sometimes compensate for relatively high wage costs.

'How do we keep ahead of our competitors?' the Managing Director of 'The Engineering Company' asks the Assistant Managing Director, 'have your investigations so far produced any ideas?' 'My Report will set out the problems we face and suggest ways forward, but we know already that we have been losing out to other firms.' 'Yes, but why?' 'We had an advantage in the past because we were an early entrant into the areas of industry we serve and we have had a strong reputation, but this has started to turn into a reputation for being behind the times.' 'Are we old-fashioned?' 'Well it may be a matter of perception, but Marketing carried out a customer survey to find out what some of our customers thought of us, and they considered that our products are good, but expensive, that we are not on the cutting edge of computer technology and this is reflected in our billing systems, our structures and our general communications.' 'We use fax and e-mail.' 'It was more to do with a feeling that we did not listen to them, they felt taken for granted.' 'So we have lost our competitive advantage and we need to regain it.' 'It may be a matter of establishing new advantages.'

Competitive advantage can also be obtained through the differentiation of the organisation's products and services. This can be achieved as a result of image and reputation, product design and development, and through marketing and distribution capabilities (Figures 6.2 and 6.3 in the previous chapter). Meeting customer needs requires knowing what these are, having the right product and making it available in the best way. Strategic marketing is an essential aspect of organisational success and, as discussed in Chapters 5 and 6, this is based on having the right product, at the right price, in the right place and having it well promoted. Products and services need to provide customer benefits and they need to be at a price and in a location where customers will know about them and make the decision to buy (see Chapter 6).

7.2 Returns on investment

Achieving competitive advantage has to be viewed in the context of returns on investment, because it arises when an organisation is in a position where it can earn returns on investment which are higher that the average for the sector. This is another way of describing an organisation which can compete successfully with its rivals in its market. All organisations have to start with some capital invested in them, whether they are a local boys' or girls' football team which hires football pitches and buys team shirts from contributions from the players' parents, a sole trader who convinces a bank manager to lend £20,000 to add to his own investment, or a major company raising hundreds of thousands or even millions of pounds through a whole variety of means, ultimately including the Stock Exchange.

The common feature of these financial arrangements is that the people involved in making the investment will expect a return. This may be, in the case of the parents of the football players, that their children enjoy well-organised games which, preferably, they win. In the case of the bank, the return it will be looking for is the repayment of the loan and the interest on it and, in the case of the Stock Exchange, shareholders will be looking for a good dividend payment and the rising value of their shares. In financial terms, the return on investment is viewed through a number of ratios which express the key relationships in a set of accounts by comparing one figure with another.

The key business ratio is the 'return on capital employed' (ROCE) which compares the profit earned to the amount of long-term capital invested in the business. The capital employed includes the capital of the company owners plus any long-term liabilities. Investors will be looking for a consistent as well as a high return, while a low ROCE will indicate to them that there are weaknesses in either the profitability or the productivity of the business. This can be assessed by considering other ratios such as 'gross profit margin' (or mark-up) which is an indication of the trading profitability of the business. The cost of the product plus the gross profit (or mark-up) will equal the price (or sale). The mark-up will vary considerably in different types of business, depending on a variety of factors such as 'what the market will bear', whether the product is a necessity or a luxury, and the extent to which the business is labour intensive. The ratio is based on the cost of goods so a labour-intensive business, such as in the building industry, which involves a large amount of 'man-hours' compared to the materials used, will have a relatively high mark-up. Examples might be a restaurant which has a 100 per cent mark-up providing a 50 per cent 'gross profit on sales' ratio, or a newsagents shop with a 19 per cent mark-up and a 16 per cent 'gross profit on sales' ratio.

A fall below expectations in these ratios may be the result of a number of factors including a reduction in the selling price (see below), a poor buying policy so that the increasing costs of purchases are not passed on in the selling price, or poor stock control so that stocks are lost or wasted. It is also possible to look at the 'net profit margin' which measures the final profit made on sales after all of the running expenses have been deducted from the gross profit. If this ratio falls while the gross profit margin has remained constant, this suggests that running costs have increased. If it is assumed that price levels cannot easily be changed because of 'what the market will bear', competition in the market or for other reasons, companies can attempt to increase their profits by looking at such factors as their running costs, their stock control arrangements and their buying policies and practices.

The other major factor which affects overall profit is productivity, and there are a number of accounting ratios used in this connection. 'Sales per employee' is used to measure the productivity of the employee of the business and reflects the importance of managers making effective use of all the people in the organisation. 'Asset turnover' measures the number of times the value of the assets employed by an organisation have been covered by sales. The 'assets' are those possessions or advantages of a business on which a money value can be placed, and include business premises, furniture and fittings, company stock, cash held by the company and money held in a bank account.

'Stock turnover' is a measure of the effective use of stock by the company. The actual turnover will depend on the type of industry in which an organisation is working. For example, a supermarket will have a wider range of products in its stock and a faster turnover than an engineering company. 'Current ratio' compares all current assets with current liabilities and indicates the ease with which a business will be able to meet its debts. Shareholders are interested in the 'dividend yield' which relates the income from shares or the dividend, to the value of the investment in the business. The result can be compared with interest rates from other types of investment, although with shares the actual share price will also be taken into account as a capital gain for the investor.

The long-term finance of a business will be provided by shareholders and long-term lenders such as banks. The 'gearing ratio' is an assessment of the extent to which a firm is financed by long-term loans. Potential lenders tend to prefer to see the owners and shareholders of a business providing a reasonably high proportion of its capital, and if more long-term lending would push the gearing ratio higher they may not be prepared to lend. The 'interest cover ratio' indicates the ability of the business to meet its interest payments. If the gearing ratio is too high, a business will have large interest costs to meet out of its gross profits. If the gearing ratio becomes too high or if interest rates rise, the interest cover will be reduced and companies may increase shareholder funds by issuing shares, or use cash assets to repay long-term loans.

Ratios of this kind can be used to compare companies in the same business and the trend of results can be monitored so that action can be taken when it is required. There are considerable differences between the ratios expected in different industries so that it is difficult to use them for comparisons between industries. For example, newsagents will have a much higher stock turnover than motor car companies so that comparisons between them are difficult, although the ROCE is used for this purpose.

The ratios will help to identify strengths and weaknesses in a business. They do not identify the reasons for these, which will be related to the particular activities and circumstances of the company and the industry. The ratios do provide an indication of successes and problems which can lead managers to take appropriate action, whether it is to encourage a successful policy or to solve a problem. An element of strategic management is to maintain an organisation's financial ratios at a favourable level in order to sustain a competitive advantage.

7.3 The location and distribution of products and services

In marketing terms, the 'place' is where the final exchange occurs between the seller and the purchaser. Managers have to make decisions about where this exchange takes place and how. Bank services, for example, were at one time usually provided 'across the counter', but in recent years they have moved to cash points and increasingly to telephone and internet banking. Place may be a physical location, such as a shop, or it may be a system of communication such as the internet or mail order. These services have altered the idea of place and location in that the services are now available in people's homes, and information can be accessed on a wide range of goods and services on a worldwide basis. Traditional retailing companies in the UK, such as Marks & Spencer and Selfridges, have introduced mail-order catalogues in order to widen the market for their goods. E-commerce companies have developed to supply customers' needs in a whole range of areas, so that consumers can order wine, books or holidays through these means of communication after carrying out their own research on the internet or through the study of catalogues and brochures in their own home, at their place of work or anywhere else where they have access to the technology.

Managers also have to decide about channels of distribution. **A distribution channel is the process that brings together an organisation and its customers at a particular place and time for the purpose of exchange**. This may be a shop, office, or via a telephone, fax or computer link. Managers have to decide how to organise their distribution channels, in terms of the number of outlets, whether to use middlemen and the preferences of their customers. The channel is a set of individuals and companies that assist in transferring the title of ownership of a particular commodity as it moves from the producer to the consumer. A car, for example, may be successively owned by the manufacturer, the wholesaler, the retailer and the final consumer. The process of transferring ownership from the manufacturer to the consumer involves buildings, equipment, transport, middlemen, salespeople, telephones, computers and administration.

The channel of distribution is designed to overcome the main gaps of time and place that separate goods and services from those who want to use them. This can be called **'logistics management', which is about having the correct product or service in the right place at the right time**.

The length of a channel of distribution reflects the number of levels interposed between the production of a commodity or service and its final exchange with consumers. The breadth of a channel of distribution is related

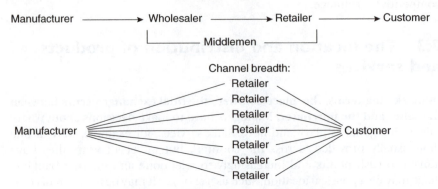

Figure 7.2 Channel length and breadth.

to the total number of different channels (such as retailers) to be used at each level (Figure 7.2). A manufacturer may decide to reduce the length of the channel of distribution for its products by cutting out wholesalers and retailers and selling directly to the consumer. Channel breadth may be reduced by selling goods through only one company of retail shops. On the other hand, it may be increased by selling through a wider variety of shops. Stamps were at one time only sold through post offices or from stamp machines, until it was decided to sell them through a variety of outlets including post offices, newsagents and confectioners.

The advantage to a customer of a direct channel of distribution, that is when it deals directly with its customers, is that the company can retain control of channel activities. It will have direct contact with customers, which can provide a better understanding of their needs and a rapid awareness of any problems that arise, and it can respond quickly to changes in the market and to particular needs of market segments. On the other hand, by using specialist middlemen, such as retailers, to sell goods a company can make use of their expertise in this particular part of the distribution chain.

'The Engineering Company' calls in 'The Communications Company' to discuss its problems in systems and communications. The consultant from 'The Communications Company' discusses the Company recommendations with the Managing Director and Assistant Managing Director. 'As you know we specialise in solving business problems through information technology, although recently we have expanded into wider "Company Health Checks", and although we started by looking at your IT systems we soon found ourselves looking at a wider picture as a result of discussion with people here.' 'It was the Health Check feature which attracted us to you,' the MD confirms. 'Your IT system is right for your purposes as far as it goes and it has been applied to all your major functions, but there are more recent systems which are faster and can provide you with an integrated programme. It would also help to support the data collection exercise being carried out by Marketing which at the moment is using its own system. However we do not see that as you main problem.'

'This is more to do with structure. It is left to each Product Division to look after their customers. This means that it is very patchy with some customers being well looked after, some not. You do not have any system of account managers, that is an individual with the responsibility of looking after a particular account or customer. Nor do you have any focused system of sales, that is people concentrating on finding new business. The Divisions are supposed to keep close to their customers and to look out for new business, but their main expertise is on production. You have both a fairly long channel of distribution and a broad one. Your suppliers have their own system of suppliers and then you distribute your products to a range of different customers. You have many small companies providing components and in comparison you have relatively few customers, so you might want to narrow the supply side of your channel of distribution. A new IT system would help you to control your supply, monitor costs and throughput and would help your new Account Managers to provide what the customers want when they want it.'

ASSIGNMENT

Draw a diagram to illustrate the channel of distribution of 'The Engineering Company' and discuss the implications of the advice given to it by the Consultant.

The choice of a channel of distribution, whether broad or narrow, long or short, direct or indirect, will depend on considerations of efficiency and effectiveness. Decisions will depend on the nature of the market and of the product/service on offer. Typically, services to individuals will benefit from relatively narrow, short and direct channels of distribution, so that the service is concentrated on the individual receiving it. Tailor-made holidays will usually be like this, where the individual holiday-maker will arrange an itinerary with the representative of a specialist holiday company. Packaged holidays, on the other hand, can be sold with a wider and longer channel of distribution. Manufactured products will often have long and indirect channels, although they may still be fairly narrow. Cars manufacturers may sell their products through wholesalers who then pass them on to specialist retailers for sale to the final buyer. In some cases this channel has been a narrow one, as customers have only been able to buy particular makes of car through a dealer registered with the manufacturer or wholesaler.

With the expansion of internet shopping, alongside telephone shopping and mail order, channels of distribution have tended to become wider, shorter and more direct. This has meant that the idea of 'place' in terms of marketing and selling strategy has changed considerably over a period of time. While these developments have greatly increased customer convenience, they have placed a premium on customer confidence. Buying consumer goods via the telephone, fax or internet means that the customer does not see them or 'handle' them until they have been bought. Customers have to be confident that the descriptions they see of the goods are accurate and that they can be easily returned if they do not satisfy the consumer needs.

7.4 Pricing strategy

In order to achieve the objectives of the company, managers have to sell its products or services, and this means not only distributing the products in the best possible way to reach consumers but also having them at a price which will attract actual purchases. Price must be consistent with the total marketing strategy for a product, although at the same time it will depend very heavily on the supply and demand for the product. If a product is available in large quantities and demand is relatively low, the price is likely to be low as well because consumers have a wide choice and can choose or bargain for a lower priced item. If in these circumstances the price is originally set by a company at a high level, it will soon fall in order to reach a point where demand is more equal to the supply. This all depends, of course, on what economists refer to as 'other things being equal', that is where consumers have wide information about the market for this commodity and where there is a high level of competition between suppliers.

The 'rules' of supply and demand suggest that provided consumers have perfect knowledge of the marketplace and perfect mobility within it, and suppliers have perfect competition, so that they have equal shares of the market and equal access to consumers, price will rise or fall until the supply of a product or service equals the demand for it. The 'equilibrium price' (Figure 7.3) is where supply and demand are equal. In practice, these perfect

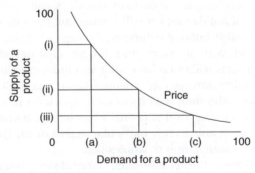

Figure 7.3 Equilibrium price.

conditions do not usually apply and although the price is greatly influenced by supply and demand, other factors will also have an effect.

Strategic managers are usually trying to create a less than perfect market-place where 'other things are not equal' and where they have a competitive advantage. Their marketing strategy is designed to differentiate the products of their company from the products of other companies so that instead of there being a large number of the same products available to consumers, there are a number of differentiated products. It can be argued that company marketing attempts to create a monopoly for that company's products so that the company can control prices by controlling the supply of the product. The Microsoft company has been an example of this approach in terms of information technology, and its success in creating a near monopoly is shown by the fact that it has been subject to the anti-monopoly (or anti-trust) laws of the United States.

In practice, markets tend to reflect various stages of imperfection in which companies have a larger or smaller share of the market, and consumer information and mobility are limited. The 'rules' of supply, demand and price do not operate perfectly in the vast majority of actual market situations, but they remain as underlying trends or tendencies which need to be taken into account. Advertising, mail-order catalogues and internet shopping are all attempts to widen information for consumers and persuade them to buy particular goods while, in practice, consumers are limited in their information by time and access and their ability to 'shop around'. Pricing strategy in fact will usually depend on the state of the market or 'what the market will bear'. Managers may want to charge a high price in order to increase profit margins, but if this policy reduces demand too much, the price will have to be lowered. In order to maximise demand, a manager may want to charge the lowest possible price, however this price will have to be high enough to provide a reasonable margin of profit.

'The Communications Company' has the advantage that its services are available to its customers on their own premises. Either the Company is able to work with their customers by telephone, by fax or by e-mail, or the Company specialists travel to the customers' premises. There is a short channel of distribution in the sense that the Company has produced the product and sells it directly to customers. The senior managers have considered franchising their product, so that they could license other companies to supply the service, but before they were able to do this, competing companies started to provide rival services. The Company product has passed through very rapid introductory and maturity stages of its life-cycle and it was discovered that rival companies were offering their services at lower prices. As a result, the Company reduced prices and attempted to add features to its service. In particular, it offered a free follow-up service once customer problems have been solved.

In the introductory stage of the product life-cycle (see Chapter 6), demand may grow rapidly and supply may be limited. Price may not be a very important part of consumers' purchasing decisions because at this stage the consumers are 'innovators' – anxious to be among the first to obtain the product. Product prices may be high at this stage as companies recoup some of their research and development costs. For example, the original personal computers were expensive as were the early wide-screen televisions and advanced photo system cameras.

At the mature stage of the life-cycle, the price of the product may be reduced in order to maintain or increase market share in what is likely to be an increasingly competitive market. At the saturation and decline stage, price will be manipulated depending on market share and sales volume. The price of a product may be raised in order to create a 'cash cow' within an established market, or the price may be lowered through sales 'promotions' in order to extend sales. Management strategy will often be to position a product in terms of price in one or other area or segment of the market. A car manufacturer may concentrate its effort on the cheaper end of the market, producing small, economical cars which can be sold at a low price. Other manufacturers may concentrate on the luxury and expensive end of the car market, or the family market, or the company car fleet market. Large manufacturers, such as Ford and General Motors, produce a range of cars which aim to cover a wide number of market segments and price ranges.

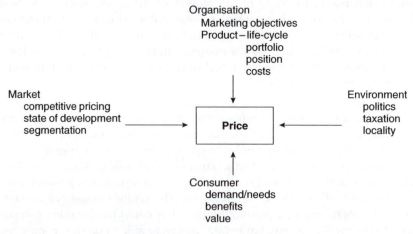

Figure 7.4   Pricing policy.

7.5   The influences on price

The actual price of a product or service is based upon a range of factors which influence decisions on it, as illustrated in Figure 7.4. It is possible to group these factors into four main areas:

- those under the control of the organisation;
- those that operate in the market in which the organisation operates;
- those influenced by customers' needs;
- those determined by the marketing environment.

Within an organisation, prices will be determined by its marketing objectives. The price of a product or service is only one of the elements in the marketing mix and it has to relate to all the other influences in the mix. The price must be consistent with the total marketing strategy devised for the product/service. Put simply, this means that if the objective is to sell large quantities of a product, putting a high price on it is unlikely to help in the achievement of this objective. On the other hand, if the objective is to market a product to a relatively small segment of consumers in the higher income bracket, setting a high price may fit in well with this approach.

Pricing strategy will also depend on the position of a product/service in its life-cycle. In the introductory and high-growth phase, demand grows fast and the product may be in relatively short supply, while the price is unlikely to be the most important factor to the consumer (Figure 7.5). So at this stage, price can be set at a high level. As more of the product becomes available and competitors enter the market, price may need to be lowered to increase the share of the market among the 'early majority' of consumers. At the saturation and decline stages, price is often reduced in order to attempt to maintain demand and sales. In some circumstances, the price may be raised at this stage, if the market share and sales volume remain robust, in order to attempt a 'cash killing' before demand runs out. Loyal customers and laggards who are eventually making the decision to buy the product may create a position where a product becoming a 'dog' has a late resurgence as a 'cash cow' as production declines and the product become relatively scarce.

Marketing objectives
Product life-cycle
Costs – cost, plus fixed costs, variable costs, marginal costs
Price of other goods
Organisational image

Figure 7.5   Organisation factors influencing price.

The price of a product/service may be influenced by the price of other goods and services in the company's portfolio. The price may need to reflect the company's image in the marketplace. If the company wants to be known as providing luxury goods, all its products may be expected to have a high price. If however a company targets lower income and economy segments of the market, it may be assumed that all its products are relatively cheap.

For example, a car manufacturer who concentrates on quality may produce a small, relatively economical car, but price it at the top of the range in terms of cars of a similar size, in order to emphasise that it may be small but it is still of high quality. In these circumstances, price may be largely a question of product positioning in the market.

On the other hand, some products/service may be priced at a lower level than other products in the company portfolio as a 'loss leader' aimed at penetrating and developing the market. Retailers will often do this in order to attract customers into their shops, and manufacturers may do this in order to establish their brand name. There is a limit to how far managers can follow this strategy, as the loss leaders may not even cover their costs. In fact, prices can be arrived at by a cost-plus process in an attempt to make sure that costs are covered by sales. In practice, costs will vary according to changes in raw material prices, fuel and transport costs, wage rises and so on. It is still possible to simply add a percentage to the costs at any time to arrive at a price and if this is large enough, variations in costs can be absorbed. This approach means that prices do not need to be changed in response to demand, and it can be considered to be a 'fair' system because the seller makes a fair return while not taking advantage of buyers when demand is greater than supply.

In order for a company to make a profit, any cost-plus or 'mark-up' system of pricing has to be based on total costs. However some prices may be based on other costs. Variable costs vary directly with the level of output, so that the greater the output of a company, the higher the costs in terms of wages and material costs. Fixed costs do not vary with the level of output; they are overheads in the form of the costs of buildings, vehicles and other fixed assets, management and finance. They have to be met whatever the level of output. Marginal costs are the costs of producing an extra unit, such as another car coming off the production line. It is possible to determine price by ignoring fixed costs, which are incurred independently of the level of output, on the basis that any price that is in excess of the unit marginal costs will make a contribution to these fixed costs. If the marginal costs of producing an extra car are more than covered by the price, then there is some contribution to fixed costs. Some products, such as 'loss leaders', may be priced on the basis of covering only fixed costs, with the variable costs covered by other sources of revenue. In the end, however, total costs must be more than covered in one way or another for a company to survive. Public sector organisations also have to cover their costs through grants and subsidies or by charging for their services. In the long run, price has to reflect this situation.

7.6 The influence of the market on price

One problem of the cost-plus approach to pricing strategy is that the price may be established independently of the rest of the marketing mix rather than an intrinsic element of it. Pricing policy (Figure 7.6) will depend on the type of

Price-skimming
Price-penetration
'What the market will bear'
The 'going rate'

Figure 7.6   Market price.

market in which the product/service is involved in terms of supply and demand. **A 'price-skimming' policy involves charging high initial prices for a product/service and then lowering prices as costs fall**. The high price will attract competitors and will limit demand, so that this can only operate where competitors will be slow to enter the market and where there is a segment of consumers (innovators) prepared to pay the high price. **A 'price-penetration' policy is based on charging a low initial price in order to attract consumers and to obtain a large market share**. This policy depends on the low price stimulating market growth and discouraging competitors.

Both price-skimming and price-penetration policies depend on the degree of elasticity of demand in the market for particular products. Demand is said to be 'elastic' when it is very responsive to changes in price, so that it falls when prices are raised and increases when prices are reduced. Demand can be said to be 'inelastic' when it is unresponsive to changes in price. Price-skimming is possible where demand is relatively inelastic, so that the initial high price does not cause a reduction in demand. Innovations in information technology have been of this nature, from computer games to the first introduction of access to the internet. Price-penetration will be possible when the elasticity of demand is high, so that the market will respond to low prices by there being high demand. Moves to increase internet services by offering free access are an example of this approach, and the expansion of the mobile telephone market also shows signs of this approach. All managers will have to consider the relative elasticity of demand in the market for their product or service in determining prices.

They will also have to consider the 'going rate' set by competitors, and they will not be able to differ greatly from this unless they can offer a clear incentive such as extra features. They will also need to consider the segmentation of the market so that they offer the appropriate product at the right price for the various segments. Prices may be fixed slightly above or below those of competitors, either to increase profit margins or to increase demand. Service stations, for example, may base their petrol price on competing service stations so that they are a penny or a fraction of a penny a litre higher or lower, depending on their location. Motorway service stations are usually able to charge higher prices because of their convenience for motorway drivers and the fact that drivers who need petrol have little choice. This is also an example of charging 'what the market will bear'. In areas where incomes are relatively high, prices will tend to be higher than in areas where incomes are lower. Village shops may decide to charge higher prices because they have a relatively 'captive' market.

7.7 The influence of the consumer on price

It can be argued that ultimately it is the customer who will decide whether or not the price of a product/service is at the correct level. When arriving at a pricing strategy, managers must consider consumers' buying decisions (Figure 7.7). When consumers buy a product/service, they exchange something of value, the price, to obtain something of value, the product/service. They pay the price with money they have earned in one way or another in order to receive the benefits from obtaining the product/service.

Effective consumer-orientated pricing strategy involves understanding the value the consumer places on the benefits received and setting a price consistent with this value, and it can be argued that the marketing-orientated approach to price is based on customers' perceptions. The 'cost' to the consumer is not only the price but any other negative outcomes of a proposed exchange. These may include problems of obtaining a product/service, such as having to wait for it or travel to obtain it. In the same way, benefits for a consumer may include not only the actual product/service but also other factors, such as the ease of obtaining it, its quality and the way it is provided. All products and service can be provided in a relatively positive or negative way. For example, large pieces of furniture, such as beds, are usually delivered within 24 hours in the United States, whereas in the UK customers often have to wait weeks for delivery. Service providers, such as travel agents, may be judged by their customers as much on the efficiency, care and consideration of their service as by their price.

Consumer demand

Perceived benefits

Perceived value

Use value

Consumer 'costs'

Figure 7.7 Consumers' influence on price.

It can be argued that price should reflect the perceived value to the consumer and, therefore, an organisation should build up the perceived value of a product/service if it wants to charge a higher price. The most important value for the consumer is the 'use value'. Unless consumers have a use for a product/service and value it at a level that provides a satisfactory margin of profit or revenue to the supplier, the supplier will not be able to continue to provide the product/service. 'Negative esteem' value means that the price is not in line with the qualities perceived by the consumer, while 'positive esteem' reflects the value in which the product/service is held.

7.8　The influence of the environment on price

Political factors may influence the price of a product or service through legislation, taxation and subsidies (Figure 7.8). Government control may impose price controls, or limit company freedom to fix prices through monopoly legislation. Government economic policy will affect raw material costs and the ease with which companies can export their goods. A highly valued currency may create difficulties for exporters by making their goods relatively expensive for foreign buyers. At the same time, their imported raw materials will be cheaper. Taxation can greatly affect the price of goods and services. Value added tax (VAT), purchase taxes and sales taxes all increase the final price. These may reflect government economic policy, in terms of the way it wants to collect revenue, or social and environmental policy. Taxation of tobacco, alcohol and petrol all reflect these polices and increase the price to the consumer by a considerable amount.

> Taxation
>
> Exchange rates
>
> Locality
>
> Political policies

Figure 7.8　Other influences on price.

The environment may also be a factor in prices in relation to locality, that is where a product is produced and sold. Different parts of a country may be relatively cheap or expensive, depending on average incomes and distribution factors. House prices, for example, vary considerably in different towns based on supply and demand and 'what the market will bear'. The price of eggs may be cheaper 'at the farm gate' than in the supermarket although, with the development of international trade and improvements in distribution channels, imported goods may undercut home-produced goods.

7.9　Pricing strategy

All organisations have to decide on their pricing objectives, which may be to maximise profits, or to increase demand and market share. Pricing strategy may be based on costs, on consumer demand or on competition, or it may be seen as a sophisticated process based on detailed market research and analysis, although often it is based on a 'cost-plus' process, on a consideration of competitors' prices and on 'what the market will bear'. Price discrimination may be a factor, with different prices charged to children or senior citizens for the same service. Discounts may be given in certain circumstances, for example when a large quantity is bought. Pricing may reflect a company's decision to 'flood' the market with a commodity in order to achieve a large market share by selling at a relatively low price, or may reflect a 'dumping' policy where goods are placed on the market at a low price simply to get rid of them.

'There are two other matters I would like to raise,' the Consultant from 'The Communications Company' tells the MD and AMD of 'The Engineering Company', 'one is the question of your pricing strategy and the other is your image. Nobody has found it easy to tell me how prices are arrived at, but as far as I can see it is decided on cost-plus. In some cases this means that you are in danger of charging more than the market can bear, and in other cases you could probably charge more and increase your profit margin. You need to consider a pricing strategy which takes into account your competitors' prices and the expectations of your customers. You may have to look at your costs and the design of your products so that they match a market price.' 'We are not going to sacrifice quality,' the MD says. 'No, but the quality should be linked to customer requirements, not some past view of standards. The other matter is your image. You are perceived as old-fashioned and set in your ways. New accounts managers could help to change this, particularly if they are supported by an updated IT system and a more prominent marketing function. Your Marketing Manager has been described by you as a "middle manager" at the same level as the Divisional Product Managers, but he is perceived to be more junior to them, with less authority because he does not have an obvious product. He has been doing some very good work, he seems to be talented and my recommendation is that his post should be upgraded to a similar level as the Head of Finance.' 'We can't afford to give him a huge pay rise,' says the MD. 'His salary is less important than his position in the structure.'

ASSIGNMENT

Consider in more detail how 'The Engineering Company' can improve its image. Can price strategy play a part in this?

High prices may be charged for luxury goods and services, either because they involve a high level of costs or because they are in short supply compared to the demand. Hotels, for example, charge according to their location, the services they offer, the size of their rooms and so on – that is, on the basis of their costs and what they are offering. However, if there is only one hotel in a desirable location it may be able to charge premium prices even though it offers limited services. On the other hand, the price of a commodity or service may be set at a high level so that it appears to be a luxury and therefore may be sought after for that reason. This approach relies on a consumer view that 'it must be good because it is so expensive', but this is a risky policy which works only while the commodity is perceived to be of high value. Fashion products, for example, do not necessarily reflect the costs of producing them in their price but depend on the demand for them because of their perceived exclusivity.

Whatever the pricing policy of a company, it plays an important part in the competitive and the promotional strategy of any organisation.

7.10 Promotional strategy

Promotion requires communication with customers and potential customers. It is obvious that people have to have heard of a product/service before they can make use of it or buy it. They need information about the product in order to decide whether or not they want it. At the same time, most companies want to create a favourable 'image' for their products in order to maintain or increase levels of demand. **The term 'image' in this context refers to people's conception of a product or service**. This image will be developed through the nature of the product, its price, the 'place' in which it is sold and through promotion. It will be created by the marketing mix of those elements and through publicity, public relations and advertising, which will also influence the corporate image, which is the individual style or 'personality' of an organisation.

Promotion can be seen as the whole collection of methods by which the task of providing information on, and creating a positive image of, organisations and their products and services may be carried out. The process of promotion will have the objective of encouraging consumers to a point where they 'demand' a product or service and 'make a decision to buy' (Figure 7.9). The process of arriving at this decision can be divided into stages of awareness, knowledge, understanding, conviction and action. At first, consumers become aware that they have a need that must be satisfied, then they discover that

Awareness – potential consumers have to become aware of the fact they have a need that must be satisfied and that there are various ways of satisfying it.

Knowledge – after consumers have realised the need exists, they develop an interest in learning more about products on offer.

Understanding – consumers begin to understand what is on offer, the alternative courses of action, the benefits available and the costs involved.

Attitude – consumers are able to compare alternative courses of action, including the option of doing nothing, and form opinions and attitudes based on their image of these alternatives.

Conviction – consumers will have a preference for a product or a course of action and also a conviction for demanding it. At this stage, consumers may have all the information and understanding required to form a strong conviction that they ought to, or they want to, demand the product/service. However, they may not be quite able to make up their minds to act.

Action – the 'closing' or 'clinching' of the sale may require the active involvement of a sales person to remove any remaining doubts and to convert the commitment of the consumer into action.

Figure 7.9 The decision to buy.

there are ways of satisfying this need, they consider the alternative methods of satisfying it, make a decision and act by buying the product. Promotional strategy will be directed at any and all these stages in order to attempt to provide information about a particular alternative way of satisfying the consumer need, and also to persuade the consumer that this is the best method.

At the awareness stage, managers will not only identify the consumer needs to be satisfied but also attempt to encourage people into believing that they have this need. The literature attached to diets and exercise regimes is based on the view that people should be 'fitter', 'more shapely', 'thinner' and so on. People who are quite content with their size and shape may be encouraged to feel that they have a 'need' to lose weight. There is then information on how this result can be achieved by following a particular diet or by using a particular piece of equipment. The consumer has to understand how this result is to be achieved and to be convinced that it will work. The action of buying will occur when the consumer feels that the cost of the product is a 'bargain' in comparison with the benefit which will be received from it.

This process assumes that potential customers pass through a hierarchy of states on the way to making a demand. The task in terms of promotional strategy is to identify the stage that the target group is at and to develop a campaign that will move them on to the next stage. In practice, this process may be truncated or telescoped so that awareness leads rapidly through knowledge and understanding to conviction and action.

7.11 Advertising

'To advertise' is to give public notice of a product or service, and advertisements are methods of doing this. **Advertising aims at informing and persuading potential customers about the benefits of a product/service**. Advertising aims to change customers' attitudes and patterns of behaviour to a product/service. At one level, advertising may be purely informative, simply describing the product, but most advertising has the objective of persuading as well as informing (Figure 7.10).

Advertising aims to change customers' attitudes and/or patterns of behaviour to a product/service. The attempt is to persuade people that certain products/ services satisfy their needs better than others. The aim is to establish a distinctive and, if possible, unique 'brand' identity that will prove attractive to potential customers. This will be linked to the quality of the product/service and the benefits that the customer can receive from it. In most cases, the ideal advertisement will build long-term goodwill between the organisation and its customers. Coca-Cola advertisements attempt to create a product image which links the product with happiness, vitality and youth, so that customers and potential customers feel good about the product. This will need reinforcement from time to time because markets are not static, and both existing

To attract attention to a product or service

To command attention and interest

To create a desire

To inspire conviction

To provoke action by consumers

Figure 7.10   Objectives of advertising.

customers and new customers need to be reminded of the availability of a product/service and the benefits that it can provide.

The specific objectives of advertising will depend on the nature of the product, the stage it has reached in its life-cycle and the strategy of competitors. Advertising may also be concerned with confirming that the product exists and is well known for the benefit of shareholders, employees and any other stakeholders. This may reassure them about the organisation with which they are involved, because they may feel that advertising is the best way to keep the attention of the public even when this may not really be the case. Much advertising is directed at a narrow band of people, for example through trade and specialised journals, who may be more knowledgeable than the general public or more important for the sales of the product. For example, sports products may be advertised mainly in the specialist magazines for a particular sport.

The advertising process can be said to involve defining the objectives of advertising so that the results can be measured. This can be summarised as **DAGMAR**:

> **D**efine
> **A**dvertising
> **G**oals, for
> **M**easured
> **A**dvertising
> **R**esults

At its simplest, measurement will involve checking to make sure that an advertisement achieves its objective. For example, an advertisement for staff should lead to a sufficient number of applications for a company to make the appointments it wants. However, many advertisements are only a part of a campaign to promote a product and it may be difficult to know exactly the part played by the advertising in general or by a particular advertisement. For example, a product may be advertised on national television and also promoted through shops receiving discounts and promotional material. Companies attempt to find out which part of the campaign was most successful, by carrying out surveys in which they ask buyers where they heard of the product or why they decided to buy it.

Advertising has been defined (by the Institute of Practitioners in Advertising) as '**the most persuasive possible selling message to the right prospects for the product or service at the lowest possible price**'. Strategic managers will want to find the most cost-effective medium for advertising, the best time to advertise and the method by which the success of the advertising will be measured. A causal relationship between advertising and sales may be difficult to establish. After an advertising campaign the demand for a product may increase and this may be as a result of the campaign, but also may be due or partly due to other factors. The campaign may have coincided with a general increase in demand, or to a change in a competitor's product, or to a change in customers' needs. The old adage that 'half the advertising is successful, but it is not known which half' tends to be true.

The result of this uncertainty about the exact effects of advertising means that a campaign may be carried out for a variety of reasons and without a very precise idea of its overall effects. Others methods of promotion may be used at the same time to provide an overall strategic campaign.

7.12 Public relations and publicity

Public relations and publicity can be seen as complementary strategies to advertising in that they are aimed at drawing attention to an organisation, its products and its services (Figure 7.11). One major difference is that they are usually free. For example, press coverage of the launch of a new model of motor car will be free in the sense that the manufacturer will not pay for the actual coverage. However, the company will have had to pay for the actual launch and this often involves an elaborately staged event with invitations to all the relevant reporters, and this in itself may be expensive. Also, of course, free press and television coverage may not always be favourable to the company or the product. The television programme *Watchdog*, for example, is built on customers' complaints about companies.

Advertising

Publicity

Public relations

Figure 7.11 Promotional methods.

Many companies use customer service as a method of promoting themselves and their products and services. They want to be known for providing high-quality products and services, and for supporting customers once they have actually made the decision to buy. **Public relations can be seen as a deliberate, planned and sustained effort by an organisation to establish and monitor understanding between itself and its public in order to improve its image**. Public relations is about any activity which is deliberately aimed at improving customers' image of a company or institution. After-sales service is one aspect of this approach. Marks & Spencer created something of a High Street revolution when they accepted undamaged returned goods with a receipt without question. This provided the company with a huge competitive advantage until other retail companies followed their lead.

Publicity is anything which creates knowledge of the organisation. This can be bad as well as good. Many organisations pass on information about their achievements to newspapers in order to obtain good publicity, but newspapers will also report on matters which organisations would rather keep quiet about. Not all organisations feel that 'all publicity is good publicity', because they consider that the creation of the right image is a delicate process. A company can develop its public relations and publicity through such factors as the company logo, the colours it uses on its outlets or transport vehicles, staff uniforms, leaflets on new products and services, sponsorship of sporting events and so on. Anything which can achieve widespread public awareness of the favourable aspects of the company can be considered.

A promotional campaign for a product or service will include advertising and publicity. At the same time, a good image of the company and a good reputation for its products and services will help to support personal selling. Selling can be seen as a 'bottleneck' through which a company's marketing strategies have to pass before their objectives can be realised, since if a sale does not take place there will have been no success, even if all the other aspects of the marketing strategy are working satisfactorily. The sales force can provide vital marketing information for a company as a result of its contact with customers. A close link between the sales force and the marketing strategy is essential if the sales force is to be committed to the marketing plan. The whole marketing and promotional strategy should support the sales force in its final direct approach to customers. For example, publicity on a new motor car or an updated model will include details of particular features which the sales people are able to emphasise when they speak to potential buyers.

The promotional strategy of an organisation and the use of advertising, personal selling, promotions, publicity and public relations will largely depend on the nature of an organisation and its products and services. A 'push' strategy may involve using the sales force and sales promotion to push the products or services through distribution channels to the customer. A 'pull' strategy involves using advertising and consumer promotion to build up consumer demand. If this is successful, consumers will ask for the product or service. The point at which the product is in its life-cycle may also play an important part in decisions about the use of various methods of promotion. At the introductory stage, publicity will be highly prized and may be relatively easily obtained, while in the growth stage 'mass' advertising may become important. As the product enters the point of saturation and then decline, promotional strategies may try to create a revival in demand, but will eventually be phased out.

7.13 Maintaining a competitive advantage

In its attempts to maintain a competitive advantage over its rivals, an organisation will have to provide products and services to customers in the places and at the prices which will persuade them to buy. The processes involved in operations management transform raw materials into a finished product or service, using the skills and competencies of the work force, which added to the distribution, pricing and promotional strategy of an organisation will have the aim of satisfying customer needs so that the objectives of the organisation are achieved.

Competitive advantage is achieved by providing a product or service which consumers want, are able and willing to buy, and do buy. In public sector terms, this means providing what the public want and are prepared to demand, and do demand. Product design and production, distribution, promotion and pricing policies are all designed to provide an organisation with a competitive advantage over its rivals.

SUMMARY OF CONCEPTS

Definition of competitive advantage – Transforming resources – Distribution of products and services – Channels of distribution – Pricing strategy – Equilibrium price – Influences on price – Market prices – Skimming and penetration – Consumer influence on price – Environmental influences on price – Promotional strategy – Image – The decision to buy – Promotion – Advertising – DAGMAR – Public relations and publicity – Maintaining a competitive advantage

---

ASSIGNMENTS

1. Discuss the importance of a sustainable competitive advantage in business strategy.
2. What are the various factors that decide the price of a new motor car?
3. Comment on the effectiveness of a recent national promotional campaign for a product or service.
4. Analyse the importance of distribution strategy in maintaining competitive advantage.
5. What are the competitive advantages of an organisation that you know?
6. How can 'The Communications Company' develop and maintain a competitive advantage?

▣ ⋈ 8 Strategic management in different organisational cultures

> **OBJECTIVES**
>
> To define organisational culture
> To analyse the role of culture in strategic management
> To consider different types of organisational culture
> To discuss the influence of culture on managing change

Definition of organisational culture – Influences on culture – Layers of culture – Differences between culture in the public and private sectors – Classifications of culture – Cultural change – Organisational beliefs – Managing cultural change – Organisational culture and strategic management

8.1 Definition

An organisation's culture can be defined as 'the way we do things around here'. It can be considered as a complex mixture of tangible factors which can be seen and touched, assumptions about how people should behave in the organisation and people's actual behaviour. Culture can be the basis of competitive advantage in markets because it may prove difficult to imitate. On the other hand, it is also difficult to change and it can be argued that organisations are 'captured' by their own cultures (Figure 8.1).

> 'The culture of any group of people is that set of beliefs, customs, practices and ways of thinking that they have come to share with each other through being and working together. At the visible level the culture of a group takes the form of ritual behaviour, symbols, myths, stories, sounds and artifacts.'
>
> (Stacey, 1996)

Tangible factors include the organisation's location, the buildings it inhabits, and the decoration and layout of the work places. For example, so-called 'hot desking' has developed as a result of a particularly informal approach to work, and stand-up discussion around a tall table has developed as a way of encouraging meetings to be short and business-like. There may be assumptions about when people arrive at work, when they leave and how many breaks they take. Although working hours may be set out in an employment contract, employees may be expected to work longer hours than those written down. The actual behaviour of employees may mean that although they are at work for long hours, they take frequent breaks so that the actual hours they work are similar to those of employees who are at work for a shorter time.

Tangible factors – physical conditions

Assumptions – expected attitudes and behaviour

Behaviour – how people actually behave

Figure 8.1   Organisational culture (TAB factors).

The ritual behaviour, symbols, myths and stories in an organisation can be analysed in order to study its culture. The way that the founder of the company behaved may create stories and myths which persist in the company long after the founder has gone, and continue to affect people's behaviour. In the same way, the style and actions of the present chief executive may set the tone for the company, even if some of the reported incidents are in fact stories or myths. A very formal approach to his working relationships by their boss may establish the style for everyone else, while an informal manner may encourage different behaviour.

Figure 8.2   Influences on 'the way we do things around here'.

Figure 8.2 illustrates some of the influences on organisational culture. Stories and myths that people in an organisation tell about what has happened in the past can provide a view of what they think is important. These may revolve around successes and failures, particular individuals and so on, and can indicate whether innovation or stability is important or whether company loyalty is highly prized. Symbols can indicate power structures in an organisation through car parking privileges, or the size of offices for different people or functions. For example, if the head of the marketing function is a middle manager, this may indicate the company view on its importance.

Power structures can influence how people behave in an organisation. The dominant group will usually be the senior management team, but marketing managers can have a powerful role in consumer goods companies and IT companies may rely heavily on individual and group knowledge. Organisational structures can also be an indication of dominant thinking in a company, with many layers of management suggesting a bureaucratic and controlled approach, while 'delayering' may not only be an attempt to cut costs but also to improve communications.

Organisational systems can be important in influencing culture. Control systems, for example, can be relatively 'hard' in that they have a financial implication, or relatively 'soft' in encouraging people to behave in certain ways. Reward systems often provide a 'carrot and stick' approach to organisational behaviour. At the same time, the way in which information is available to people may be of significance. Information systems and learning systems can indicate whether the organisation has an open structure which encourages learning and development, or a more closed structure where information and learning are held by individuals or groups as a form of power.

Stories about the leader of an organisation and his insistence on good timing will influence attitudes towards time-keeping by all the employees, even if these stories are exaggerated. In practice, within a company different functions or departments may have different cultures which reflect both the people who work in it and expectations about it. For example, there may be a marked difference between the finance and the design departments, with the people working for finance dressing relatively formally and with a clearly hierarchical structure, while the design department employees dress much more informally and operate on a consensus basis.

The managing director of a small packaging company knows all his employees by their first names and insists on them calling him by his first name. He also insists on good time-keeping and a high level of output. He does not have a reserved parking space in the staff car park and every day he walks through the factory talking to the workers and telling them about any changes in the work that are about to occur and listening to their concerns. The physical conditions in the factory are not particularly good because it is in an old building with limited staff catering and social facilities, but the atmosphere is informal, relaxed and efficient.

It can be argued that **successful organisations have 'a way of doing things', or culture, which supports their strategy, and strategic management has to take into account different organisational cultures**. The culture of an organisation will tend to consist of three layers:

- **Values**, which may be written down as part of the organisation's mission or vision statement. They are often vague statements of intent, such as 'serving the community' or 'conserving the environment.
- **Beliefs** tend to be more specific in the sense that they may be about such matters as which suppliers the company is prepared to use. For example,

a company like Body Shop wants to have suppliers with good environmental and human rights records.

- **Assumptions** are at the core of an organisation's culture. They are often difficult for employees to explain, but they affect the day-to-day working of individuals and groups within the organisation.

The assumptions which are taken for granted are at the centre of an organisation's culture and, although these may not be articulated, they are understood by all the employees. These assumptions will be surrounded by beliefs which are more specific and values which may be strongly held but more difficult to put into practice (Figure 8.3).

In the packaging factory, the employees take it for granted that they can talk freely to the owner about their problems at work and for that matter at home. They believe that they can trust the owner to react in a way that will provide them with a sympathetic hearing. The employees greatly value the trust that exists between them and their boss. These values, beliefs and assumptions are thrown into confusion when a new owner takes over the company and insists on a reserved car parking place, is seldom seen on the factory floor and introduces changes in the employees' work without any discussion with them.

Written statements by companies attempting to explain their culture can be misleading, because they usually describe aspirations or strategic intent

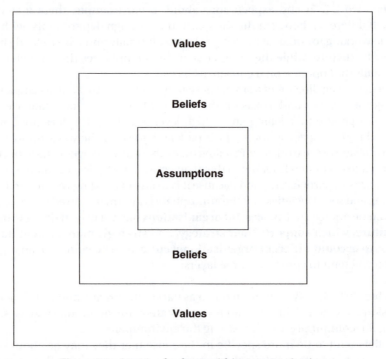

Figure 8.3 Layers of culture within an organisation.

rather than the actual way the company operates. At the same time, there are often subcultures within a company created by different working groups or different locations. Merging different branches of a company, or bringing the staff from an outlying office into the head office, can cause a clash of cultures in terms of the way they are used to working. There may be 'a head office culture' which is more formal and autocratic than the relatively informal way of working at the outside office.

Many industries and public services have a shared approach to managing organisations in the firms and institutions of which they are comprised, and it may be difficult for individual organisations to ignore this. The advantage of these influences is that it can maintain standards and consistency between individual providers. Some industries have trade associations which help to reinforce these industry norms, such as ABTA, the Association of British Travel Agents. Public sector services and professions tend to have very strong cultures in this sense, often reinforced by a central organisation. The British Medical Association regulates areas of the health service, and funding councils exert control over universities and colleges.

The dominant culture varies between one industry and another and although managers are able to move between industries, they can face difficulties if the industry cultures are very different. For example, managers making the transition from a private sector company to a public sector institution can find that there are different traditions and expectations.

Differences in cultural influences between the private and public sectors are detailed in Figure 8.4.

Private sector	Public sector
Profit	Service
Shareholders	Stakeholders
Products and services	Services
Personal gain	Public service
Customer sovereignty	Patients, students etc.
Individual choice in the market	Collective choice by government
Demand, supply and price	Need for resources
A competitive market	A controlled market

Figure 8.4 Factors influencing different cultures.

The differences between the private and public sectors illustrate the differences between sectors and areas of activity. In the private sector, the market conditions establish the boundaries in which an organisation is working, while in the public sector, boundaries are established by government legislation and regulation. Public sector 'customers' are not only clients of the public sector organisation, but also members of the public who are represented either directly or more indirectly in the organisation itself. Shareholders are looking for financial returns on their investment, while stakeholders in the public sector are looking for returns such as the public interest and the level of the service being provided. These differences between the two sectors do make a difference in the culture of the organisations involved, with different approaches to appraising people's performance, a different level of job security, and a different approach to risk-taking and decision-making, which have to be taken into account in the development and implementation of strategy.

8.2 Types of culture

In practice, the ability of strategic managers to organise, control and change their organisations will depend to a great extent on the culture that exists. There have been a number of studies which identify a range of cultures, none of which necessarily fit an organisation exactly but may provide an overall impression. For example, if an organisation is said to have a macho culture it does provide an image of it even if it is not the whole story about the organisation. One way of describing cultures is to divide them into power, role, task and person cultures (Figure 8.5).

A **power** culture is typically found in small entrepreneurial companies controlled by powerful figures. People in this culture share a belief in individuality and in taking risks; they believe that management should be an informal process with few rules and procedures. This type of culture suits people who thrive on political situations and are confident about the use of power.

Power – individuality and powerful managers

Role – bureaucratic and formal

Task – focus on work and teamwork

Person – serving personal interests

Figure 8.5 Handy's classification.

A **role** culture is associated with bureaucracies where people's functions are defined in a formal way and they specialise. People here share a belief in the importance of security and predictability, and they equate successful management with rules and regulations. In this culture, people will tend to be slow to change and they value security and predictability. The civil service is an example, and banking certainly in the past if not today. A **task** culture is found where people focus on their job or on a project, and share a belief in the importance of teamwork, expertise and in being adaptable. This is often the culture preferred by middle and junior managers because they know what they have to do and they can build up teams. The **person** culture occurs where people believe that the organisation exists so that they can serve their own personal interest, for example barristers and architects, and many other professionals.

'I've been thinking about what that Consultant from 'The Communications Company' was saying,' the Managing Director of 'The Engineering

Company' tells the Assistant Managing Director. 'He is suggesting that we make a number of changes and I know from what you have said in the first draft of the Strategic Report that you agree with him.' The AMD nods his head in agreement. 'Whatever we do is going to be difficult,' the MD continues, 'people don't like change, particularly to the way they work. We need to flag up what change is coming in some way and we can start with something we can do fairly easily. I would like you to look at our organisational structure and the titles we use in it. I know that changing people's job title does not alter their responsibilities or the way they work, but it will be a sign that changes are being made.'

ASSIGNMENT

Consider other examples of changes in names in organisations and the reasons for them. The Managing Director of 'The Engineering Company' does not mention the culture of the Company. How could it be described? Discuss whether a change in organisational structure and job titles could alter this culture.

Cultures tend to follow the life-cycle of organisations, so that the power structure is often found in the early stages of a company's life when its structure is simple. At this stage there is a single source of power from which influence spreads throughout the organisation like a web. The internal organisation is highly dependent on trust, empathy and personal communications. Later the organisation will tend to change to the role culture as it grows and installs a functional structure, and then it will develop a task culture to fit in with a structure based on sections and teams.

Another classification of cultures has been produced by Deal and Kennedy (1982) after the examination of hundreds of companies (Figure 8.6). They identified the **macho** culture which exists when an organisation is composed of individualists who are frequently called upon to take high risks and receive rapid feedback on the quality of their actions and decisions. These cultures were felt to focus on speed and the short-term, and place enormous pressures on individuals because they are risk-taking cultures in which those who succeed have to take a tough attitude towards their work and their colleagues. Many sales organisations cultivate this type of culture which can be highly successful in high-risk quick-return environments, but they are unable to benefit from co-operative activity and tend to have a high turnover.

Macho – high-risk, quick-feedback

Work-hard/play-hard – low-risk, quick-feedback

Bet-your-own-company – high-risk, long-feedback

Process – low-risk, slow-feedback

Figure 8.6 Deal and Kennedy's classification.

The **work-hard/play-hard** culture is a low-risk, quick-feedback culture which emphasises fun and action. Individual sales will not damage a member of staff and so production systems have many checks and balances built into them to neutralise the occurrence of big risks with rapid feedback on staff. These types of organisation are often customer-focused sales organisations or companies, such as the fast food chain McDonald's, which encourage competitions and systems of acknowledging good performance in order to maintain morale. These are often achievement cultures but they may displace volume for quality and concentrate heavily on the present rather than the future.

> 'The Communications Company' was established by two friends and the first people they employed were treated as if they were also friends. They were expected to do whatever was required to help the new Company to survive and to succeed even if this meant working long and unsociable hours. The informal implication was that the reward for this work would come when the Company was firmly established. The atmosphere of the offices was very informal and work tended to merge with everybody's social life. There was general agreement that everybody should work hard, while enjoying an active social life, although the rapid feedback on decisions and actions emphasised the risky nature of the enterprise. As the Company expanded and a wider range of people were employed, more formal working conditions had to be arranged. The atmosphere of the Company offices became less convivial and the original members of the Company became more concerned about their rights in terms of hours of work and pay, as they saw new employees working set hours for a set wage.

The **bet-your-own-company** culture exists in environments where the risks are high and the feedback on actions and decisions takes a long time. These companies invest in large-scale projects that take years to reach a conclusion. Decisions tend to be top-down, reflecting a hierarchical structure and a focus on the future. Employees are co-operative with colleagues and respect authority and technical competence. The **process** culture is a relatively low-risk and slow-feedback approach. Employees work with little feedback and so they focus on how they do something rather than on what they do. There is often a rigid hierarchy with a considerable emphasis on job titles and formality, with relatively cautious employees who may be protective about their work and focused on technical perfection in the performance of their duties. Both the bet-your-own-company and the process cultures are slow to respond to change.

Another classification (by Scholz, 1987) divides cultures into five primary types: **stable, reactive, anticipating, exploring** and **creative** (Figure 8.7). A **stable** culture is one that is averse to risk, backward-looking, 'introverted' and does not accept change. A **reactive** culture is one where risks are accepted, provided they are small, and it is orientated to the present and accepts only minimal change. An **anticipating** culture accepts familiar risks, is still

Stable – 'don't rock the boat'

Reactive – 'roll with the punches'

Anticipating – 'plan ahead'

Exploring – 'be where the action is'

Creative – 'invent the future'

Figure 8.7 Scholz's classification.

orientated to the present but accepts incremental change. An **exploring** culture is 'extroverted', orientated to the present and the future, operates on a risk against gain trade-off and accepts radical change. A **creative** structure is orientated to the future, actually prefers unfamiliar risks and seeks novel change. These five culture types can be epitomised in terms of slogans such as 'don't rock the boat' (stable), 'roll with the punches' (reactive), 'plan ahead' (anticipating), 'be where the action is' (exploring) and 'invent the future' (creative).

The problem with any classification of cultures is that organisations do not fit neatly into one or other type, although they may have dominant elements of one culture or another. Also, within organisations there may be different cultures so that often the finance department of a business is thought of as being a 'stable' or a 'process' culture with a 'don't rock the boat' approach, while the sales department may be considered to be more like an 'exploring' and perhaps 'macho' culture, with a 'be where the action is' approach. The classification of culture does encourage consideration of this aspect of an organisation in strategic management, while the actual effect may depend on the relative strength of the culture. For example, the introduction of professional managers into hospital trusts has often created a clash between the professional approach adopted by the medical staff and the business-like approach which the managers introduce. Figure 8.8 illustrates a summing-up of the various classifications in terms the main organisational beliefs.

Around the basic assumptions and values in an organisation, there are a number of views about such matters as attitudes to time and the working environment, innovation and learning, risks, power and control (Figure 8.8). For example, organisations need to be learning organisations so that the competencies of individuals, sections and the whole organisation are improved and

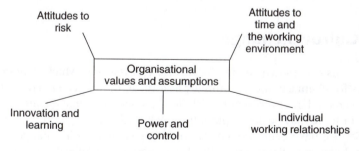

Figure 8.8 Summary of organisational beliefs.

maintained. This learning is in the sense that an organisation needs to learn faster than competitors so that it can meet customer needs better. It can be argued that this is not only a major strategic advantage, but perhaps the only sustainable long-term advantage. Working relationships are a feature of all organisations which can have a marked effect on the efficiency and effectiveness of their operation. In practice, companies try all sorts of approaches to create the desired culture in organisational relationships. Such approaches include team-building techniques such as 'outward bound' type courses, re-organising offices so that they are based on units of people working together, or are open plan, or where there is some form of 'hot-desking', and longer-term programmes to encourage a productive interaction between individuals and groups.

Where people need reassurance and certainty, there may be a strong culture or the culture that exists may appear stronger. For example, the doctors and nurses in a hospital trust may close ranks and emphasise the importance of medical considerations as against those of business efficiency. Organisations with weak socialisation practices employing people on a part-time basis, such as supermarkets, will usually be weak in terms of both the degree of consensus in terms of culture and the degree of intensity.

Other organisations may evolve high-consensus cultures which are not felt very deeply, so that a management is supported by all its employees but they would be likely to support another management if they were taken over. A high-intensity, low-consensus culture would be one in which the management was passionately supported by some employees, but by no means all of them. Japanese companies which have employed people for life in the past and provide a wide range of benefits and strong socialisation programmes are an example of companies with a high intensity and a high consensus.

The main problem with thinking about the intensity of a culture or the degree of consensus in an organisation is that these are difficult factors to measure. However, when an organisation is subject to change for one reason or another, these factors do need to be considered. The change in the National Health Service over the last twenty years is a good example of this, with clear cultural difference between the medical staff and the professional managers, with both having strongly felt, but different, views of the culture in which they would like to work. In these circumstances, adjustments may be required by both groups.

8.3 Cultural change

Organisations experience change for a variety of reasons, which may include pressures for change within a company as a result of financial needs, external pressures created by government legislation, changes in exchange rates or competition, or there may be developments in technology. Changes in the National Health Service have been brought about by legislation, while changes within IBM have been caused by competitive forces and technological developments, and travel agents have been influenced by changes in the exchange rate. In dealing with these changes, strategic managers may be able to alter rules and procedures without too much difficulty and alter staffing structure and job descriptions with rather more difficulty, but the most difficult task they face is likely to be altering the organisational culture.

One approach to organisational change is through a process of 'unfreezing' and 'refreezing' (see Kurt Lewin, 1951, Chapter 10). Strategic managers in an organisation decide that there is a need to change because of external pressures of one kind or another. A company's profitability may have declined or there are clear indications of a falling market share. Senior managers know that changes are needed in order to ensure organisational survival. The strategic managers' problem is to convince everybody else in the organisation that change is necessary and that the present culture needs 'unfreezing':

- **Unfreezing** – the need for change is made so obvious that individuals and teams can easily recognise this need and accept it.
- **Leadership** – managers foster new values, attitudes and behaviour through a process of consultation, retraining and communication.
- **Refreezing** – the new practices are locked into place by supporting and reinforcing mechanisms so that they become the norm.

Many people will feel that 'the way we do things around here' is the best possible way, so that changes will not help. Meetings and other forms of communication may help to explain the need for change and persuade employees to accept change. External consultants can be introduced in order to provide an objective assessment of the need for change, and because of their distance from the internal culture they may be able to criticise individuals, systems and practices, and explain what other organisations have had to do in order to remain competitive. More direct signs of change, such as the replacement of senior managers, redundancy among employees, changes in location and the introduction of new equipment, may help to convince people that changes are happening but may also mean that there is a retreat into the familiar culture. For example, the replacement of managers who had worked their way through the system in the National Health Service by professional managers encouraged doctors and nurses to emphasise the medical culture in which they worked.

At this stage of culture change there will be strong forces for maintaining the status quo. There will be a fear of change among many employees, who may be worried about their position in the organisation or at having to learn new skills, or simply because they are used to the present situation and they are not convinced that any change is necessary. Managers have to reassure people that they will be able to master the new skills required and also that the change is necessary. Encouragement and support can be backed by training and retraining programmes. The purpose of change is to move an organisation from its present point to a different one which is more desirable in meeting its objectives. The gap between the starting point and the desirable conclusion can be bridged by reminding everybody about the direction of the organisation and outlining how the change is to be achieved. Strategic managers have to clarify 'where we are going' and 'how we are going to get there', and then, by monitoring the change, point out 'this is how far we are now'.

In this process, cultural change is often the most fundamental problem and the most difficult to overcome. Many people may be unable to fully understand the cultural implications of the changes that are being introduced, possibly because of the vocabulary being used, a difficulty of putting into words what is required or a resistance to it.

In many public sector organisations, the people who use the service are referred to by a term which is understood by everybody in the service. For example, in universities and colleges the people who use their educational services are referred to as 'students', while in the National Health Service the people who use the medical service are referred to as 'patients'. When there is an attempt to introduce 'business-like' approaches to these services, the people who use the services may be referred to as 'customers'. This is particularly the case when a 'customer-orientated' marketing function is introduced. When private sector marketing managers are employed by the public service, they may use terms such as 'customer service', 'after-sales service', or 'customer focus', instead of terms such as 'student services' and 'patient care'. Resistance to these terms may be more fundamental than simply vocabulary, in that the terms may represent strong cultural differences between managers and other employees.

In the public health service, cultural and other gaps between managers and medical staff are emphasised by the fact that the managers negotiate contracts and may have performance-related earnings, while the organisation's other staff will have to execute these contracts and may be on fixed earnings. Doctors will use the language of medicine and caring while managers use the language of business, so that patients are customers, the art of medicine becomes a business and the act of medicine becomes a product. At the same time, attempts are made to measure performance, the professional duty of medical staff becomes a job and trust becomes negotiated consent.

Changes in the public sector in recent years have been radical and the same has been true in the private sector. The development of global competition and new technology has brought about considerable changes within many companies in the way they have provided products and services, and in their structure and composition. Take-overs and mergers bring together two or more cultural traditions with all the difficulties this produces. At the same time, the restructuring of companies has given rise to a vocabulary of change in such terms as 're-engineering', 'down-sizing' and 'out-sourcing'.

'The Communications Company' finds that as it expands the work atmosphere becomes more formal. It has to introduce clear-cut personnel policies after one of the new employees threatens to take the Company to the Equal Opportunities Commission because she feels she has been discriminated against when a new job was given to another employee without an advertisement or formal interview. A personnel manager has to be appointed in order to make sure that the Company complies with equal opportunities, health and safety, and other regulations and legislation. It also has to introduce formal procedures in a range of areas which have previously been organised informally and relying on word of mouth rather than written contracts and agreements. These changes are strongly opposed by some of the original members of the Company who are heard to make comments such as: 'next thing we'll all be wearing suits and sitting in little offices.'

During the 'refreezing' stage of cultural change, individuals will look for ways of ending the uncertainty and instability that the changes have brought to their working life. Individual members of staff start to redefine what is required of them and how they should carry out their work. Refreezing only occurs when the new culture is understood and accepted, and when the new rules and regulations and the new assumptions are accepted as 'the way we do things around here'. This may be a long process which can take years to be fully introduced while two cultures live awkwardly with each other. In order to help this process, strategic management can provide a structure which helps change by providing training programmes and information about the reasons for change and the results of changing, and also the consequences of not changing, so that good communication between managers and other employees becomes even more important. For a successful change, the new culture must be seen as the factor responsible for solving the initial crisis.

8.4 Managing cultural change

The difficulty of managing cultural change in an organisation depends on the strength of the existing culture and the size of the proposed change. The National Health Service is an example of an attempt to impose a new culture on a strong existing one and expecting a large change. The existence of a number of subcultures within an organisation will make change even more difficult. Strategic managers need to be sure that strategy requires shifts in values and assumptions, or whether changes can be achieved within the present culture. Successful organisations tend to have a way of doing things which support their strategy. In order to achieve this, managers can introduce a structure which encourages behaviours that do support organisational strategy. This includes the promotion and rewards structure, and other policies which provide a clear message.

Organisations can perpetuate their cultures through a variety of **socialisation** mechanisms as well as more formal approaches (Figure 8.9). The **recruitment** process can be used to select people who will 'fit in' with the culture of

Socialisation

Recruitment policies

Induction processes

Reward systems

Promotion policy

Leadership

Training and development

Figure 8.9   Factors in the management of cultures.

the organisation, and questions can be asked which help to create an awareness of what is important in the organisation. The **induction** process can be
used in the same way to reinforce what is expected of the new recruit, not only
in terms of rules and regulations but also in terms of company policies and
less formal expectations. Individuals will be at their most receptive to new
ideas and ways of behaving at the early stages of their employment, and companies such as IBM have used this early stage to provide their new employees
with something of their history and philosophy.

The Managing Director of 'The Engineering Company' has a meeting
with the Chief Personnel Officer. 'I know that the Assistant Managing
Director has discussed with you the personnel implications of the strategic
review he is carrying out and I want you to give him all the help you can.'
'Of course, of course,' the CPO agrees. 'We need to make structural changes
and alter the way we work. I don't underestimate the difficulties we face
and we will have to lose some people while rewarding others.' 'Do you
mean redundancies?' asks the CPO. 'You have already overhauled our early
retirement programme and we may have to go further. At the same time, we
have to try to maintain morale and not destroy the loyalty that many people here feel towards the Company. We need to beef-up our training and
development programme, we need to have a series of meetings to explain
what we are doing and of course we have to talk to the unions.'

The **reward system** in an organisation sends a clear message to employees
about what types of behaviour are expected and acclaimed by senior management. For example, if large bonuses are paid to teams rather than individuals
this will encourage team-building, and loyalty to the team. If bonuses are
a small proportion of individuals' total remuneration, this may encourage
a relatively cautious culture. At the same time, if a company rewards the
finance director to a much greater extent than the marketing director, this
sends a message to everyone about the relative importance to the company
of the two functions. Large corporations may have multiple reward systems,
reflecting the demands of different business situations or traditional differences between groups of employees. These systems may perpetuate multiple

cultures and mean that managing cultures through reward systems may be difficult in large organisations.

Different salary systems can create or reinforce organisational cultures, so that one way of managing the culture is to adjust the reward system. Where length of service is the most important criteria for salary increases, an organisation is likely to end up with large numbers of long-serving middle and senior managers, highly deferential to organisational norms and unlikely to show initiative or take risks. Where salary increases are determined by a rigid pay system, then order and predictability will tend to become ingrained within the organisation; while where pay increases are a matter of discretion on the part of senior managers, the formation of cliques and self-serving activity may develop. If pay is linked to measured performance, such as the level of completed sales, conflict and antagonism may be encouraged.

'The Communications Company' originally employed people on a 'who do you know?' basis, so that the first employees were friends or acquaintances of the original group. When it had to introduce more formal recruitment systems, it still attempted to select people who would 'fit in' with everybody else. The Company had started with a vague idea about profit-sharing schemes, but as more people were employed this had to be formalised. It was decided by the senior managers that only the original group plus a few others would be on a profit-sharing scheme. This created a situation where there were two groups of employees, those on the scheme and those not on it, who tended to see themselves in different ways. The original group had become used to socialising together and they developed 'in-jokes' about the origins of the Company and the 'early days'.

In a similar way to the reward system, the **promotion process** can also influence the culture of an organisation. A policy of internal promotion will encourage loyalty and consistency, while basic assumptions about the 'way we do things' are unlikely to be questioned. On the other hand, a policy of looking for external appointees is more likely to result in cultural diversity and can more easily lead to cultural change. The use of promotion to develop people and to indicate the organisation's commitment to its staff can contribute to an organisation with a common culture. In organisations with a highly competitive internal structure, promotions may be used to ensure that people with a particular viewpoint are in positions of influence.

Leadership is an important element in managing culture. Leaders can 'set a good example' in terms of their working habits. They can communicate important messages to employees, call meetings and shape agendas, and praise and reward members of staff who are considered to have worked well. Leaders can also act as barriers to culture change in that the leader may be the most resistant to change. For example, the founders of successful organisations may believe that they have a winning formula which they are very reluctant to change. The classic example is Henry Ford who had to be persuaded that the idea of 'a Model T car in any colour so long as it was black' was no longer a good idea when rival car companies began to produce cars of different colours.

Training and development may be used to try to introduce a change in the culture of an organisation. This approach involves explaining the reasons why a change is necessary, 'why things need to be done differently around here', and then trying to convince people so that this becomes part of their beliefs. This is particularly difficult unless all the other factors which can assist the management of culture are supporting the new approach. These means that, for example, the reward system, promotions and so on all point in the same direction in terms of cultural change. Above all, management leaders at all levels need to show by example the importance to them of the changes. Programmes of staff-training, appraisal systems and coaching can combine to send a powerful message to everybody, but still may face the difficulty of overcoming basic beliefs and values. An example of the problems to be overcome is clearly seen where professionals are expected to start to behave as if they are running a business, in the way that doctors and consultants have in the UK National Health Service and lecturers have in the UK university system.

8.5 Organisational culture and the formation of strategy

An organisation's culture may exert an influence over the strategies it pursues. People are often locked into traditional or habitual ways of doing and seeing things, and this affects their ability to consider new options and new solutions. Two organisations in the same industry may interpret their environment significantly differently because their different cultures promote different perceptions, and this may give rise to radically different strategies.

Provided with the same environmental changes in terms of both regulations and the benefits being sought by customers, banks tended to react in one way, while building societies reacted in another. While banks were generally slow in reacting to customer needs, building societies tended to move more quickly. For example, building societies have developed more flexible opening times to meet customer needs, while banks have been slower to do so.

The formation of strategy is dependent on how an organisation gains information from the environment. Where there are cultural assumptions which lead strategic managers to believe that the environment is stable and well known, strategies will be different from a situation where strategic managers believe that the environment is unstable. The difference in these views may arise because organisational assumptions vary and they focus attention on some areas of information and away from other areas. Different organisations also prefer their information to come in different ways. Some pay most attention to objective and statistical data, others prefer more qualitative information and base their strategic decisions on specialists, or on 'what they have heard' and 'hunches' rather than sets of 'facts'.

The information that an organisation receives about its environment has to be interpreted and then it has to decide how it is going to act on it. Business information is often incomplete and ambiguous, and provides scope for different interpretations. Some organisations will have a bias towards making as few changes as possible, believing that their strength lies in the loyalty of their employees and in the methods they have tried and tested in the past. Other organisations will have a bias towards change and adaptation in order to meet the challenges of the environment is which they work and to remain ahead of their competitors. These organisations will have a preference for flexibility among their staff and their ability to learn new skills.

In the past, British car companies (such as British Leyland and Rover) have often maintained the production of their models for very many years so that they did not have to invest in new production lines and retrain their staff, while their rivals from the United States (such as Fords and General Motors) have ended the production of their models in a much shorter time span, investing in new designs, new plant and the retraining of staff. In terms of the British market for motor cars, both groups of companies were competing in the same environment and had similar information about it, and yet their strategic response was different. At least part of the reason for this difference was the cultural assumptions of the companies involved.

It can be argued that organisational culture is the key to understanding why some firms succeed in implementing their strategies, while others fail. The important factor is that successful companies have a culture which supports the strategy they are pursuing, so that it is a positive factor in the management of strategic change rather than a barrier to the implementation of change. It is difficult to introduce a strategy which ignores the prevalent culture of the organisation, unless it is a new company which has not had time to develop a strong culture or there has been a major change in the people who are employed by it.

Another option is to attempt to manage around the culture, which can be justified when a strategy which is vital to the success of an organisation clashes with its culture. Modifying the culture to fit the strategy is a long-term and difficult process, while adapting the strategy to fit the culture is easier. This may be necessary if there are considerable cultural blocks in the way of strategy, as there may be, for example, after a merger of two companies.

One approach to the clash of cultures within the National Health Service hospital trusts was to separate the medical functions of the organisation from the business functions, so that the two cultures would not need to come together. The difficulty with this was that the performance of the trusts was measured by such matters as the occupancy of hospital beds and the length of waiting-lists, and the resources available to the trusts depended on their performance. While the medical staff would want a hospital bed for any patient they diagnosed as needing one, the business managers were not always able to supply these. On the one hand, the medical staff measured their own performance in terms of improving the health of each patient and, on the other, the business managers wanted to achieve their more precise performance targets.

Large corporations which control a number of businesses, such as holding companies, have to consider the culture and strategy of each of its businesses as well as the overall corporate structure. In practice, the different businesses can enjoy different cultures provided these do not conflict with the overall objectives of the corporation. For example, a corporation may decide that each business should achieve a certain level of profit and, provided this is reached, the actual culture of each business does not matter. If one of the businesses fails to reach its profit target, questions may be asked about its culture as well as about its strategic management.

8.6   The importance of the link between strategic management and organisational culture

Strategy is a focus for an organisation and the people within it to understand the purpose of the organisation, where it is going, how it is going to reach that goal, and for the individual their role in the life of the organisation. Strategy can also provide individuals with long-term objectives with which they are able to identify and value, and it can also provide a link between company policies and a context for company actions. This means that strategy can be more than a means of matching internal resources to meet external opportunities and to deal with external threats.

Strategic management and strategic plans are influenced by the needs of customers, competitive forces and other environmental forces. They are also affected by the culture of the organisation and help to reinforce or mould this culture. In order for an organisation to be successful it must have more than a strong and appropriate culture, it must also be able to continuously adapt to its environment. An adaptive culture is likely to be one in which people will take risks against a background of trust, teamwork and confidence in their own abilities and those of their colleagues, and have enthusiasm for their jobs.

Adaptability enables an organisation to be effective by:

- recognising and responding to its external environment;
- an ability to respond to internal constituencies so that different teams and departments interact positively with each other;
- responding to either internal or external influences with the ability to restructure and re-institutionalise behaviours and processes as appropriate.

At the same time, if an organisation takes too many risks it may find itself in difficulties, and change can lead to instability and a loss of direction. Ideally, the culture of an organisation should be one which values and supports all the stakeholders in an organisation, such as customers, shareholders and employees, and in the case of the public sector, government agencies and the public as well. The culture can provide employees with non-economic reasons for investing their efforts in supporting the success of the organisation.

Organisational culture influences strategy formulation in a number of ways:

- it acts as a filter for people's view of their environment;
- it affects the interpretation of information;
- it establishes moral and ethical standards;
- it provides rules and norms for behaviour;
- it influences power and authority and how decisions are made.

Strategy formulation can be described as:

'a cultural artifact which helps employees understand their role in the organisation, is a focus for identification and loyalty, encourages motivation, and provides a framework of ideas that enables individuals to comprehend their environment and the place of their organisation within it'.

(Brown, 1998, p. 195)

An organisation's culture influences how its strategy is implemented. The more closely the strategy is in tune with the prevailing culture, the more effectively the strategy will be put into practice. It can be argued that the most effective cultures are those which actively involve large numbers of individuals in consultative and decision-making bodies. Also some cultures allow an organisation to exploit an environment more effectively than others and are therefore more strategically appropriate. Organisational strategies and structures and their implementation are shaped by the assumptions, beliefs and values which can be defined as culture, and culture can constrain or support the ability of an organisation to succeed.

SUMMARY OF CONCEPTS

Organisational culture – The 'way we do things around here' – TAB factors – Influences on culture – Layers of culture – Values, beliefs, assumptions – Culture in private and public sector organisations – Types of culture – Different classifications – Cultural change – Managing cultural change – Freezing and unfreezing – Links between organisational culture and strategic management

---

ASSIGNMENTS

1. Discuss the organisational culture of different companies.
2. Analyse the advantages and disadvantages of different types of culture.
3. What are the cultural problems of managing change in organisations?
4. What effects does organisational culture have on the formation of strategy?
5. Analyse the culture of an organisation that is known to you.
6. Describe and discuss the culture of 'The Communications Company'.
7. What approaches can 'The Engineering Company' take to alter its culture?

▮ Ⅴ **9** Strategic leadership

OBJECTIVES

To understand the importance of strategic leadership
To discuss the characteristics of leaders
To consider the styles of leadership
To analyse the sources of leaders' power

The importance of leadership in strategic management – Attributes, characteristics and styles of leadership –Strategic vision – The sources of power of leaders – Leadership in modern organisations

9.1   **The importance of strategic leadership**

Leadership can be described as the process of motivating other people to act in particular ways in order to achieve specific goals. The captain of a sports team, for example, attempts to motivate the team members to play in such a way that the team wins. The word 'leader' derives from the word meaning 'path' or 'road', and suggests the importance of guidance on a journey. Leadership is a vital ingredient in developing the purpose and strategy of organisations because strategic management is concerned with the way forward for an organisation. **Strategic leadership is about motivating people to move in a particular direction in order to achieve particular objectives**.

The people who develop a strategy may or may not be the same as those who take a lead in managing strategic change. Some managers may be especially good at creating a vision for the future, but may need to rely on others to take a lead in implementing the changes. **A 'change agent' is the individual or group that effects strategic change in an organisation**. Senior managers need both leadership and management skills; they need, either as individuals or as a team, to be change agents as well as managing the change. They need also to be creative in order to achieve the continual renewal required for the long-term success of an organisation.

Managers deal with the physical resources of an organisation, its capital, raw materials, technology and the skills of employees. They are concerned particularly with efficiency; they 'make the organisation work' by resolving problems and bringing together the 'factors of production', the capital, raw materials, designs and skills in order to produce a product or service which satisfies the customers. Leaders are more concerned with effectiveness; they provide the direction and the goals, and the means to head towards them. It can be argued that while managers deal with the physical resources of an organisation, leaders deal with its emotional and spiritual resources. Strategic management involves both management and leadership and this distinguishes it from other forms of management. It is concerned with effective leadership to produce change that moves the organisation in a direction that is in the long-term best interest of the organisation.

'Managers are people who do things right and leaders are people who do the right thing. The difference may be summarised as activities of vision and judgement – effectiveness, versus activities of mastering routine, efficiency.'

(Bennis and Nanus, 1985)

Warren Bennis and Burt Nanus wrote (in 1986) that leadership remains the most studied and least understood topic in all the social sciences. They argue that, like beauty, we know it when we see it but we cannot easily define it or produce it on demand. However in *Leaders: The Strategies for Taking Charge* (1985) they studied leaders in the United States, established that leadership is not a rare activity and considered that all sorts of people in a whole variety of jobs and voluntary work practise leadership. They saw this in private companies, public sector institutions, sports clubs and recreational societies. Leaders provide a direction, develop fresh ideas and look for new opportunities. Bennis and Nanus found that leaders are not generally born, they make themselves. They thought that most people could become leaders but the ability to lead could be improved through practice and because of a motivation. Outstanding leaders may be very rare, like outstanding people in any walk of life (great footballers, or authors, or pianists), but most people have leadership potential and leadership can be learned.

Bennis and Nanus found that leaders were of all sorts and sizes and there was no one 'leader type'. They found that few leaders could be described as 'charismatic' (that is, 'having a personal quality or gift that enables them to impress and influence other people'), they were ordinary people who had 'made themselves into leaders' through practice and having the motivation. Also, although leadership clearly existed at the top of organisations and was a responsibility of the Board of Directors and the Chief Executive, it was required at the functional as well as the business and corporate level. In summary:

- leadership is not a rare quality;
- leaders are not born, they make themselves;

- there is no one leader 'type';
- leadership is not just required at the top of organisations;
- leadership can be 'learned'.

If leadership can be learned and leaders are not simply 'born', it is important to know how to learn the skills required. Research has shown that when informal groups are asked to choose a leader, they tend to select someone who most represents the group's needs and values, so that for example a sports team will often choose the best player. The problem with leaders of larger and more formal organisations is that they cannot hope to represent the aspirations and needs of all the groups involved, so that they must have characteristics other than simply representing group aspirations. Research findings suggest that leaders of complex organisations must have a strongly held vision, which they are able to communicate, and they should be able to convert their vision into reality (Figure 9.1).

Strongly held vision

The ability to communicate that vision

The ability to convert the vision into reality

Figure 9.1   General attributes of leaders.

9.2   Strategic vision

For leaders to be credible they must have a mission or vision for their organisation which is also believable and achievable. If the vision is really a wish based on what a leader would like rather than on what the organisation is, it will not appear to have any reality. The vision needs to be grounded on where the organisation is and on its strength. The time scale in which the vision can be achieved has to be one to which the people in the organisation can relate. If the work of the organisation is usually thought of in terms of a year rather than five or ten years, then the vision has to be seen to be achievable in this period of time. For organisations which offer lifetime employment and are relatively stable, the time scale of a vision can be much longer. IBM, for example, offered lifelong employment, at least in the past, while e-commerce companies can only offer employment for a period of weeks or months because they do not have a track record of long-term employment and stability. However short or long the overall time scale, it needs to be broken down into shorter-term milestones on which employees can concentrate. These milestones can be particular aspects of the vision, or a stage in its achievement.

The strategic vision needs to offer an attractive and challenging future that is better in some ways than the present situation (Figure 9.2). The guarantee of continued employment is attractive to some extent but in a rather negative way, while increased pay or greater profitability would be more attractive incentives.

Based on organisational strengths
Offering an attractive and challenging future
Communicated by leaders
Reinforced by senior managers
Integrated into the organisation and culture

Figure 9.2   The strategic vision.

In one way or another the vision has to be communicated by the leader so that the people in the organisation share it, and this means that it has to resonate with the values of the employees, indicate how each individual can contribute to its achievement and encourage the idea that success will bring rewards.

The vision and objectives of an organisation can be reinforced and encouraged by all managers and particularly by senior managers. It has been found that the work of managers can be characterised by brief segments of action, many of them involving interactions with people, the majority of whom are working in the organisation. For example, while a salesman is working with customers on particular sales projects and a portfolio of accounts, the sales manager spends time dealing with the salesmen who are accountable to him and the sales director is involved with all the sales managers and with a number of other directors and managers in the company. Senior managers have been found to spend much of their time in many fairly short interactions with other people in the organisation, with many opportunities to communicate and reinforce the organisational vision.

The vision can also be communicated through the organisation and culture of the company, so that so-called 'hot-desking' (where no-one has an established work area in an office) can indicate and reinforce the need for flexibility, and 'stand-up' (where people stand around a high table) meetings can encourage efficiency. The vision can be encapsulated in a short phrase or slogan which is relatively easy to remember. 'The world's favourite airline' and 'Solutions for Business' are two examples of this approach (for British Airways and Coopers and Lybrand) which were supported by more detailed statements of the vision, corporate objectives and action plans to turn the visions into reality. The aim of an organisational vision is to motivate people so that they have a sense of achievement or a desire for achievement, however the problem with a slogan is that it may be remembered when it no longer provides a clear objective within the organisation's grasp. The problem faced by British Airways was that soon after their slogan was adopted in the 1980s, other companies developed strong customer-care programmes and cut-price airlines entered the market. They were all attempting to become the 'favourite' airline either through improved customer services or by providing cheap air fares.

The vision has to be reinforced by encouraging the adoption of it through the organisation's culture. In many ways it is a more difficult process than 'selling' the vision, which involves persuading people that it is what they should want or what they should feel. Strategic leadership involves enlisting people into the process by showing them that the organisation's vision fits in with their beliefs and values. Posters and logos can all help to reinforce the vision, while videos and meetings can attempt to answer people's questions and concerns. Above all, 'actions speak louder than words' so that the example set by managers in what they actually do may be more important than anything else. If, for example, a customer service approach is the new vision of an organisation, the sight of the chief executive dealing with customers in a sympathetic way may be more important than all the memos, voice-mails and e-mails put together.

'The Communications Company' was founded by two friends and to start with they employed mainly people that they already knew. As the Company expanded, it employed a wider range of people with different skills and from a variety of backgrounds. The founders originally developed the Company on a laissez-faire basis, as a group of professional friends working together on an innovative project. As the Company grew, more formal structures had to be introduced because some of the new employees found it unsatisfactory that they were not told what they should be doing. The two founders had to split their roles, so that one of them concentrated on developing new ideas and new products and services for the Company, while the other concentrated on organising the work of the Company. The latter came to be considered both within it and by customers and suppliers as the leader of the Company, and when formal structures were introduced became the Managing Director.

The employees of the Company looked to the Managing Director for leadership when the Company had to move into new products and services and develop in new ways as the original products and services were overtaken in the market. The MD discussed the future of the Company with the other founder and with a few key staff before coming up with the idea of a business solutions company. This was developed into a strategic direction and vision for the Company, which was discussed in detail with key staff. It was clear that the Company needed to develop innovative products and services in order to provide business solutions, and it was decided that all aspects of the organisation must be altered to meet this objective. The Design Section, with one of the founders in charge, was put at the centre of the Company and physically moved to the best accommodation. All those involved with innovative solutions met frequently and regularly with the MD to have brain-storming sessions in the form of a think-tank. When these meetings became too long, the old table and chairs were removed from the room in which they met and a table at standing height was purchased. The MD took time to walk around the offices, talking to all employees and asking them if they knew what the objectives of the Company were and if they had any new ideas about the business.

Most people at work are concerned with their day-to-day, week-to-week or month-to-month tasks, and the idea of 'mission' and 'vision' are not uppermost in their thoughts. However, Peter Drucker pointed out as long ago as 1955 that there are more or less productive ways of working. He outlines the story of the three stone-cutters (or stone-masons) to illustrate the point. When asked what they were doing, the first replied 'I am making a living', the second said 'I am doing the best job of stone-cutting in the entire country', the third looked up and said 'I am building a cathedral'. It could be argued that the first man has his feet firmly on the ground, he works and he is paid, the rest he leaves to managers and supervisors. The second man is a craftsman with a pride in his work and believes he is accomplishing something by his expert stone-cutting, but if his work does not help in the completion of the building it may be useless. The third man has an understanding of the objective of his work and the part he is playing in its accomplishment.

Increasingly, organisations want people to know what their objectives are and how to achieve them, because otherwise they may not be achieved. It is difficult for an airline to become the world's 'favourite' unless the checking-in staff are polite and helpful to travellers, the baggage handlers are careful with people's luggage and the cabin crew look after the needs of passengers, while the actual flight is efficiently and effectively carried out. A 'people come first' programme to support the slogan can emphasise employees' natural helpfulness, new employees may be recruited who understand the importance of an efficient, effective and caring service, and people can be helped to understand that this approach will enable the company to be profitable and employees' jobs to be secure and better paid.

9.3 Characteristics of leaders

There are three main approaches to understanding and analysing leadership:

- **Trait theories** suggest that the purpose of an organisation will be based largely on the decisions of an individual. These theories argue that certain types of individuals can be identified who will provide leadership in most situations. It has been argued that such individuals will be intelligent, self-assured and able to see beyond the immediate issues. Recent evidence suggests that these theories are inconsistent and incomplete as an explanation of leadership.
- **Style theories** suggest that individuals can be identified who possess a general style of leadership that is appropriate to the organisation. Two contrasting styles would be the authoritarian and the democratic, with leaders of the former style imposing their will from the centre, while democratic leaders allow free debate before developing a solution. Research suggests that this approach has some validity, but that leadership is more complex than this approach indicates. Organisational relationships, culture and internal politics all need to be considered.

- **Contingency theories** explore the idea that leaders should be promoted or recruited according to the needs of the organisation at a particular time. The choice of leaders is contingent on the strategic issues facing the organisation at that time and, if the situation changes, then the leaders should be changed. These theories could again be considered to oversimplify the leadership task.

Research findings suggest that there is no one leader 'type' characterised by particular physical or personality traits. Charles de Gaulle and Abraham Lincoln were both tall, Alexander the Great was of medium height, Napoleon Bonaparte and Mahatma Gandhi were below average height. Some views suggest that leaders are of above average intelligence or are more decisive than other people but research has failed to produce a consistent position. There is also a cultural bias in terms of leaders, so there may be a bias towards people of above average height or towards men rather than women. The so-called 'glass-ceiling' experienced by women in many societies has prevented women from becoming senior managers in some companies, in spite of research that shows that when women do become senior managers they are just as effective leaders as men.

From a strategic perspective, the contingency approach to leadership has the most to offer because it emphasises the importance of the relationship between leaders and other people in the organisation and it identifies the importance of the strategic situation as being relevant to the analysis of leadership. At the same time, research into what leaders do suggests that there are a number of characteristics which are felt to be required to convert a vision or a sense of direction into reality. These are characteristics which help to align the strategy of the organisation with the actual behaviour of the people working in it (Figure 9.3).

Integrity
Respect for others
Energy
Perseverance
Courage
Team-building skills
The ability to encourage others
The ability to learn from experience
The ability to see patterns and anticipate trends

Figure 9.3 Some characteristics of leadership.

It is considered that integrity is important for leadership because a leader needs to be able to see the 'whole picture' and act consistently. Leadership requires a consistent interpretation of the vision, so that the leader is considered to be reliable and can inspire trust in other people. This trust is dependent on the leader showing respect for other people, in the sense that the leader recognises people for what they are, treating them with courtesy and showing a positive rather than a negative attitude towards them.

> 'We need to have a business plan,' the Assistant Managing Director of 'The Engineering Company' tells the Managing Director. 'We've got one, the Board agree it every year, orders, profits, investments, everything's there.' 'Sorry, I meant that we need to have a new company plan which includes our objectives, how we are going to achieve them and so on in more general terms than the facts and figures we put into the business plan.' 'You can't get away from facts and figures.' the MD observes 'Of course not, but 'The Communications Company' describes itself as providing business solutions through the application of IT, although it is now emphasising simply providing business solutions.' 'So this is a strategic plan which sets out our position and our direction and so on?' 'Yes, and includes facts and figures as support.' 'You are right,' agrees the MD, 'we need to be clear about our business strategy and make sure that our marketing strategy supports it. We have to convince everybody in the Company that this is the way forward.'
>
> ASSIGNMENT
>
> Discuss the leadership style of the Managing Director of 'The Engineering Company'.

Leaders tend to have more than an average amount of energy and perseverance. They need to be resilient in the face of opposition and should not need constant approval. The relatively high-profile position that leaders are in means that they will experience failures and there will be opposition to their policies, and they will need the courage to persevere in spite of this. In fact it can be argued that leaders do not consider setbacks to be failures, they are learning experiences from which they move on with improved understanding. Leaders position themselves, or take up a position, so that a failure or a mistake does not undermine their whole strategy.

Leaders build up teams of people to deal with problems and developments; they are able to delegate to people and to teams and imbue them with a strategic vision. They make people feel more confident than previously and therefore able to achieve more. Rather than dictate the details of how to achieve particular objectives, strategic management allow others to be creative and to use their skills and expertise. In terms of strategic management, leaders are able to look ahead and to discern patterns in their environment, and they can see trends developing so that they are able to anticipate changes.

9.4 Leadership styles

The styles of leaders have been categorised in a number of ways. One approach is to consider them in terms of whether or not they are 'task-orientated' or 'people-orientated'. **Task-orientation** is concerned with the organisation and its procedures, while **people-orientation** is concerned with the feelings and attitudes of people in the organisation. Very task-orientated leaders with little consideration for the feelings of the people around them can be described as 'autocratic'. The opposite type of leader would have people's feelings as their main concern and little concern for the task, and this can be described as a 'human relations' style. Those leaders who are both task- and people-orientated can be described as 'team' leaders, and those who not very concerned with either tasks or people can be described as 'laissez-faire' leaders. 'Middle-of-the-road' leaders show a moderate amount of concern for both people and tasks and believe in compromise, so that decisions are taken only if they are endorsed by employees (see Figure 9.4).

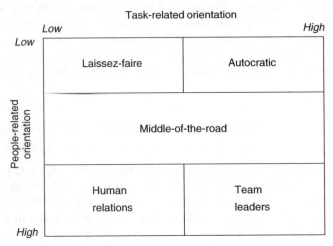

Figure 9.4   Styles of leadership.

Research has shown that, as might be expected, employee turnover rates were lowest and job satisfaction rates highest under managers who were rated high in consideration for people. Conversely, high grievance rates and high turnover were associated with managers who were rated low in consideration for people and high in task-orientation. However, it has also been found that employees' ratings of their leader's effectiveness depended not so much on the particular style of the leader as on the situation in which the style was used. For example, managers who worked in manufacturing and who exhibited high concern for task completion and low concern for people were rated as more efficient than employee-centred managers, while in service-based organisations the reverse was true.

Various factors have been noted which influence the manager's choice of leadership style. These include the manager's own background, experience, confidence and inclinations. It also includes the characteristics of other employees, how willing or unwilling they are to accept responsibility and take decisions, while groups of professionals and experts may have to be managed in a different way from groups of relatively unskilled employees. Managers also need to recognise the situation in which they find themselves in terms of corporate culture, the nature of the tasks to be performed and time pressures.

The **'situational' view of leadership** suggests that the type of leadership required depends on the situation. For example, new employees will tend to be very task-orientated in the sense that they want to know how to do the job. A non-directive manager can cause anxiety by not instructing new employees about the tasks they are to perform. As employees become more familiar with their work they may seek greater responsibility and leadership styles can become more participatory, and in time a point may be reached where there can be a high level of delegation (see Figure 9.5).

Autocratic ——————————————— Democratic —— Laissez-faire				
Manager makes decision and announces it	Manager presents ideas and invites questions	Manager presents problem, receives suggestions, and makes decision	Manager permits employees to function within limits defined by senior managers	Manager allows employees complete freedom of action

Figure 9.5   Situational leadership.

The idea that the situation plays an important part in leadership style provides a flexible view of leadership which suits modern strategic management. Depending on the situation, a manager may be more or less autocratic. In different circumstances, a manager may make a decision and announce it, present ideas and invite suggestions, ask a group to make a decision within defined limits, or allow a high degree of freedom of action. Some problems, those for example which involve everybody, may be best dealt with through laissez-faire leadership; other problems, involving a few experts, may be best dealt with through a more autocratic style. In practice, within the scope of contingency theories of leadership, there is a view that leaders and subordinates should reach a compromise on strategic ideas so that they can move forward. There may be a difference of views but a way forward to the organisational objectives will be achieved by some agreement between them.

9.5   The sources of power in leadership

Leadership in strategic management involves persuading people to work towards a particular objective. There are a number of ways of doing this, depending on the basis of a manager's power (Figure 9.6). Power may be 'coercive', based on punishment and threats, or 'expert', based on the leader's possession of skill and knowledge. The source of power may be 'legitimate', based on the hierarchy of the organisation and the perception of employees that they should obey the orders of senior managers, while 'referent' power is based on other people's admiration and wish to identify with the leader. 'Reward'-based power is determined by the leader's ability to provide rewards, while 'connection' power is based on the leader's relationships with influential partners.

The power of managers over employees can be described as 'social power' because it is derived from the social interaction of leaders and their followers.

Coercive power

Expert power

Legitimate power

Referent power

Reward power

Connection power

Figure 9.6   Sources of power.

Unless 'followers' are prepared to follow, the leader cannot lead; and in a more flexible and informal society, managers rely more than in the past on expert, referent and connection power than on coercive, legitimate or reward power. Leaders now tend to use personal power rather than positional power as management structures have become flatter and management practice more open. Information is now shared more widely than in the past and management is seen as a form of partnership in order to achieve agreed objectives. There are still, of course, organisations and individual leaders who base power on coercion and reward.

9.6   Modern strategic leadership

New forms of technology, communications and enterprise have led to new forms of organisation, new corporate cultures and new forms of leadership in strategic management. The so-called 'learning organisation' is an example of the new trends. This has arisen from the idea that while people learn throughout their lives in one way or another, many organisations are based on the idea of control. This means that employees may be rewarded for performing particular tasks rather than cultivating their natural curiosity and impulse to learn.

The idea that the top of the organisation 'thinks' and establishes the strategic direction, while lower down the organisation people 'act' by carrying out orders, is out-of-date in relation to many new businesses. Learning companies look for adaptive learning within the organisation so that they can cope with environmental change, but they also look for generative learning so that they can create new ways of facing change and solving problems. For example, at one level, quality control means that a company concentrates on making a product that is reliable so that it will do what the designers have intended and what the customers have been led to expect. The next level is a focus on understanding better what customers want and then providing products that reliably meet these needs. The third level is to seek to understand the 'latent' need of the customers – what they will truly value but have not really thought of – and meet this need.

'I have read the final draft of your report on our strategy,' the Managing Director of 'The Engineering Company' tells the Assistant Managing Director, 'and I have looked at the organisational structure you suggest.' 'Can I just say that it is not my report so much as the result of discussions with numerous people, including you of course,' the Assistant Managing Director points out. 'Well whatever, you have done a really good job and it is time we put some of it into action.' 'We haven't finished all the consultations yet.' 'We can't wait for ever, I have discussed it with the Chairman. We'll announce the new organisational structure next week. That will give us time to discuss it with the people involved. We will advertise immediately for Account Managers who will work closely with the Divisions but will report directly to you along with the Divisional Product Managers. The Marketing Manager will become Head of Marketing, while the Chief Personnel Manager will become Head of Human Resources and they will both report directly to me along with the Head of Finance. We might think of new names for all these posts, perhaps the three reporting to me should be called directors?' 'I'll come up with some suggestions.' 'The main decision we have to make is about our products and markets. There is one Division that stands out as by far the weakest, don't you agree?' 'Yes, what do we do next?' the AMD asks. 'I'll talk to the DPM and see what he has to say.'

Generative learning requires new ways of looking at the world, whether in understanding customers or in understanding how to manage a business better. The major example of this in the past has been the contrast between European and North American manufacturers and Japanese production companies. The Western approach was based on strong control over production levels and forecasts, and also over stock levels. The Japanese approach was to eliminate delays in the production process by improving cost, productivity and service. They built strong relationships with suppliers, redesigned physical production to reduce delays and based stocks on what were needed. They saw the process of order entry, production scheduling, materials procurement, production and distribution as an integrated system, and therefore were able to see that delays between the various stages were a major problem. They saw the 'systems that control events', the 'bigger picture', and unless this is seen then improvements and innovations in organisations are dealing with symptoms rather than with the underlying causes of the problems.

The developments of dot com, e-commerce enterprises are frequently examples of people looking afresh at an area of the economy, understanding the systems involved and finding a way to improve on the present organisation. The traditional view of leaders has been as people who set the direction, make the key decisions and motivate people. This could be described as an individualistic and non-systematic view which views leadership in terms of great men and women who become prominent in times of crisis. This view reinforces a focus on short-term events and charismatic heroes rather than on systematic forces and collective learning. Leadership in a learning organisation relies on leaders building a shared vision, challenging prevailing mental models and fostering more systematic patterns of thinking. Their responsibility is to build organisations where people are continually expanding their capabilities to shape their future.

> 'The wicked leader is he who the people despise.
> The good leader is he who the people revere.
> The great leader is who the people say, "we did it ourselves" '.
>
> (Loa Tsu)

This age-old saying has often been quoted and still helps to illuminate the needs of modern management. Leaders in learning organisations have to be designers, teachers and stewards. In these roles they require new skills, such as the ability to build a shared vision, and to foster more systematic patterns of thinking, and through these attributes and skills they are responsible for learning. They first need to have a clear view of the strategic direction of the organisation, where it wants to be, and also have a clear view of where it is now. This gap creates a tension which leaders have to resolve, the gap between the vision and the present reality. This tension can be resolved either by raising current reality towards the vision, or by lowering the vision towards the current reality. Strategic management aims at raising the present situation in the direction of the vision. This is not just problem-solving, where there is an attempt to improve the present situation rather than moving away from it. Many organisations are only motivated to change when their problems are so bad that they have to change. Strategic leadership motivates people to change before this situation arises.

Strategic leaders are also responsible for building a foundation of purpose and core values. They can do this through long-term policies and fostering strategic thinking. While plans may be a useful guide for an organisation, they need constant adjustment and this is only possible with strategic thinking. The production of a forecast of the future business environment may be useful but it does not in itself lead to an organisation actually preparing for changes that could occur. One way of doing this is through 'scenario analysis' or 'planning as learning', where decision makers are asked to consider their reaction to a range of possible future situations. This means that when a change does occur they have already thought through ways of dealing with it.

At the start, the leaders of 'The Communications Company' obtained their power to lead through their 'expertise'. They had started their Company in their homes so they knew exactly what they wanted to do when they began to involve other people. As the Company expanded, they maintained a 'referent' power because the people that the founders employed admired them for their enterprise, their expertise and their hard work. Further expansion meant that more and more employees did not know the two leaders as founders of the Company and were not inspired by the original pioneering fervour of the organisation. They wanted to be paid well for completing a good job. The founders of the Company continued to use personal power, rather than exerting the power they had from being the senior managers of the Company, because this suited their image of good management. Luckily for the future of the Company, it began to emerge that one of them was very task-orientated and began to lead innovation and development within the Company, while the other was more people-orientated and became the managing director with the task of motivating everybody working in the Company as well as satisfying customers and stakeholders.

As 'The Communications Company' developed into business solutions based on innovation, it had to become a learning organisation. It began to focus on what customers wanted and then providing it. The senior managers of the Company encouraged everybody in the organisation to learn about the Company business and consider ways of improving and developing it. The MD did this by talking to each employee regularly and frequently, and also began to experiment with rewarding innovation and good results. While the Company's focus was on trying to provide what customers wanted, there was also some thought about the latent needs of customers and how far customer requirements matched the capabilities of Company employees.

The modern strategic leader also has to be a teacher or a coach in the sense of bringing to the surface people's assumptions and challenging them. People will have or develop over a period of time a range of assumptions about their work. These might be that the industry they are in is very stable and that their jobs are very secure. Leaders as teachers may want to change these impressions by emphasising that this apparent stability and security have only been achieved by remaining ahead of the competition in an environment that has remained unchanged for an unusually long period of time. Reality for many employees means the pressures that must be borne in a job, crises that must be reacted to and limitations which must be accepted. Strategic leaders help people to restructure their views of reality, to see beyond the superficial conditions and events into the underlying causes of problems, and therefore to see new possibilities for shaping the future.

Many organisations are focused on events in the sense that this or that happens and there is a reaction to it. This is a 'media' approach to some extent, in that television and newspapers report dramatic events and people's reaction, and then move on to the next event and reaction, so that 'there is nothing older than yesterday's news'. Organisations also focus on patterns of behaviour by identifying long-term trends and assessing their implications. This enables them to respond to changing conditions but not necessarily to be innovative in this response. This requires an organisation to encourage structural explanations that consider the underlying causes of behaviour at a level at which these patterns can be altered. While many organisations are reactive or responsive, structural explanations enable them to be generative, in the sense of looking at generic or underlying factors which can promote innovation. Leaders of learning organisations focus on all three explanations and they can then teach, largely through example, everyone else in the organisation to do the same.

The strategic leadership of a learning organisation requires new management skills. These include the encouragement of a personal vision by employees so that they have a direction in which to aim and attempt to build this up into a shared vision. This requires a constant questioning of people's vision and its validity, and asking 'what do we really want to achieve?' It is much more than simply producing a mission or vision statement to include in the corporate plan, it is a constant and evolving process which has to combine external factors and internal objectives.

Objectives that are limited to defeating a competitor can lead to a defensive approach once this objective has been achieved; while setting new standards for customer satisfaction, or creating innovative products, can encourage innovation. If organisations concentrate simply on survival there will be a tendency for a negative approach to developments, while if organisations concentrate on aspirations these can be positive and continuing sources of learning and growth. The technology-based companies may adopt a hierarchical and heavily structured approach to their management, at least once they have passed the initial setting-up stage. However, they do provide an opportunity for modern management styles based on what can be called the 'democracy of information' brought about by the internet.

9.7   Strategic leadership in context

The gulf between the theory and practice of leadership is wide partly because there are so many examples of leaders and because research has indicated that leadership is not a rare ability, leaders are made rather than born, there is no one leadership type, leaders exist throughout organisations and leadership can be learned. At the same time, leaders must have certain characteristics and certain attributes in order to have a strategic role. They must have an idea of the direction in which they want the organisation to move, aspirations about what it can attain, and they must be able to communicate these ideas and turn them into reality.

Strategic leaders must have an accurate view of reality and they need some form of power in order to bring about change. Peter Drucker wrote in 1992 that leadership has little to do with 'leadership qualities' and even less to do with charisma:

> 'Leadership is not itself good or desirable. Leadership is a means. Leadership to what end is the crucial question. History knows no more charismatic leaders than this century's triad of Stalin, Hitler and Mao – the misleaders who inflicted as much evil and suffering on humanity as have ever been recorded.'

The features which distinguish what Peter Drucker refers to as the 'misleaders' from the leaders is their goals. He argues that charisma can be the undoing of leaders because it makes them inflexible, convinced of their own infallibility and unable to change with the needs of the organisation. He felt that charisma did not on its own guarantee effectiveness as a leader, giving the example of John F. Kennedy as perhaps the most charismatic person ever to occupy the White House, but who achieved very little.

The strategic perspective suggests that the direction of a company is a dynamic development from where it is now, by a process of testing the boundaries, through experiment and trial and error, by being entrepreneurial and taking every opportunity that arises. The company does not know exactly what will happen as it moves forward from the familiar area of work it knows about into new areas. This does not mean that it has no idea where it is going, but it does mean that the direction is set from where it is now and that it does not know exactly where it will end up. The direction is provided by leaders with a strategic view. They decide which direction is most likely to make the best use of the organisation's skills and abilities, to match the organisation's values and most likely to produce the best rewards.

> 'How the leader views experimentation, accepts failure, rewards success, takes an interest in the conduct of experiments, has some vision of how the experiments relate to each other and the existing business, and uses the meetings of the top team, will all have a major bearing on the extent and the consequences of experimentation in the organisation. The leader sets many of the challenges, creates a sense of urgency to do something about them and expresses the determination to succeed.'
>
> (Ralph Stacey, 1996)

Strategic leadership is not about a plan in the sense of an architect's plan, which predetermines every action. It is about a clear, continuous and coherent process designed to explore and extend the boundaries of the existing business which are agreed to be the most fruitful by senior managers. If there is a plan, it is based on the abilities of the organisation and the forward thinking of the strategic managers. It is not about any trial and error, which will provide little or no sense of direction, it is trial and error in areas where the organisation has the capabilities to be successful, so that there is a sense of direction.

SUMMARY OF CONCEPTS

The importance of strategic leadership – The meaning of leadership – Change agents – Attributes of leaders – Strategic vision – 'People come first' – Theories of leadership – Characteristics of leaders – Leadership styles – Task- and people-orientation – Situational Leadership – Leaders' sources of power – Modern strategic leadership – Generative learning – Coaching – Learning organisations – 'Misleaders' – Leadership in context

---

ASSIGNMENTS

1. What is the importance of leadership in the strategic management of an organisation?
2. Discuss the leadership style that would be best for an e-commerce company.
3. What are the characteristics of leadership?
4. How do leaders maintain their power?
5. Describe and discuss leadership in an organisation that you know.
6. Compare leadership styles in 'The Communications Company' and in 'The Engineering Company'.

■ Ṽ 10 Managing strategic change

OBJECTIVES

To provide an understanding of strategic change
To analyse the process of change
To consider the management of strategic change
To discuss the methods of achieving change

The importance of understanding strategic change – Analysing the process of change – Considering the management of change – The methods of achieving change

10.1 What is strategic change?

Previous chapters, such as those on marketing, satisfying customers and maintaining a competitive advantage, all stress the importance of recognising that the only factor that is a certainty in both the private and public sectors is that 'things will change'. Change can be thought of as a journey rather than an event, with slow organisational change fitting the description of a journey, while sudden and rapid change is more likely to appear to be an event.

Change is necessary for all organisations because, however much there may be a desire to keep things as they are, everything around the organisation is moving. Competitors are seeking for ways to achieve their own competitive advantage, global changes take place as organisations are established, expand, contract or collapse, and the economies of countries across the world rise and fall. Government legislation and actions affect some organisations more than others, as do climatic conditions and so on. For whatever reason, organisations experience change in their business environment and unless they change in response they will experience strategic drift, so that they move further and further away from providing what is wanted by customers and stakeholders. At the same time, there are inevitable movements within an organisation caused by ageing buildings and equipment (and people!), changes in personnel, changes in management and so on.

Strategic change is the implementation of new strategies that involve sub-stantive changes beyond the normal routines of the organisation. There may be slow change where change is introduced gradually in small incremental steps, so that the roles of the senior managers may be changed, middle managers may be given slightly different responsibilities, or an extra task may be added to every-one's job. There is likely to be little resistance to slow change which involves the changing roles of managers and a slight change in tasks for other employees. Sudden organisational change will encounter more resistance however carefully it is handled, so that, for example, closing down a department in a company, an office or a factory cannot be carried out without some resistance as people lose their jobs or the circumstances in which they work alter. So a distinction can be made between incremental change and transformational change:

- **Incremental change** does not alter underlying organisational cultural beliefs or values because it is about doing things a little differently and the cause of it is easily seen by everybody.
- **Transformational change** does involve change in organisational cultural assumptions because it is about doing different things or doing things very differently, and the cause of the change is not very clear to everyone.

Incremental change is the most frequent type of change in most organisa-tions and is often initiated by employees who are directly involved with the organisational processes and customers. They may introduce it themselves or it may be introduced after discussions with managers. On the other hand, **transformational change** is associated with strategic leadership, so it is a top-down process initiated by senior managers. It may be possible to look back on a series of incremental changes to see that together they constitute a transfor-mational change. Whether it is incremental or transformational, strategic change is concerned with changes which are necessary to maintain the link between the organisation and its environment so that it remains competitive and able to meet the needs of its customers.

10.2   The process of strategic change

In order to maintain strategic 'fit' or 'stretch', or to maintain a competitive advantage, an organisation has to manage the process of change. It is strate-gic change, rather than operational change, when a new strategy is required in order to ensure the success of the organisation. In practice, the reasons for strategic change becoming necessary include the development of new tech-nology, changes in the availability or quality of raw materials, changes in the control of the organisation as well as competitive factors. The pressures not to change include anxieties about the results of change, an unwillingness to alter established work patterns and worries about the loss of well-established skills.

Managing strategic change is not necessarily as easy as following through a rational sequence of actions and decisions, it is often complex and messy because it involves people and their behaviour.

The Managing Director of 'The Engineering Company' arranges a meeting of his divisional and functional managers. These include the Head of Finance, the Head of Human Resources, the Head of Marketing and Divisional Product Managers. 'I have explained to all of you that the Company faces problems because of increasing competition,' he says, 'the main problem is that firms who specialise in particular industries are able to produce machinery more cheaply than we are. Although they are smaller operating units than we are overall, they are larger when it comes to particular industrial sectors. This means that they are able to take advantage of the economies of scale and to focus on the needs of that one industry better than we do. Our strategy in the past was based on diversification, so that we used our expertise in making machinery for one area of industry in order to move into another area. This is no longer a viable strategy and I have asked each of you what we should do about this.' He pauses to see if there is any comment; when there isn't he continues. 'For the Company to remain viable, we have to make a strategic choice. You have all received copies of the Strategic Review prepared by the AMD and you have all made an input into this. I hope you have all read it and noted that it discusses both the competition we face in each of our markets and the analysis of our internal structure.' He pauses again to see if anybody will admit that they have not read the report. 'The fact is that we cannot ignore this report because our profits have fallen and if we continue to work as we do now, they will continue to fall. We have started to alter the structure, which is the easy part, the difficult part is changing what we do and how we do it.' He pauses again to make sure that he has everyone's attention. 'This includes rationalising, that means reducing, the number of products we offer.'

At the beginning of a period of change, the organisation could be said to be in a state of equilibrium where any reasons for change are balanced by reasons for not changing. Everything seems to be going along smoothly, people have settled into their jobs, supplies to the organisation are well established, and customers are satisfied with the products and services they are receiving. Some 'trigger' then upsets this equilibrium. There may be a break-through in technology, a competitor introduces an updated product, overseas companies start to have an impact on the home market, the government introduces new health and safety legislation, there is a merger with another company, a new chief executive takes over the company, or something or other breaks up the smooth arrangements which have worked in the organisation up to that time.

As far back as 1951, Kurt Lewin argued (see also Chapter 1) in terms of equilibrium, 'unfreezing' and 'refreezing':

- **equilibrium** – factors or forces encouraging change balanced by factors or forces resisting change;
- **unfreezing** – a 'trigger' upsets the equilibrium and people begin to accept the new situation;
- **refreezing** – as a new equilibrium is achieved.

In the '**unfreezing**' stage, people accept the new situation either willingly or through persuasion so that the organisation can return once more to an equilibrium. For example, employees in a company that is the subject of a merger may accept, however reluctantly, that this has created a new situation and that there are likely to be changes. They may not fully understand why the merger has come about, so they may have to be persuaded that it is in the best interest of the company.

A **new equilibrium** has to be achieved where new arrangements have to be made in terms of management, tasks, suppliers, customers and so on, so that these become the established and accepted 'way of doing things'. In order to survive, the new equilibrium must be more appropriate than the previous one to the new environment in which the organisation is operating. There may then be a '**refreezing**' as the new equilibrium is achieved. This unfreezing and refreezing process is bound to be disruptive to some extent so that ideally an organisation becomes, at least to some degree, a learning organisation where the forces for change are relatively strong compared to the forces resisting change, so that it can adapt to a new trigger which upsets this new equilibrium.

'The Communications Company' passed through a period of incremental changes when it expanded the range of services it was offering as competition increased. It became a business solutions company, offering an information technology-based service to solve business problems. As a result of the Company's success in providing IT solutions, it was asked more and more frequently to provide solutions to problems outside the scope of IT. The pressure was on it to become a management consultancy company, extending its service to areas of production, finance and human relations. With the expanded use of the internet and the development of a range of e-commerce companies, the senior management of 'The Communications Company' decided that it had to expand into management consultancy areas. This was more than an incremental change, it required a re-thinking of the role and the skills of all employees. Up to that point the people working in the Company had thought of themselves as IT experts, usually working with other experts or people with less expertise. This change meant that they would be working in areas where they were less confident and where they would be working with people with specialisms in which they were unfamiliar.

The unfreezing process begins with the loosening of the hold of the established behaviour because there is a feeling that change is needed and is possible. The feeling that change is needed may arise because profits are falling or demand is clearly being reduced week by week or month by month. People also have to be convinced that changes are possible, so that there are reasonably clear ways of doing things differently which will improve the situation. The actual change involved will be easier if it is not very fundamental, and will be more difficult where it is.

A small change in behaviour will be easier to introduce that a change in people's values, although a change in values will be a more long-lasting change. At the same time, if a change is imposed rather than occurring with the agreement and support of the people involved, it is likely to be less successful; so that strategic leadership involves making it very clear why change is necessary and helping everybody to understand this. In the refreezing of an organisation and a return to an equilibrium, people need to be convinced that the changes have been worthwhile – that they do lead to increased customer satisfaction or higher profits.

It can be argued that almost everyone feels some opposition to change because they are moving into an unknown situation where they are not sure how things work. The feelings that many people may have when faced with change have been considered in five stages:

- denial;
- defence;
- discarding;
- adaptation;
- internalisation.

Most people feel some sense of **denial** when changes are proposed, even if it is in a mild form such as saying 'are you sure it's necessary?' A stronger denial may be in the form of asking why change a pattern of work which has worked well for a long time, or pointing out that things have always been done in a particular way. A **defensive** approach may arise once people start to become convinced that change is going to take place. People, sections and departments defend their position against any change which they see as a loss of power. Individuals may feel that their skills are going to be down-graded, while departments may think that their position in the organisational structure is being attacked. Both denial and defence are focused on the past, and change is only taking place once these stages have been passed and people reach the discarding stage.

In this third, **discarding**, stage of the coping process, the focus is moved on to the future, so that the past is discarded and people start to look forward. In order to reach this stage, managers have to convince everybody that change is necessary and inevitable and therefore that the past has to be discarded. People can be reassured up to a point by encouraging them to experiment with new operations and to visit other organisations which are already operating in a new way. The low point in the change process may be passed as people gain confidence in resolving problems and start to take the initiative.

'The Communications Company' experienced a considerable change in becoming a management consultancy. New employees were taken on who were not necessarily experts in information technology but did have skills in other areas such as finance, management and human resources. Above all, they were experts in the inter-personal skills required for advising other companies. Some of the original Company staff became very defensive about the changes taking place, particularly because the new staff had to be fitted into the same office space. A number of them insisted on a meeting with the two senior executives of the Company to ask why the changes were necessary. When this was explained to them and they became convinced that the changes were going to take place whatever they said, they wanted to know about their positions in the Company, their roles and practical matters such as office space. They were assured that the Company was actively looking for new larger offices and they were told that the Company was not giving up its previous contracts and areas of work, it was simply expanding into new areas. They were asked by the senior managers to co-operate with the new members of staff and to support them.

The fourth stage of the coping process is **adaptation** as individuals adapt to the new working practices and the new practices are adapted as people learn about them. At this stage, managers can concentrate on the outcomes; provided these are satisfactory, individuals, teams and departments can be given control of the processes.

Internalisation corresponds to the refreezing process when individuals internalise the changes so that they begin to feel that the new ways are the normal ones, the new 'way we do things around here'.

The change process as far as individuals are concerned often follows the marketing model (see Chapter 6) where there are **innovators** who embrace the change at an early stage with enthusiasm. Then there are **early adopters** who accept it once they see it in action and then **the majority** who work their way through denial and defence. Finally there are the **laggards** who accept the change because everyone else has and there is no longer a choice. Strategic managers will concentrate on the innovators in the early stages of change and on the early adopters, so that they can set an example for the majority.

10.3 Competition and strategic change

In 1985 Michael Porter argued that strategic change may arise because of alterations in one or more of five competitive forces (Figure 10.1) or factors which exist within an organisation's operating environment (see Chapter 6):

- capital requirements and the scale of the enterprise;
- the bargaining powers of buyers and purchasers;
- the bargaining power of suppliers;
- the threat of substitute products;
- rivalry among competitors.

In **capital**-intensive industries, where expensive equipment is needed to set up a company, new companies are likely to find it difficult to start up, while in service industries where the need for capital may be small, starting up a new company may be relatively easy. For example, at least some of the e-commerce companies have been established with very limited capital, while engineering companies usually require capital investment in expensive machinery before they can start operating. Service industries (such as retailing) are more likely to face relatively frequent changes, as a result of new entrants, than manufacturing industries (such as the motor car industry).

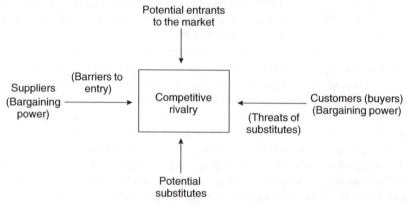

Figure 10.1   The organisational operating environment.

Buyers, whether they are final consumers or company purchasers, are in a better bargaining position when they know the full range of product and price options, and where there are a range of options available. Advertising, consumer groups and an increase in competition have all helped to add to consumer information and to increase the bargaining power of buyers. The fall in the price of motor cars in the UK has been the result of these factors, when consumers realised that cars were cheaper in other countries in Europe.

The bargaining power of suppliers will depend on the availability of substitute suppliers; so a sole supplier will have great power while if there are a number of suppliers, their bargaining power will be less. **The threat of substitute products** is most powerful where there are alternatives and substitutes for a company's product. Changes in opinions about the environment, costs and so on may influence the demand for these products. For example, consumers in the UK realised that they could buy cars from other countries in Europe more cheaply than from suppliers in the UK, and this reduced the bargaining power of the UK suppliers. They were eventually forced to reduce their new car prices in response to this situation.

'The Communications Company' found that it had to introduce strategic change because competing companies were being established all the time. Some of them did not last long but the others nibbled away at the Company's customer base. Accounts had been lost to companies providing a wider service, as well as to companies providing a cheap service through the internet. One company established itself simply by opening a website and offering 'Computer Solutions', charging customers the cost of the internet link. As well as opening its own website, 'The Communications Company' started to develop a comprehensive business solutions and management consultancy service, including a hands-on service in companies' own premises. It realised that they were in an industry where entry was very easy and price differentials were considerable, but where a quality service was difficult to find, so it decided to concentrate on providing an efficient, effective, customer-based service.

Rivalry among competitors appears in all sorts of forms, such as through price, advertising or product differentiation. Companies have to adjust to rivals' strategies in order to remain competitive. Porter has argued that these competitive forces may influence the changes to which an organisation is exposed. If it is operating in an area of low barriers to entry and where its bargaining powers are small, changes may be relatively frequent and organisations may attempt to find a competitive advantage through product differentiation or cost leadership. Product differentiation involves branding products and adding distinctive features to make the products different from those of other companies, while cost leadership involves reducing prices in order to undercut competitors.

Where barriers to entry to an industry are high and an organisation has a relatively strong bargaining position in relation to suppliers and customers, changes may be slow to occur. The bargaining power of an organisation in relation to the threat of substitute products and to rivals will also make its competitive position more or less strong. Any changes in these competitive forces will be a factor in an organisation's environment leading to change.

10.4 Change tactics

Timing can be a very important factor in strategic change, particularly when the change required is transformational. If there is an actual or perceived crisis, everybody in the organisation will be able to understand the high risk of maintaining the present processes and the importance of change. Obvious threats such as a take-over or a major fall in profits can be understood by everyone, but smaller changes in profitability or market share can either be shrugged off by senior management or stressed as a potentially disastrous downward trend.

The Managing Director of 'The Engineering Company' tries to involve the meeting of his divisional and functional managers in the process of strategic change. 'We have established the need for change; we cannot carry on as we are, profits are falling and the company is becoming less and less viable. We have analysed our working structures, our financial systems and our costs and we have considered the markets we are in and their future.' He pauses to provide a chance for a discussion of his summary of the Company situation. 'We have to make choices,' he continues, 'which involves reducing our costs, improving our systems and streamlining our activities. Over the last few months these choices have been discussed with you, and you have been invited to contribute and to discuss these in your divisions. We have taken into account all the feedback we have had and now we have to act. The communication and information systems in the Company are to be updated and 'The Communications Company' has been contracted to help us to do this. We have invested in updating our technology so that it is less labour intensive. We have offered early retirement across the Company. The hardest choice has been to decide on which areas of industry we should concentrate. I can tell you now that the Board has supported a move to concentrating on three main industrial areas where we believe we can compete successfully. You all know about our redundancy policy. We have had discussions with the unions and we have agreed to improve our redundancy package.'

There may be 'windows of opportunity' for change which again may be obvious to most people. For example, a new chief executive will be expected to make changes, or the introduction of a new product may need clear changes. All change will cause anxiety and it may be possible to reassure people by making changes to personnel before changing other processes such as work routines. These changes can then be seen as improvements resulting from a management shake-up. Changes are often assumed to cause job losses and often do, so anticipating a change may help to reduce opposition to it. For example, a well-funded early retirement policy may be seen as an opportunity rather than a threat; on the other hand, a slow process of compulsory redundancies will create tensions and anxiety. It is often better to have one round of heavy reductions in the number of jobs rather than a slow process of job losses. A well-organised and caring approach to job losses can reassure remaining employees that the organisation cares about them and has good reasons for the policy it has introduced.

The implementation of strategic change will require many detailed actions and tasks even though the overall process is a relatively long-term one. It is important that short-term actions are seen to be effective and successful so that it becomes accepted that the change process is an improvement on the old systems.

10.5 The management of strategic change

In one way or another, changes in any organisation have to be managed. Where operational change is involved, this can be left to the unit or team most involved and management responsibility may be mainly in terms of overall policy. For example, any changes to jobs must adhere to industrial relations agreements and equal opportunity policies, while technical changes have to consider health and safety policies. Strategic change will be more fundamental and requires much more management involvement in the whole process of seeing through the appropriate change. A simple model of change has a starting point that there is usually a degree of inertia in an organisation and something prompts change:

- there has to be a sufficient number or strength of senior managers who feel dissatisfied by the way things are and who want to do something about it;
- they need to have an idea of the direction in which the organisation should be moving;
- they need to have some fairly simple first steps in order to start the process of change;
- finally, these factors multiplied together must exceed the perceived costs of changing.

This means that there is not very much point in developing a strategy for managing change if senior managers are satisfied with present strategy for one reason or another, or if they lack the confidence to make the necessary changes. In times of crisis, developing a strategy for change is more straightforward because everyone can understand that something needs to happen. There is a tendency in these circumstances to introduce well-tried cost-cutting strategies, such as budget reductions, the elimination of layers of management, closing plants and making people redundant. Everybody understands these actions, however unpopular they may be. While these actions may become necessary they can also be considered to be negative approaches to strategic change, often taken because senior managers have not anticipated the need to change.

Andrew Pettigrew (and others) in a number of books have considered the management of strategic change in terms of the content, process and context of change. In these books, strategic change has been seen as occurring in a '**context**' and as a result of pressures on an organisation which were either external or internal or both, and can be described as the 'why?' of change, the reason for it becoming necessary. The '**content**' can be seen as the 'what?' of change, the actual changes that have to be made. The '**process**' is the 'how?' of change, the way in which these changes are made depending on the strategy introduced by the organisation. The strategy would depend on the need for change by the organisation and its capability to respond to this need. This capability depends on the competencies of the people involved, the available resources and finances, the land and buildings under the organisation's control, and the information it has at its disposal. How capable an organisation was in meeting the need to change also depends on its structures and the values and attitudes held by its employees.

The 'incremental' approach to managing change suggests that managers have an intended destination for their organisation, but they discover how to reach it by taking logically connected decisions step by step. Managers do not make major changes but build incrementally in a consistent manner on what they already have. This approach reduces conflict and opposition, but it can lead to 'strategic drift' (Figure 10.2). Managers may build on their understanding of their organisation and the situation in which it is working, so that the incremental changes are adding to the accepted 'way we do things around here'. This means that the organisation moves further in a particular direction, which may be the wrong direction in terms of its survival in the future.

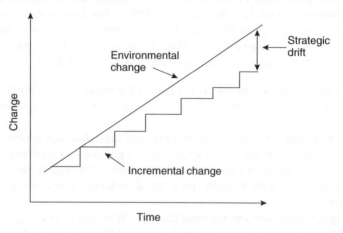

Figure 10.2   Strategic drift.

The incremental approach can lead to strategic drift. **'Strategic drift' arises where an organisation is driven down the same, familiar, path by its own momentum, becoming more and more out of line with its environment**. This means that while the industry is changing in a new way, the organisation is developing in the old way. The introduction of information technology created this gap or drift for many companies – where they continued to use their old manual systems, rivals were developing the new technology. The gap between the company and its rival will widen until it is forced to make sudden changes in order to survive. Examples of this have been seen with IBM's relatively slow move into the production of Personal Computers, while other companies were rapidly developing them, and Marks & Spencer's slow acceptance of credit cards and cheap ranges.

Strategic managers have to manage the main causes of strategic change, which can be identified as the environment, business relationships, technology and people:

- **the environment** – shifts in the economy, competitive pressures and changes in legislation can all lead to major strategic change;
- **business relationships** – new acquisitions, partnerships, competition and other significant developments may require substantial changes in the organisational structure;
- **technology** – new developments can have a substantial impact on organisations and 'ways of working';
- **people** – new employees may have different expectations, which is especially important when the leadership of an organisation changes.

Pettigrew and Whipp (1991), in *Managing Change for Competitive Success*, studied strategic change at four companies – Jaguar cars, Longman publishing, Hill Samuel merchant bank and Prudential life assurance – and made a general examination of the industries in which these companies were operating. Their conclusions were that there were five interrelated factors (Figure 10.3) in the successful management of strategic change:

- **Environmental assessment** – every part of the organisation should be constantly assessing the competition, so that strategy can emerge constantly from this process.
- **Leading change** – the type of leadership required depends on the particular circumstances of the organisation, which provides a constraint on leaders. They may be most effective when they move the organisation forward at a comfortable, if challenging, pace, because bold actions can be counterproductive.
- **Linking strategic and operational change** – this may be prescriptive in the sense of a strategic manager providing a specific strategy for the organisation, or it may be partly emergent in the sense of allowing for the evolution of strategy over time.
- **Strategic human resource management** – human resources constitute the knowledge, skills and attitudes of the organisation, and some individuals are better than others at managing people.
- **Coherence in the management of change** – the goals of the organisation must not conflict with each other, the process of change must respond well to the environment, a competitive advantage must be achieved and the strategy must not provide unsolvable problems.

Overall, the organisation needs to be able to develop a balanced approach to change that is both focused and efficient.

Coherence

Environmental assessment	Leading change
Strategic human resource management	Linking strategic and operational change

Figure 10.3 Five factors in the successful management of strategic change.

10.6 Styles of managing strategic change

There are more or less appropriate styles of management for the people man-aging change (Figure 10.4). One approach is through 'education' and **commu-nication** in the sense of explaining the reasons for and the means of strategic change. This communication has to be in a form that enables people to assim-ilate the information and to understand it. Putting up notices, issuing leaflets and holding briefing meetings may not be sufficient, because these are top-down approaches to the problem.

Communication

Collaboration

Intervention

Direction

Coercion

Figure 10.4 Styles of strategic change management.

'**Collaboration**' and participation is a process of involving those most affected by strategic change in the identification of strategic issues, the setting of the strategic agenda and the strategic decision-making process. This can help to involve people in the process of change so that they do assimilate and understand the changes taking place. The risk is that solutions may arise in the form of the present situation so that fundamental change is not achieved. Workshops and cross-organisational working groups will involve people in the process but can lead to limited solutions or disagreement. This means that some 'intervention' may be required.

'**Intervention**' involves co-ordination and control over the process of change by so-called 'change agents'. These are the people who effect strategic change in an organisation, whether they are external consultants or managers within the organisation. The advantage of using external consultants is that they can appear relatively objective in their approach to change. They are outside the various power and influence structures of the organisation and they can introduce a breath of fresh air into the process of change. They also have experience of dealing with strategic change in other organisations which they can pass on. At the same time, they may introduce a discordant note into what may be considered to be an internal process. They may be seen as people employed by senior managers to do something the managers should be doing themselves, or they may be seen as people who are highly paid to 'borrow your watch to tell you the time', so that they simply tell people in an organisation either what they already know or they can easily find out.

The Managing Director of 'The Engineering Company' has a meeting with his longest serving Divisional Manager who has been with the company for many years and is reluctant to introduce any changes. 'Look,' the MD says, 'the gap between what we have been doing and what the industry wants has been widening. Orders are down and the future does not look bright. We have to change and we have set this in motion. The alterations we have made in our systems and technology have already had an impact and we have had our first round of early retirements. You need to talk to the key people in your Division, make it clear that the changes taking place are inevitable and are not going to be reversed. The future of your Division depends on lower costs, greater productivity and producing what your customers want. You must persuade your key people that this is the way forward so that they can persuade everybody else.' 'They won't like it,' the Divisional Manager says, 'they have been used to working in one way and they are reluctant to change.' 'You will have to persuade them, by pointing out the need for change and making clear the way forward,' says the MD, 'they already know that one of the Divisions is closing, involving both the early retirement programme and redundancies. The bottom line is that strategic change is necessary, if there are not changes your Division will close.'

While some managers may be skilful in developing a strategy they may have to rely on other people, particularly people who could be described as 'change agents', to introduce the changes. These are people who are able to cope with what may appear to be two conflicting ways of managing – the present one and the new one. They have to understand the required changes and the need for them, while being able to take action to challenge the present situation and to carry people with them. So they have to be able to explain complex issues of strategy in everyday ways and to demonstrate the means to achieve change.

Whether they are senior managers or junior team leaders they need to be clear about the need for change, sensitive to different people's concerns while also being able to network with a variety of contacts and to build teams to bring together key stakeholders and establish effective working groups. They also have to have communication skills and personal enthusiasm, while holding a 'helicopter' perspective in the ability to stand back from the immediate task and take a broad view of priorities. The people who have all or some of these qualities can make or break the process of change by helping people to understand the need for change, to develop an enthusiasm for it and to understand the actions required to introduce it.

Change can be introduced by **direction** or even **coercion**. Direction involves managers using their authority to establish a clear future strategy and how change will occur. In a crisis, managers may use coercion to impose change. These methods of introducing strategic change are based on a top-down leadership approach which may be appropriate for transformational change but suffers from the problem that while employees may go along with the changes, they may do so with little enthusiasm. In practice, the different styles may be applied in different circumstances, used to satisfy different stakeholders, or used together in various combinations. A major change may be introduced by direction in order to achieve a rapid transformation in the interests of satisfying shareholders, suppliers and customers; then more participative methods with the encouragement of change agents may be used in an attempt to satisfy employees.

10.7 Strategic change and the culture of the organisation

By definition, change involves moving from a previous strategy so the starting point for the change process may be seen as an attack on the existing strategy. This approach is likely to produce resistance to change, particularly from those who introduced the previous strategy or who feel they have benefited from it. Ideally, the culture of the organisation helps in the process of change by being a 'change culture'.

The culture of an organisation is 'the way we do things around here' (see Chapter 8); it is the beliefs, customs, practices and ways of thinking that are dominant in an organisation. If the strategic change attempts to alter these patterns of behaviour, customs and beliefs then opposition to it may be fierce. Transformational leadership can be seen as a form of 'culture busting' where people are persuaded to change their set of beliefs and patterns of behaviour. On the other hand, there is the view that cultures are so embedded in an organisation that they are not easily manageable, so if the success of a given strategy depends on the ability to manage the organisational culture then this culture may make or break that success. For many organisations the 'old' ways of doing business cannot continue if they are to survive in today's high-technology-based global market.

As 'The Communications Company' expanded it had to employ administrators and other support staff without the same expertise as the original
(Continued)

group of employees. This created a split between the two groups of staff – those with the capabilities to meet the prime objectives of the business and those who were supporting their efforts. The support staff called the technology experts 'prima donnas' and 'egg-heads', while the technology group called the support staff 'drones' and 'wooden-tops'. Two cultures developed in the company, epitomised by the situation where the technology group was expected to work for 'as long as the job required', while the support group worked set hours. There were also clear pay differences, with the technology group on better pay and profit-sharing schemes. The expansion of the company into management consultancy involved the employment of new staff with different skills. These were people with capabilities in management consultancy who had skills, particularly with people, that were quite different from those of the technology group. Both the original groups had to come to terms with this new group of staff, who became known as 'the likely lads'.

For many years, organisations thrived and prospered by focusing their efforts on their 'core' competence, that is doing one thing and doing it well. These organisations supported this business focus by emphasising issues such as structure, procedures and loyalty to the organisation. A hierarchical structure, with layers of management each responsible for a specific area of the business, was very effective in this environment. The increasing speed of communication as a result of developments in information technology and the emergence of new countries as major competitors have altered the nature of many industries, with a greater emphasis on flexibility and on satisfying customer needs quickly and efficiently.

In the traditional UK manufacturing culture, each production unit worked without necessarily communicating to any extent with other units. The focus was on employee discipline, production targets and communication skills, and consideration of customer needs was often felt to be the job of someone else. A successful strategic change process has to work with the prevailing culture unless a way can be found to change it. A merger of two companies often brings about a conflict of cultures, because the two companies may have different ways of 'doing things around here'. At first the two companies may be able to operate fairly separately in their own ways but, as time goes on one or other culture may become dominant, so a new way of 'doing things around here' may be achieved. In the process there is likely to be a shake-up in personnel as some people feel that they cannot work under the new systems.

The Managing Director of 'The Engineering Company' has another meeting with his longest serving Divisional Product Manager. 'People are very reluctant to make any changes,' the DPM admits, 'they understand that some changes are needed, but they don't like this new Accounts

Manager who has been brought in. He is younger than most of them and he is telling us what we should do. What does he know about our products? Also they feel that cutting costs and demanding higher productivity will simply mean lower standards.' 'Are you convinced about the changes that are necessary?' the MD asks him. 'I am not sure we have to go as far as you have suggested.' Later the MD talks to the Assistant Managing Director. 'I have had another look at the structure we are introducing and I am now convinced we have not gone far enough. Apparently there is at least one company that might be interested in taking us over. I have spoken to the Chairman and we agree that a merger or take-over is not a viable strategy for us because we would be absorbed and just disappear. Meanwhile, we have been trying to contain the change within our existing basic organisation. What we have to do is to close all the Divisions and streamline our operation so that we have a single product division using the technology we are introducing across all the products.' 'What happens to the Divisional Product Managers?' the AMD asks. 'We part company with some, the others work together under you.'

ASSIGNMENT

Consider merger and take-over as a strategic option. Discuss the MD's most recent proposals for change.

A clash of cultures was seen in the National Health Service (NHS) when business managers were introduced to run Hospital Trusts. Their 'business-like' approach clashed with the medical professionals' approach to problems and different priorities. Medical priorities did not always coincide with financial priorities and in many NHS organisations the two cultures have co-existed uncomfortably together for many years. If people cannot be persuaded to embrace strategic change they may have to be accommodated, especially if they are key workers as in the NHS Hospital Trusts. Ideally, however, an organisation is open to change and sees changes as positive challenges. In order to be fully effective, an organisation should learn to welcome change. It should regard strategic change as a positive challenge and manage itself accordingly. This can only be achieved if it is a learning organisation, that is one that constantly learns from experience and expects change to be the only consistent factor in its development.

10.8 Introducing strategic change

One practical way of introducing strategic change is to alter people's **routines**, the way they do things. This can be achieved by introducing flexitime where it has not previously existed, by moving offices and equipment, or by organising cross-company working groups. In recent years, many companies have attempted to introduce a greater customer focus by encouraging their employees to provide a customer service efficiently and with a smile. The 'Customer comes first' programmes have been introduced, sometimes with financial incentives, and training programmes have been introduced to help employees understand the customer needs.

Symbols can also play a part in strategic change, because they express more than their obvious content whether they are objects, events, acts or people. The selection interview process, for example, may provide a signal to those being interviewed about the nature of the organisation. A very formal and efficient interview procedure may signal a rather hierarchical organisation where efficiency is a major priority, whereas an informal and rather chaotic procedure may indicate a relaxed but not particularly efficient organisation. Different selection procedures may mean that different people are appointed. At the same time, more obvious symbols may indicate change, such as the location of the head office or the organisation of work space. If someone who is made redundant has their work place cleared of all their belongings in a very short time, this makes a clear statement about their position.

The behaviour of the change agents may be a particularly important symbol of change. If change requires alterations in the behaviour of employees, managers must show the way by changing their behaviour because, for most people, their work situation is not a matter of written or spoken abstractions but of deeds and actions. The manager of a large retail store which prides itself on customer care needs to reinforce this message by talking to customers and employees. Middle managers play an important part in the implementation of change because they provide the link between the senior management and employees. They can make sure that resources are allocated correctly and controlled appropriately, they can monitor performance and above all they can communicate the strategic view of senior managers to the employees they are managing.

10.9 Stakeholders

Strategic change has to be managed according to the needs of the various organisational stakeholders. The key players are those with a high level of interest in an organisation and a high level of power. For example, major shareholders are likely to have a strong interest in a company and also a high level of power. They need to be satisfied that strategic changes are being made at the correct time and that the changes are the right ones. They will have a particular interest in making sure that the changes encourage a higher yield and a rise in the share price.

On the other hand, small shareholders may have a strong interest in the organisation but have little power on their own, so that the company will be less concerned about informing them of changes or making changes that they approve of. In the same way, key workers will need to be treated carefully in the change process, with adequate rewards for any changes they have to make, while workers who can easily be replaced will need fewer incentives to change.

Employees may well be reluctant to change because they have a vested interest in the present ways of doing things. They have their established power bases, the skills to do the job and they know where they are in the work situation. Change in an organisation tends to be either a reactive change brought about by a sudden or unplanned event, or planned change which is a systematic, deliberate change in the way part or all of the organisation functions. The sudden foot and mouth outbreak in British agriculture in early 2001 created a rapid change in the tourist and holiday industry which created a downturn in many small and medium organisations as they reacted to the situation, while a change in technology may result in a planned and systematic change.

Strategic change will alter the way in which the organisation operates in one way or another, and existing employees may not see this as being for the better. Using outsiders as change agents can be productive where these feelings of opposition are strong, so that, for example, a new chief executive from outside the organisation can bring a new perspective on the organisation which is not constrained by past routines and organisational culture. An example of this approach was seen in the year 2000 when British Airways appointed a new chief executive in order to improve the company fortunes. Consultants can be used as facilitators in strategic workshops or can be used as a reference point in order for managers to be able to claim that other people apart from them are recommending change. Their very cost may indicate that something is wrong in the organisation which requires experts to identify and to help in implementing change. They also bring a dispassionate view to the process, since they have a different perspective from people in the organisation and they may have valuable experience from working in other organisations.

'Structural change' involves altering organisational design, levels of decentralisation, lines of communication, the distribution of authority within an organisation, span of management, job design and/or the scheduling of activities. These changes will be designed to improve organisational performance. Decentralisation has been a major area of change with, for example, 'delayering' to reduce the number of management strata and improve communications. 'Out-sourcing' has meant that specific functions and activities in an organisation are no longer provided internally but are moved to an external organisation. This type of change alters the working arrangements in an organisation, that is the way it operates.

'Technological change' refers to alterations in the equipment, processes, materials, and knowledge with which an organisation creates and provides its products and services. For example, work processes may be altered by introducing computer-controlled machinery to replace some of the functions on the assembly line. This alters 'the way things are done around here' and creates resistance among the workers on the line as their jobs are changed. 'People change' refers to alterations in the behaviours, attitudes, skills and expectations of employees so as to improve organisational performance. These changes are usually undertaken through such methods as employee training and development, in order to instruct people in new skills, behaviour and expectations, or there may be a recruitment campaign to attract the desired personnel into the organisation.

Another approach to 'people change' is through organisational development (OD). The role of employees as stakeholders has changed in the UK in recent years, with concepts such as 'a job for life' and 'company loyalty' increasingly being replaced by the concept of individual 'ownership' of skills and careers. People offer their skills to companies on the understanding that they will be loyal to the firm so long as it satisfies their need for financial rewards and job satisfaction. These employees are still stakeholders in the company, in that they have an interest in it, but it is not a vital interest, in the sense that if necessary they will move their skills elsewhere. There are, of course, many people who do rely on an organisation for their careers for a variety of reasons, such as an old-fashioned feeling of loyalty, inertia, family ties in a location, a lack of confidence in their ability to find other work and so on. These employees have a vital interest in the company because they are relying on it, and therefore any strategic change affects them as stakeholders.

Organisational development is usually a process of recognising a problem which requires a need for change, diagnosing the situation in order to understand what changes are required, obtaining recognition for the problem among all employees so that people believe that it exists, and selecting a solution. It is important, in order to achieve a relatively smooth change, for employees to accept that there is a problem and that a change is necessary. The idea of 'ownership' is that people recognise that a problem exists, they understand their contribution to the problem or the impact it has on them, and they become committed to doing something about it. It is then possible to plan the change and implement it. Ideally, in the strategic management of an organisation, the organisational development process introduces techniques which can be applied continuously so that change is the accepted 'norm' rather than an occasional and rare phenomenon.

The techniques which can be introduced to make change a normal process include training to update skills and to alter behaviour. Customer-care programmes, for example, have been introduced into many companies in order to enhance the service that they provide. Team building can increase the cohesiveness of particular units and of the whole organisation. For example, cross-organisational teams can help employees from different departments and sections of an organisation to understand each others' problems and to co-operate with each other. Communication can be improved so that people understand the reason for continuous change, and consultation about changes and their implementation can help both managers and other employees to understand and acquire ownership of changes.

10.10 Coherence in managing change

Strategic change is much more likely to work if it is coherent across all aspects of the organisation:

- There needs to be a consistency between the intended strategy, the stated strategic objectives, the operation changes introduced and the behaviour of managers.
- The direction of strategic change should be consistent with that is happening in the environment, and the way in which this is understood in the organisation. It should also be managed with due regard to stakeholders, including suppliers and customers, on whom the organisation is critically reliant.
- The strategy should be feasible in terms of the resources it requires, the structure of the organisation, and the changes that need to occur in organisational culture and operational routines.
- The strategic direction should be clearly related to achieving competitive advantage or excellent performance, and internally it should be understood how this is so.

Overall, this coherence means that there needs to be an ability to hold the organisation together as an efficient, successful entity, while simultaneously changing it. Many of the studies on the reasons why some organisations are more successful than others suggest that the clarity of strategy direction and its relevance to the changing environment are crucial. Techniques of analysis, evaluation and planning can all help organisations to understand the foundations of success; but it is the processes of management, the skills of managers and their ability to relate to the external environment, their internal culture and the people around them that ensure success.

The starting point for a strategic change programme is clarity regarding the changes required. This may relate back to the organisation's objectives, but also relates to what is possible. The questions that have to be considered in the organisation of a programme are:

- What areas of change are available?
- What areas are to be selected and why?
- Who will resist change? How can this be overcome?
- What are the effects on the culture and politics of the organisation?

The areas of change available include changes in working arrangements, such as routines and organisation, monitoring and control, organisational structure, the introduction of new techniques and new technology. In terms of the areas to be selected, areas will be chosen which can help to create the prime conditions for change, such as recognition of the need for change, setting standards and monitoring performance. Teams that have achieved successful change can be highlighted and praised as role models, while individuals can be rewarded for their success.

It is virtually certain that there will be some opposition to change, so the process has to be managed. This can be helped by involving people who resist change in the change process itself and building support networks, particularly between those who support the change and those who are resistant. At the same time, communications and discussions about the changes, encouragement and support can all help in the process, with extra incentives and the use of managerial authority. The culture and the politics of an organisation have to be considered in the process of change. A change programme needs to identify potential and influential people and groups, and persuade them to support the new strategy. The main areas of opposition need to be identified and attempts made to change opinions, or at least to neutralise them and to build the maximum consensus for the new strategy.

The senior managers of 'The Communications Company' noticed the problems that were being caused by introducing a new group of employees. They decided to introduce a staff training programme in order to encourage all the Company staff to understand the new direction of the Company and the fact that each group of staff was dependent on the others for its success. They also introduced a new Company structure with teams of staff working on a group of accounts. The teams included people from all three groups, so that each team consisted of technology experts, management consultants and support staff. They were to be judged by the success of the team, and the reward structure was also altered to reflect this. It took some time for these changes to settle down, but when it did the Company continued to be successful (and everybody lived happily ever after!).

Hamel and Prahalad, writing in the *Harvard Business Review* (March/April 1993), have argued that organisational success arises from organisation-wide intention or strategic intent, which is based on a challenging shared vision of the future leadership position of the organisation, on an obsession for winning which is not secured by long-term plans but by achieving a broad, stretching and challenging intention to build core competencies. They considered that the gap between more successful and less successful companies was the gap between the resource base and the aspirations of the company. This was the degree of ambition and aspiration, and the degree of 'stretch' in getting the most from their resources and capabilities. They suggested that 'creating stretch is the single most important task of senior management', and this could be achieved by an accelerated product-development cycle, tightly-knit cross-functional teams, a focus on a few core competencies, and programmes of employee involvement and consensus.

Hamel and Prahalad argue that in the search for less resource-intensive ways to achieve ambitious objectives, 'leveraging' resources provide a very different approach from down-sizing, delayering, restructuring and retrenchment. Strategic managers leverage resources by concentrating them more effectively on key strategic goals, accumulating them more effectively, and complementing one kind of resource with another to create higher order value, thus conserving resources.

The role of strategic managers is not so much to stake out the future of an organisation as to help accelerate the acquisition of market and industry knowledge. In this way, risk will recede as knowledge grows and with it the company's ability to develop and succeed. The learning organisation is an essential element in modern organisations, whichever sector they are in, if they are faced with competition. With improvements in the availability of information, competition has tended to become more fierce rather than less so in most areas of work and in order to cope with this, successful company employees need to embrace new technology, new ideas and the process of strategic change.

SUMMARY OF CONCEPTS

Strategic change – The process of change – Equilibrium, freezing and unfreezing – Individual reaction to change, from denial to support – Competitive forces on strategic change – Change tactics and the management of change – Models of strategic change – Content, process and content – Causes of strategic change – Styles of managing change – Cultural influences – Symbols, behaviour – Stakeholders – Coherence in managing change, how to survive strategic change – Stretch, leverage, down-sizing, core competencies, learning organisations

---

ASSIGNMENTS

1. What is strategic change?
2. How can strategic managers assist in the process of strategic change in an organisation?
3. Discuss the importance of competition in causing strategic change.
4. What is meant by a 'learning company'? Why is it that this type of organisation might be in a strong position to cope with strategic change?
5. How has an organisation that you know coped with strategic change?
6. How have 'The Communications Company' and 'The Engineering Company' dealt with strategic change?

▼ Bibliography

Adair, J. (1998) *Leadership in Action*, Penguin, London

Bartlett, Christopher and Ghoshal, Surmatra (2000) 'Going global. Lessons from late movers', *Harvard Business Review*, March/April

Bennis, W. (1966) 'The coming death of bureaucracy', *Think*, November/December

Bennis, W. and Nanus, B. (1985) *Leaders: The Strategies for Taking Charge*, Harper & Row, New York

Bergman, Bo and Klefsjo, Bengt (1994) *Quality: From Customer Needs to Customer Satisfaction*, McGraw-Hill, New York

Bhote, Keki (1997) *What Do Customers Want Anyway?* American Management Association, March

Brown, A. (1998) *Organisational Culture*, Pitman, London

Deal, T.E. and Kennedy, A.A. (1982) *Corporate Cultures: The Rites and Rituals of Corporate Life*, Addison-Wesley, Reading MA

Drucker, P. (1955) *The Practice of Management*, Heinemann, London

Drucker, P. (1992) *Managing for the Future*, Butterworth-Heinemann, Oxford

Drucker, P. (1998) *Managing in a Time of Great Change*, Plume, London

Drucker, P. (1999) *Management Challenges for the 21st Century*, HarperCollins, London

Fayol, Henri (1949) *General and Industrial Administration*, Pitman, London

Finlay, Paul (2000) *Strategic Management*, Prentice Hall/Pearson Education, London

Garvin, David (1993) 'Building a learning organisation', *Harvard Business Review*, July/August

Hamel, Gary (1996) 'Strategy as revolution', *Harvard Business Review*, June/August

Hamel, Gary and Prahalad, C.K. (1993) 'Strategy as stretch and leverage', *Harvard Business Review*, March/April

Hamel, Gary and Prahalad, C.K. (1994) *Competing for the Future*, Harvard Business School Press, Boston MA

Handy, C. (1989) *The Age of Unreason*, Business Books, London

Handy, C. (1990) *Understanding Organisations*, Penguin, London

Harrington, H. James (1996) *The Complete Benchmarking Implementation Guide: Total Benchmarking Management*, McGraw-Hill, New York

Harvey-Jones, J. (1993) *Managing to Survive*, Heinemann, London

Heskett, James, Sasser, W. Earl and Schlesinger, Leonard (1997) *The Service Profit Chain: How Leading Companies Link Profit and Growth to Loyalty, Satisfaction and Value*, Free Press, New York

Jelinek, Mariann (1979) *Institutional Innovation*, Praeger, New York

Johnson, G. and Scholes, K. (1993) *Exploring Corporate Strategy*, Prentice Hall, Englewood Cliffs NJ

Joyce, Paul (1999) *Strategic Management for the Public Services*, Open University Press, Buckingham

Joyce, Paul (2000) *Strategy in the Public Sector*, John Wiley and Sons, New York

Lewin, Kurt (1951) *Field Force Theory in Social Sciences*, Harper & Row, New York

Lewis, R. (2000) *When Cultures Collide*, Nicholas Brealey, London

Lynch, Richard (2000) *Corporate Strategy*, Prentice Hall/Pearson Education, London

Mescon, Michael H., Albert, Michael and Khedouri, Franklin (1985) *Management: Individual and Organisational Effectiveness*, Harper & Row, New York

Mintzberg, Henry (1994) *The Rise and Fall of Strategic Planning*, Prentice Hall, Englewood Cliffs NJ

Peppers, Don and Rogers, Martha (1997) *The One to One Future: Building Relationships One Customer at a Time*, Doubleday, New York

Peters, T. (1992) *Liberation Management*, Macmillan (now Palgrave), Basingstoke

Peters, T. and Waterman, R. (1982) *In Search of Excellence*, Harper & Row, New York

Pettigrew, Andrew, Ferlie, Ewan and McKee, Lorna (1992) *Shaping Strategic Change*, Sage, London

Pettigrew, A. and Whipp, R. (1991) *Managing Change for Competitive Success*, Blackwell, Oxford

Porter, Michael (1985) *Competitive Strategy*, Free Press, New York

Porter, Michael (1996) 'What is strategy?', *Harvard Business Review*, November/December

Porter, Michael (1998) *Competitive Advantages: Creating and Sustaining Superior Performance*, Free Press, New York

Prahalad, C.K. and Hamel, Gary (1990) 'The core competence of the corporation', *Harvard Business Review*, May/June

Raynor, Michael (1998) 'This vision thing: do we need it?', *Long Range Planning*, June

Scholz, C. (1987) 'Corporate culture and strategy – the problem of strategic fit', *Long Range Planning*, August, pp. 78–87

Segal-Horn, Susan (1998) *The Strategy Reader*, Open University Press/Blackwell, Oxford

Stacey, Ralph D. (1996) *Strategic Management and Organisational Dynamics*, Pitman, London

Books by Tim Hannagan

Marketing for the Non-Profit Sector, Palgrave, Basingstoke, 1992
Work Out Statistics, 3rd edn, Palgrave, Basingstoke, 1996
Mastering Statistics, 3rd edn, Palgrave, Basingstoke, 1997
The Effective Use of Statistics, 2nd edn, Kogan Page, London, 1999
Management: Concepts and Practices, 3rd edn, Pearson Education, London, 2001

◪ Glossary

Action plans – are concerned with turning objectives and priorities into reality

Advertising – the most persuasive possible selling message to the right prospects for the product or service at the lowest possible price

Ansoff Matrix – the marketing strategies for a product/service portfolio linked to market penetration, and extension and product development and diversification

Benchmarking – the process of comparing a firm's offers and processes with those of comparable firms in order to identify where improvements can be made

Boston Matrix – a classification of products and services within a portfolio linked to their cash usage based on relative market share and market growth rate

Brand – a name, symbol or design used to identify offers from one seller and to differentiate them from competitive offers

Change agent – the individual or group that effects strategic change in an organisation

Chaos theory – the organisational world is so turbulent and chaotic that it is not possible to predict what is going to happen and when

Competitive advantage – when a company receives a return on an investment that is greater than the norm for its competitors for a period long enough to alter the relative standing of the company among its rivals

Consumer surplus – the difference between the price that a consumer is prepared to pay for a product or service and the price that they actually pay

Core competencies – skills and knowledge essential for the success of an organisation

Cost leadership – when an organisation places an emphasis on cost reduction at every point in its process

Critical path analysis – a technique for planning projects by breaking them down into their component activities and showing these activities and their interrelationships in the form of a network

Critical success factors – those components of strategy where the organisation must excel to outperform competition

Customers – whoever receive benefits from an organisation's products and services

Customer benefits – customers are not so much looking for particular products and services, but rather for the benefits that these may be able to provide

DAGMAR – define, advertising, goals, for measured, advertising, results

Decision trees – rank strategic options by progressively eliminating options one at a time

Deliberate strategy – strategy that has been accomplished and was intended

Distribution channel – the process that brings together an organisation and its customers at a particular place and time for the purpose of exchange

Emergent strategy – strategy that was not intended but emerges over time

Entrepreneurial organisation – one with a single or a few dominant managers directly controlling the operative labour force

Environment (natural) – external conditions influencing development or growth of people, animals or plants

Environment (organisational) – everything around an organisation that affects it and that can influence its success or failure

Environmentalism – concern about the environment and its preservation from the effects of pollution

Equilibrium price – where the supply of a product or service is equal to the demand for it

Experiment – involves the manipulation of an independent variable to see the effect this may have on the dependent variable

Federal organisation – a variety of individual organisations or groups of organisations allied together by a common approach and mutual interest in order to obtain some of the advantages of large companies

Fit (organisational) – the attempt by managers to match the resources and capabilities of the organisation to the environment in which it works and to the opportunities open to it

Focus strategy or strategy focus – occurs when an organisation focuses on a specific market niche and develops its competitive advantage by offering products especially developed for that niche

Forcefield theory – these are forces for change and forces resisting change in an organisation

Forecasting – a systematic way of combining managerial judgement with market research data to say something useful about the future

Imposed strategy – strategy imposed on an organisation by an outside body

Incremental strategy – a process of taking actions and gradually blending these initiatives into a coherent pattern of actions

Innovative organisation – with specialist and highly trained staff, with control exercised through expertise and need

Intended strategy – strategy that indicates the desired strategic direction of an organisation

Interviews – a conversation with a purpose

J-shaped organisation – characterised by organisational knowledge and expertise, controlled by project-groups under a central hierarchy

Learning organisation – an organisation skilled in continually seeking out new knowledge, acquiring, creating, spreading and managing knowledge, and expert at modifying its behaviour to reflect its new knowledge

Levels of strategy – corporate strategy, business strategy and functional (departmental, team) strategy

Leveraging resources – using the resources that a company already has in new and innovative ways in order to reach new 'stretching' goals which require the company to use resources to the full

Life-cycle analysis – products and services, after they are introduced, tend to pass through periods of growth, relative stability and decline

Logistics management – about having the correct product or service in the right place at the right time

Machine organisation – where a large middle-management control the organisation through standardised processes

Management – the organisation, supervision and control of people so that there is a productive outcome to work

Market – the group of actual or potential customers who are ready, willing and able to purchase a commodity or service

Market-based strategy – is based on market options

Market extension – occurs when an offer is introduced into a market segment other than the one where it is currently positioned

Marketing – is the management process responsible for identifying, anticipating and satisfying customer requirements profitably

Marketing mix – the appropriate combination, in particular circumstances, of product, price, place and promotion (and people, process and physical evidence)

Market-orientation – in which the marketing function is at the centre of the structures of an organisation, integrating the work of all the other functions

Market penetration – involves either increasing sales to existing users or finding new customers in the same market

Market positioning (see *Positioning*) – often seen in terms of market share as a precursor to profits

Market research – the planned, systematic collection, collation and analysis of data designed to help the management of an organisation to reach decisions about its operation and to monitor the results of these decisions

Market segmentation – the identification of specific parts of a market and the development of different market offerings that will be attractive to these segments

Market segmentation analysis – seeks to identify similarities and differences between groups of customers and users

Mission – represents what an organisation is about, its basic purpose

Models – simplifications of reality with unnecessary detail discarded so that the fundamentals can be seen clearly

Network analysis (see *Critical path analysis*)

Niche marketing – differentiation by a company selection of a small market segment and concentration on satisfying the customers in this market

Operations management – the process of transforming an organisation's resources from one state, such as raw materials, to another, such as a finished product

Organisational culture – 'the way we do things around here', the set of beliefs, customs, practices and the ways of thinking that have come to be shared between employees through being and working together

Out-sourcing – the practice of handing over the management and operation of certain functions to a person or organisation outside the company

Passive strategy – when an organisation continues to do what it is already doing

PESTLE – political, economic, social, technological, legal and environmental factors in an organisation's environment

Place – where the final exchange occurs between the seller and the purchaser

Positioning (organisational) – where the organisation sees itself and its products and services in the market

Price-penetration – charging a low initial price in order to attract consumers and to obtain a large market share

Price-skimming – charging high initial prices for a product/service and then lowering prices as costs fall

Products – tangible objects whose sale involves a change of ownership

Products and services – anything that can be offered to a market for consumption that satisfies a want or need

Product development – involves modifying the product/service in terms of such factors as quality and performance

Product differentiation – the development of unique features or attributes in a product or service that positions it to appeal especially to a part of the total market

Product diversification – involves both product development and market extension

Professional organisation – characterised by a large number of professionals and controlled by their knowledge and skills

Public relations – a deliberate, planned and sustained effort by an organisation to establish and monitor understanding between itself and its public in order to improve its image

Questionnaire – a list of questions aimed at discovering particular information

Random – each unit of the statistical population being studied has the same chance as any other unit of being included

Realised strategy – patterns of strategic action that have been accomplished

Resource-based strategy – considers the opportunities available to a company to add value to its products and services or to cut costs

Risk management – where there are several possible outcomes and the probability of their occurrence is unknown

Sample survey – anything less than a full survey of a statistical population

Scenario planning (or building) – a 'what if?' approach based on possible changes in an organisation's environment

Scope (organisational) – the range of an organisation's activities, its offer of products and services

Service – an intangible process that does not result in a change of ownership

Shamrock organisation – this has three interlocking parts composed of three distinct groups of workers who are treated differently and have different expectations

SPECTACLES – social, political, economic, cultural, technological, aesthetic, customers, legal, environmental and sectoral factors in an organisation's environment

Stakeholders – the individuals and groups who are affected by the activities of the organisation

Statistical population – the group of people or items about which information is being sought

STEP factors – social, technological, economic, political factors in an organisation's environment

Strategy – is about a sense of purpose, looking ahead, planning, positioning, fit, leverage and stretching

Strategic analysis – the complexity arising out of ambiguous and non-routine situations with organisation-wide rather than operationally specific implications

Strategic business plan – outlines the process of allocating resources in an organisation in order to achieve its strategic objectives

Strategic change – the implementation of new strategies that involve substantive changes beyond the normal routines of the organisation

Strategic content – what is or will be the strategy for an organisation

Strategic context – the set of circumstances under which the strategy content and the strategy process are determined

Strategic control – to identify whether the organisation should continue with its present strategy or modify it in the light of changed circumstances; it is the continuous, critical evaluation of plans, inputs, processes and outputs to provide information for future action

Strategic decisions – are concerned with achieving an advantage for an organisation in the long-term

Strategic drift – the actual strategy of an organisation drifts further and further away from the strategy needed for success

Strategic fit – the matching of the activities and resources of an organisation to the environment in which it operates

Strategic leadership – motivating people to move in a particular direction in order to achieve particular objectives

Strategic management – the decisions and actions used to formulate and implement strategies that will provide a competitively superior fit between the organisation and its environment to enable it to achieve organisational objectives

Strategic marketing – about moving the organisation from its present position to a more competitive one where it has a competitive advantage

Strategic options – the broad choices open to a business

Strategic pathway – those strategic options chosen by a business

Strategic process – is how strategy is formulated, implemented and controlled

Strategic resources – an advantage a company enjoys because of the structure of the competitive area in which it is involved, such as location, reputation, external relationships

Stretch (organisational) – developing an organisation's resources and capabilities to meet the opportunities and challenges it faces

SWOT analysis – highlights the internal strengths and weaknesses of an organisation from the customers' point of view as they relate to external opportunities and threats

Triple-I organisation – based on Intelligence, Information and Ideas, representing the intellectual capital possessed by the core workers

Unrealised strategy – when intended or deliberate strategies are not accomplished

Value – the price of a product or service plus the consumer service

Value chain – the set of conversion processes between the beginning of a process and the final product

☑ Index